Colloquial
Gujarati

The Complete Course for Beginners

Jagdish Dave

Routledge
Taylor & Francis Group
LONDON AND NEW YORK

Second edition published 2012
by Routledge
2 Park Square, Milton Park, Abingdon, Oxon OX14 4RN

Simultaneously published in the USA and Canada
by Routledge
711 Third Avenue, New York, NY 10017

Routledge is an imprint of the Taylor & Francis Group, an informa business

First edition published by Routledge 1995

British Library Cataloguing in Publication Data
A catalogue record for this book is available from the British Library

Library of Congress Cataloging in Publication Data
Dave, Jagdish.
Colloquial Gujarati : the complete course for beginners / Jagdish Dave. — 2nd ed.
p. cm. — (Colloquial series)
Includes bibliographical references and index.
1. Gujarati language—Textbooks for foreign speakers—English. 2. Gujarati language—Spoken Gujarati. 3. Gujarati language—Self-instruction.
4. Gujarati language—Sound recordings for English speakers. I. Title.
PK1845.D38 2011
491.4′782421—dc22

2011013939

ISBN: 978-0-415-58063-2 (pbk)
ISBN: 978-0-415-58065-6 (audio CDs)
ISBN: 978-0-415-58064-9 (pack)
ISBN: 978-0-415-58067-0 (MP3s)
ISBN: 978-0-203-85093-0 (ebk)

Typeset in Avant Garde and Helvetica
by Graphicraft Limited, Hong Kong

FSC www.fsc.org MIX Paper from responsible sources FSC® C004839

Printed and bound in Great Britain by
TJ International Ltd, Padstow, Cornwall

Dedicated to all my students/teacher-trainees in India since 1950, in the United Kingdom since 1984 and worldwide since 1995.

Jagdish Dave

Contents

Preface

We are delighted to present our readers with this revised edition of *Colloquial Gujarati*, first published in 1995. That original edition, followed by three reprints, was used widely by both teachers and students. The Language Centre at the School of Oriental and African Studies (SOAS), University of London, adopted *Colloquial Gujarati* as its textbook. This current edition incorporates improvements which we trust will make study both easier and more enjoyable.

Gujarati is spoken by some 50 million people in the State of Gujarat and a further estimated 20 million around the world, mostly in the United Kingdom and the United States.

Gujarati belongs to the Indo-Aryan group of languages – a subgroup of the Indo-European family. Modern Gujarati, along with Rajasthani and Braj (Western Hindi), has its source in Shaureseni Apabhramsha, which fell into disuse around the twelfth century. The language comprises four principal dialects – Pattani, Surati, Charotari and Kathiawadi – of which the standard written form (used in education, the media and literature) is by far the most common. The script is derived from Devnagari (the name of the Sanskrit script; many of the Indian scripts are derived from Devnagari).

Some sounds in Gujarati have no equivalent in English. The information contained in this book will demonstrate how to closely simulate those sounds, but at best they are an approximation. It is only by listening to the spoken language that correct pronunciation can be achieved. Radio, television, video and films offer an excellent way of achieving this end, and two audio-discs are available with this book. One of the best solutions to this difficulty is to spend time with native Gujarati speakers whenever possible.

The course assumes no prior knowledge of Gujarati and is designed to lead the student to a good working knowledge of the written and spoken language. It is divided into 15 lesson units, covering grammar and colloquial quirks of the language, with dialogues, exercises and related vocabulary. All lessons are presented in Gujarati with English translation and transliteration. A new alphabet chart in large letters is provided in this edition along with a list of Gujarati websites and a list of books for further reading and information. Also included is a 2,000-word Gujarati–English/English–Gujarati glossary, and a thematic glossary.

Acknowledgements

I wish to thank Swamishri Sachchidanand, Professor Gunvant Shah, Mr Rajni Vyas, Professor Bernard Comrie, Mr K. N. Trivedi, Ex-Director of Languages, Gujarat State, Father Vallace and Navjivan publishers for permitting me to use their material in this course.

I would especially like to thank Dr H. C. Bhayani, eminent linguist and honorary fellow of SOAS, for going through the entire manuscript and making valuable suggestions; my friend, philosopher and guide Mr A. D. Chappa for his constant help and guidance; Ms Maria Calivis for giving me very helpful comments during the writing process, especially in the Reference grammar; and Simon Bell, all of whose continuous help was a great asset in the first edition in 1995.

For the second edition I thank the editor Ms Andrea Hartill, and assistant editors Sonja van Leeuwen and Samantha Vale Noya, who suggested many of the improvements contained in this new edition. I would also like to thank Upendra Dave for typing, providing photographs and giving me many useful suggestions, Pathik Shah and Chandrakant Patel for corrections, Raghav Dave for help in the tapescript.

Last but not least, I would like to thank my students from various colleges in India whom I taught from 1950 until 1984, when I settled in England. While in England, I have had both the pleasure and privilege of teaching at the Institute of Education, University of London, the School of Oriental and African Studies, Language Centre, University of London, the Academy of Vedic Heritage, Harrow, the Gujarati Literary Academy (UK) and the Chandaria Foundation. I thank all my students and teacher-trainees (about 2,000) in England and around the world where I could go and teach them as the project director, Gujarati Teaching Worldwide (a project sponsored by the Chandaria Foundation). Also during 1990–92, in *Gujarat Samachar* (a prominent weekly published from London) my 'Learn Gujarati' column was serialized which gave excellent feedback from the reader-learners.

The valuable suggestions from all of them made this new edition more meaningful.

I am indebted to each and every one of them.

Jagdish Dave

Abbreviations

a (*v*)	adjective variable
a (*inv*)	adjective invariable
adv	adverb
conj	conjunction
f	feminine noun
inf	infinitive
m	masculine noun
n	neuter noun
prep	preposition
pron	pronoun
vi	verb intransitive
vi, *t*	verb intransitive and transitive
vt	verb transitive

Gujarati alphabet chart

Vowels (CD1; 2)

અ	આ	ઇ	ઈ	ઉ	ઊ	એ	ઐ	ઓ	ઔ	અં
a	ā	i	ī	u	ū	e	ai	o	au	am

Consonants (CD1; 3–8)

ક	ખ	ગ	ઘ	
k	kh	g	gh	
ચ	છ	જ	ઝ	
ch	chh	j	jh	
ટ	ઠ	ડ	ઢ	ણ
ṭ	ṭh	ḍa	ḍh	ṇ
ત	થ	દ	ધ	ન
t	th	d	dh	n
પ	ફ	બ	ભ	મ
p	ph	b	bh	m
ય	ર	લ	વ	
y	r	l	v	
શ	ષ	સ		
sh	Sh	s		
હ	ળ			
h	!			

Gujarati alphabet and script

Vowels chart

	Front	*Central*	*Back*
High	i		u
Mid	e	a	o
Low	E	ā	O

Vowels

Letter	*Pronounced as*	*Letter*	*Pronounced as*
a	*u*p	**e**	m*ay*
ā	*ar*m	**ai**	p*ai*n
i, **ī**	*i*t	**o**	g*o*
		au	*ou*nce
u, **ū**	p*u*t		
		E	c*a*t
		O	b*o*x

Consonant chart

			Velar	*Palatal*	*Cerebral*	*Dental*	*Labial*	*Glottal*
Stops	Voiceless	unaspirated	k		ṭ	t	p	
		aspirated	kh		ṭh	th	ph	
	Voiced	unaspirated	g		ḍ	d	b	
		aspirated	gh		ḍh	dh	bh	
Affricates	Voiceless	unaspirated		ch				
		aspirated		chh				
	Voiced	unaspirated		j				
		aspirated		jh				
Fricatives	Voiceless		sh		s			
	Voiced			z				h
Lateral					ḷ	l		
Flapped/trilled						r		
Nasal				ṇ	n	m		
Semi-vowel				y			v	

Consonants

Letter	*Pronounced as*
k	pic*k*le
kh	*kh*aki
g	fo*g*
gh	like **g** above, but with an aspirated 'h'
ch	vou*ch*er
chh	like **ch** above, but with an aspirated 'h'
j	*J*ack
jh	like **j** above, but with an aspirated 'h'
ṭ	but*t*er
ṭh	like **ṭ** above, but with an aspirated 'h'
ḍ	*d*ull
ḍh	like **ḍ** above, but with an aspirated 'h'
ṇ	**n** with strong aspiration
t	as in *t*ête (French)
th	*th*ird
d	*d*e (French)
dh	*th*us
n	*n*ut
p	u*pp*er
ph	*f*irm (but following closed lips)
b	*b*urn
bh	a*bh*or
m	*m*ug
y	*y*es
r	*r*ush
l	*l*uck
v	*v*erge
sh	*sh*ut
s	*s*upport
h	*h*ush
ḷ	no equivalent

Script

Many Indian languages are rooted in Sanskrit, from which they derive words and grammar. Written Gujarati is a modification of the Sanskrit script (known as Devnagari).

Pronunciation in Gujarati corresponds closely to the written letter (unlike the many variations in English, e.g. the 'u' in 'but' and 'put').

The simplest and most effective way to learn the Gujarati script is by dividing it into groups according to letter shapes. We will start with the first three groups:

Group 1

ડ	**ḍa**	as in *d*ull
ક	**ka**	as in pic*k*le
ફ	**pha**	as in *f*irm
હ	**ha**	as in *h*ush
ઠ	**ṭha**	(no equivalent in English; see Introduction)

Group 2

ત	**ta**	(no equivalent in English; French *tête*)
ન	**na**	as in *n*ut
મ	**ma**	as in *m*ug
ભ	**bha**	as in a*bh*or

Group 3

પ	**pa**	as in u*pp*er
ષ	**sha**	as in *sh*ut
ય	**ya**	as in *y*es
થ	**tha**	as in *th*ird

Practise writing the following words.

kaḍak	**ḍaph**	**kaph**	**haṭh**
ṭhak	**kaṭh**	**hak**	

We can now combine letters from groups 1 and 2:

mat	**nam**	**man**	**kaphan**
bham	**maphat**	**tak**	**kam**

And finally from all three groups:

pakaḍ	**kap**	**paḍ**	**bhay**
math	**nath**	**thaḍ**	

Group 4

ટ	**ṭa**	as in *butt*er
ઢ	**ḍha**	(no equivalent in English)

Group 5

લ	**la**	as in *l*uck
બ	**ba**	as in *b*urn
ખ	**kha**	as in *kha*ki
વ	**va**	as in *v*erge
ળ	**ḷa**	(no equivalent in English)

Group 6

ર	**ra**	as in *r*ush
સ	**sa**	as in *s*upport
શ	**sha**	as in *sh*ut

The pronunciation of ષ in group 3 and શ in this group is the same, 'sh', although written differently in different words.

Write the following words and pronounce them loudly:

naṭ **kapaṭ** **ṭapak** **maṭ**

To form additional words we can combine letters from groups 1–5.

નખ	**nakh**	લટ	**laṭ**
લડ	**laḍ**	લત	**lat**

ટળ	**ṭaḷ**	બટન	**baṭan**
વન	**van**	વતન	**vatan**
હળ	**haḷ**	બડબડ	**baḍbaḍ**
બળ	**baḷ**		

Now combine letters from all six groups to form more words.

રસ	**ras**	સફર	**saphar**
સરસ	**saras**	બરફ	**baraph**
તરસ	**taras**	નરમ	**naram**
વર	**var**	રમત	**ramat**

For those sounds that have no equivalent in English, listen to the audio for the correct pronunciation.

Group 7

દ	**da**	(no equivalent in English)
ઘ	**gha**	as in *gh*ost
ધ	**dha**	as in *th*us
છ	**chha**	as in *ch*urch
ઈ	**i**	as in s*i*t

Write and then pronounce the following words (the letters are all from groups 1–7).

das	**dhan**	**chhat**	**ghan**	**iyaḷ**
had	**ghar**	**vadh**	**kai**	

Group 8

જ	**ja**	pronounced like *Ge* in *German*

There are no other letter shapes similar to જ in Gujarati.

Write and then pronounce the following words:

pharaj	**jaḍ**
sapharjan	**bhaj**
jay	**jash**
jam	**taj**

Go to the glossary for the meanings.

Group 9

ગ	**ga**	as in *f*og
ણ	**ṇa**	(no equivalent in English)
ઝ	**jha**	(no equivalent in English)
ચ	**cha**	as in *vouch*er
અ	**a**	as in *u*p

Write and pronounce the following words:

gaṇ	**paṇ**
jhagaḍ	**rach**
chaḍ	**gaḍh**
aḍak	**ananas**
jagat	

Group 10

ઉ, ઊ **u**, **ū** as in p*u*t

The difference between ઉ and ઊ exists in the script only. The pronunciation is the same.

Now we can combine all the letters from groups 1–10 to make some new words:

ઉપર	**upar**	ઊંચક	**ũchak**
ઊઠ	**uṭh**	ઊખડ	**ukhad**
ઊન	**un**	ઊછળ	**uchhal**
ઊતર	**utar**	ઊજવ	**ujav**
ઉઘાડ	**ughād**		

Gujarati vowels are shown by the addition of signs above, below, before or after the consonants. The ten Gujarati vowel signs are:

◌ા	**ā**	◌ે	**e**
◌િ	**i**	◌ૈ	**ai**
◌ી	**ī**	◌ો	**o**
◌ુ	**u**	◌ૌ	**ou**
◌ૂ	**ū**	◌ં	sign for nasalization

For example:

ક	**ka**	ખ	**kha**	ગ	**ga**
કા	**kā**	ખા	**khā**	ગા	**gā**
કિ	**ki**	ખિ	**khi**	ગિ	**gi**
કી	**kī**	ખી	**khī**	ગી	**gī**
કુ	**ku**	ખુ	**khu**	ગુ	**gu**
કૂ	**kū**	ખૂ	**khū**	ગૂ	**gū**
કે	**ke**	ખે	**khe**	ગે	**ge**
કૈ	**kai**	ખૈ	**khai**	ગૈ	**gai**
કો	**ko**	ખો	**kho**	ગો	**go**
કૌ	**kou**	ખૌ	**khou**	ગૌ	**gou**
કં	**kam**	ખં	**kham**	ગં	**gam**

The traditional order of the alphabet used in Gujarati dictionaries largely follows the Sanskrit alphabet.

Vowels: અ આ ઇ ઈ ઉ ઊ એ ઐ ઓ ઔ અં

Consonants:	ક	ખ	ગ	ઘ	
	ચ	છ	જ	ઝ	
	ટ	ઠ	ડ	ઢ	ણ
	ત	થ	દ	ધ	ન
	પ	ફ	બ	ભ	મ
	ય	ર	લ	વ	
	શ	ષ	સ		
	હ	ળ			

Copy the following sentences as neatly as possible:

શરદ, જમણ જમ.
અકબર,ગરમ મગ ઝટ જમ.
કનક, ઉપર ન ચઢ.
રમણ, ઇયળ ન પકડ.
અહમદ, પગ પર મલમ ઘસ.
લતા બાગમાં કામ કરે છે.
રવિવારે રજા હોય છે.
વૈદની દવા સારી અસર કરે છે.
મરચું તીખું લાગે છે.
આ મારો અંગૂઠો છે.

Conjuncts

The joining of two consonants in Gujarati is achieved in various ways.

1 As previously mentioned, the Gujarati script is derived from the Devnagari script, in which there are two letters which, although they appear to be individual, are in fact conjuncts. The Gujarati script has retained both these letters. They are:

ક્ષ **ksha** જ્ઞ **gna**

The first letter, ક્ષ, is made up of the two consonants **ka** and **sha**. The second is a combination of **ga** and **na**.

2 In English the complete letters are always used even when the sounds run into one another: for example, the letters *n* and *c* in the words *pencil* do not change even though together they form a close-linked sound. In Gujarati, however, the sound created by their conjunction is reflected in the written word, with the first letter losing half its shape.

The word **pensil** (the same in Gujarati as in English) is written પેન્સિલ. You will see that ન has lost its ા-like shape before joining with સ. All those letters which contain this ા shape lose it before joining to another full letter.

ખ	ગ	ઘ	ચ	ણ	ત	થ	ધ	પ
ભ	મ	ય	લ	વ	શ	ષ	સ	ળ

3 The remaining twelve letters of the alphabet are:

ક, છ, જ, ઝ, ટ, ઠ, ડ, ઢ, ડ, ફ, ૨, હ.

With the exception of દ, ૨ and હ, the letters follow a simple rule: always write them as close to one another as possible:

અક્કલ	**akkal**
જ્યાં	**jyā̃**
દાઝ્યો	**dājhyo**
વાટ્યું	**vāṭyũ**
ઊઠ્યો	**uṭhyo**
ઊડ્યું	**uḍyũ**
વઢ્યો	**vaḍhyo**
ફ્લ્યુ	**phlu**

4 When ટ, ઠ, ડ and ઢ are involved in conjunctions the letter is repeated, slightly smaller, underneath itself:

ટટ્ટુ	**ṭaṭṭu**
અઠ્ઠાઈ	**aṭṭhāi**
ઊડ્ડયન	**uḍḍayan**
ઢડ્ઢો	**ḍhaḍḍho**

5 દ combines in different ways with different letters:

દ + ય	**da + ya**	=	દ્ય	e.g.	વિદ્યા	**vidyā**
દ + વ	**da + va**	=	દ્વ	e.g.	વિદ્વાન	**vidvān**
દ + દ	**da + da**	=	દ્દ	e.g.	ઉદ્દામ	**uddām**
દ + ધ	**da + dha**	=	દ્ધ	e.g.	ઉદ્ધાર	**uddhār**

The sign ્ (known as **khoḍo**) is written underneath દ when it joins with the remainder of the letters. e.g.

દ + ગ	**da + ga**	=	દ્ ગ	e.g.	ઉદ્ગમ	**udgam**
દ + ઘ	**da + gha**	=	દ્ ઘ	e.g.	ઉદ્ઘાટન	**udghāṭan**

6 The letter હ joins in the following ways:

હ + ય	**ha + ya**	=	હ્ય	e.g.	ડાહ્યો	**dāhyo**
હ + મ	**ha + ma**	=	હ્મ	e.g.	બ્રાહ્મણ	**brāhmaṇ**

With all other letters the **khoḍo** sign is used.

7 There are at least six ways of joining the half letter:

(a) A ^ sign under the letter represents half ર:

ટ્ર	**ṭra**	e.g.	રાષ્ટ્ર	**rāshṭra**

(b) A ⸝ sign is added in the following way:

ગ્ર	**gra**	e.g.	ગ્રાહક	**grāhak**
પ્ર	**pra**	e.g.	પ્રવેશ	**pravesh**
ક્ર	**kra**	e.g.	ક્રિકેટ	**kriket̤**

(c) When the **r** sounds like **ru** a ૃ sign is used under the letter:

પૃ	**pru**	e.g.	પૃથ્વી	**pruthvi**
કૃ	**kru**	e.g.	કૃતિ	**kruti**

(d) When the half ર is used between two consonants, a ˁ sign (known as **reph**) is written above the following letter:

આશીર્વાદ **āshirvād**
ધર્મ **dharm**

(e) When ર joins with શ it is written as શ્ર:

શ્રી **shri**
શ્રમ **shram**

(f) Joined with ત, it is written ત્ર:

ત્રિકોણ **trikoṇ**
ત્રીસ **tris**

Some of these conjuncts appear only infrequently, the others you will come across more often and learn gradually.

Script revision

The purpose of this section is to look back over what we have learned about the script. The examples given will also contain new grammatical constructions which will be explained fully in future chapters. The main objective is to familiarize yourself with the letter shapes and vowel signs. Repeated practice of these examples will facilitate reading in the forthcoming units.

The examples are divided into vowel groups and are introduced in a graded way. Group A contains only the vowel અ, while group B adds આ. Each new group will include those vowels already studied, e.g. in addition to the introduction of new vowels group D will also contain those from groups A, B and C. This system is designed to help you proceed easily and systematically.

As Indian names are likely to be unfamiliar to some students there follows a list of all the proper nouns contained in this section:

Magan, Nayan, Akbar, Kanak, Amar, Manhar, Ratan, Latā, Mahmad, Ramā, Ramaṇ, Mamtā, Rām, Niti, Vijay, Saritā, Nirāli, Ramṇik, Punam, Sulemān, Anurādhā, Bhairavi, Kailās, Kanaiyālāl, Shailesh, Sheelā, Saiyad, Chaulā, Gauri.

Group A

All sentences in this group are made of words containing the vowel **a** અ:

1 મગન, વજન કર. **magan vajan kar.** Magan, weigh this.
2 નયન, સરસ ગરમ મગ જમ. **nayan saras garam mag jam.** Nayan, eat good hot moong (lentils).
3 અકબર, સરસ રમત રમ. **akbar saras ramat ram.** Akbar, play a good game.
4 કનક, પગ પર તરત મલમ ઘસ. **kanak pag par tarat malam ghas.** Kanak, rub the ointment on your leg quickly.
5 અમર, સરસ ભણ. **amar saras bhaṇ.** Amar, learn well.
6 મનહર, છ રકમ લખ. **manhar chha rakam lakh.** Manhar, do (*lit.* write) six sums.
7 રતન, હરણ ગણ. **ratan haraṇ gaṇ.** Ratan, count the deer.

Group B

This group has **a + ā**, અ + આ, ા:

1 આજ રજા, કાલ પણ રજા. **āj rajā kāl paṇ rajā.** Today is a holiday, tomorrow is also a holiday.
2 લતા, દાળભાત પાપડ ખા. **latā dāḷ bhāt pāpaḍ khā.** Lata, eat dal (a lentil soup) rice and a papadam.
3 મહમદ, દાડમ લાવ. **mahmad dāḍam lāv.** Mahmad, bring a pomegranate.
4 રમા, ઝાડ પર ચડ. **ramā jhāḍ par chaḍ.** Rama, climb (on) the tree.
5 રમણ, બરાબર કામ કર. **ramaṇ barābar kām kar.** Raman, do your work properly.
6 મમતા, મારા હાથ પકડ. **mamtā mārā hāth pakaḍ.** Mamta, hold my hands.
7 રામ હરણ પાછળ ગયા. **rām haraṇ pāchhaḷ gayā.** Ram went after the deer.

Group C

This group has the additional vowels **i**, ઇ ઈ િ ી:

1 નીતિ, બસની ટિકિટ આપ. **niti basni ṭikiṭ āp.** Niti, give (me) the bus ticket.
2 શનિવાર તથા રવિવાર રજાના દિવસ. **shanivār tathā ravivār rajānā divas.** Saturday and Sunday are holidays.

3 વિજય, આવ. **vijay āv.** Vijay, come in.
4 સરિતા, હિસાબ ગણ. **saritā hisāb gaṇ.** Sarita, do (*lit.* count) the accounts.
5 શિકારી નદી આગળ હતા. **shikāri nadi āgaḷ hatā.** The hunters were near the river.
6 નિરાલીના વિચાર સાચા હતા. **nirālinā vichār sāchā hatā.** Nirali's thinking was correct.
7 રમણીક, ઇયળ ન પકડ. **ramṇik iyaḷ na pakaḍ.** Ramnik, do not pick up (catch) the worm.

Group D

Together with the previous vowels this group contains **u, ū** ઉ ઊ ુ ૂ:

1 પૂનમ ઉપરથી ખમીસ લાવ. **punam uparthi khamis lāv.** Punam, bring the shirt from upstairs.
2 પૂનાથી કાકાના કુશળ સમાચાર હતા. **punāthi kākānā kushaḷ samāchār hatā.** There was news from Poona that uncle was well.
3 સુલેમાન સકીનાને વધુ દૂધ ન આપ. **sulemān sakināne vadhu dudh na āp.** Suleman, do not give any more milk to Sakina.
4 ભસતા કૂતરા કરડતા નથી. **bhastā kutrā karaḍtā nathi.** Barking dogs do not bite.
5 તબિયત માટે ઉપવાસ સારા. **tabiyat māṭe upvās sārā.** Fasting is good for (your) health.
6 કુદરતી ઉપચાર કર. **kudrati upchār kar.** Use natural medicines.
7 અનુરાધા વધુ આરામ કર. **anurādhā vadhu ārām kar.** Anuradha, rest (some) more.

Group E

The vowels **e ai** એ ઐ ે ૈ are added:

1 ભૈરવી કેરી લે છે. **bhairvi keri le chhe.** Bhairavi takes a mango.
2 કૈલાસ વિચાર કરે છે. **kailās vichār kare chhe.** Kailas is thinking.
3 વૈદ વૈશાલીને દવા પાય છે. **vaid vaishāline davā āpe chhe.** The doctor is giving medicine to Vaishali.
4 વરસાદ છે એટલે કેટલાક ન પણ આવે. **varsād chhe eṭle keṭlāk na paṇ āve.** As it is raining, some (people) may not come.

5 કનૈયાલાલ મુરલી વગાડે છે. **kanaiyālāl murli vagāḍe chhe.** Kanaiyalal plays the flute.
6 કાલે શૈલેષ અને શીલા અમેરિકા જશે. **kāle shailesh ane shilā amerikā jashe.** Shailesh and Sheela will go to America tomorrow.
7 સૈયદને ઐતિહાસિક નવલકથા ગમે છે. **saiyadne aitihāsik navalkathā game chhe.** Saiyad likes historical novels.

Group F

This group deals with **o, au** ઓ, ઔ, ો, ૌ:

1 ભારતનો શિયાળાનો તડકો ઘણો સરસ હોય છે. **bhāratno shiyāḷāno taḍko ghaṇo saras hoy chhe.** India's winter sunshine is very nice.
2 રોહિતને સાથે લઈ ચૌલા બહાર ગઈ. **rohitne sāthe lai chaulā bahār gai.** Chaula went out with Rohit.
3 પોપ નૌકા જોઈ ખુશ થયા. **pop naukā joi khush thayā.** The Pope was delighted to see the ship.
4 અમર ઓટલેથી પડી ગયો. **amar oṭlethi paḍi gayo.** Amar fell from the verandah.
5 કાલે મારા મોટાભાઇ નાયગરાનો ધોધ જોવા જશે. **kāle mārā moṭābhāi nāygarāno dhodh jovā jashe.** My elder brother will go to see the Niagara Falls tomorrow.
6 નાઈલ નદી સૌથી મોટી છે? **nāil nadi sauthi moṭi chhe?** Is the Nile the biggest river?
7 ગૌરી સરસ ગીતો ગાય છે. **gauri saras gito gāy chhe.** Gauri sings beautiful songs.

Group G

Nasalization, indicated in the English transliteration by the sign ˜, is shown in the Gujarati script by ˙ above the relevant letter:

1 ચિંતા ન કરશો બધું સારું થઈ જશે. **chintā na karsho badhũ sārũ thashe.** Do not worry, everything will be all right.
2 હું ઘરમાં ગયો ને મેં ગંગાનો સંદેશો જોયો. **hũ gharmā̃ gayo ne mẽ gãgāno sãdesho joyo.** I went inside the house and saw Gaga's message.

3 હિંમત રાખ ગોવિંદ. **himmat rākh govind.** Be brave (*lit.* take courage), Govind.
4 મંગળવારે બધું મંગળ જ થશે. **mangaḷvāre badhũ mangaḷaj thashe.** Everything will be auspicious on Tuesday.
5 રવિવારે બેન્ક બંધ હોય છે. **ravivare bẼk bandh hoy chhe.** The bank is closed on Sundays.
6 નાનું છોકરું ઊંઘી ગયું. **nānũ chhokrũ ũghi gayũ.** The young child fell asleep.
7 અહીં મારાં દાદીમાનો ફોટો છે. **ahĩ mārā̃ dādimāno phoṭo chhe.** Here is the photo of my grandmother.

Group H

This group gives some of the Gujarati conjuncts:

1 અક્ષરજ્ઞાન સૌથી મહત્વનું છે. **akshargnān sauthi mahatvanũ chhe.** Literacy is very important.
2 જોડાક્ષરો ચોખ્ખા લખવાનો અભ્યાસ કરો. **joḍāksharo chokkhā lakhvāno abhyās karo.** Practise writing the conjuncts clearly.
3 વાક્ય શબ્દોનું બનેલું છે. **vākya shabdonũ banelũ chhe.** A sentence is composed of words.
4 સ્વરો અને વ્યંજનો પ્રથમ શીખવાં જરૂરી છે. **svaro ane vyanjano pratham shikhvā̃ jaruri chhe.** It is essential initially to learn the vowels and consonants.
5 ગુજરાતની અસ્મિતા માટે ગુજરાતી ભાષા શીખો. **gujrātni asmitā māṭe gujrāti bhāshā shikho.** Learn Gujarati to understand the identity of Gujarat.
6 ઈશ્વરલાલ ઈચ્છાબેન સાથે ગયા. **ishvarlāl ichchhāben sāthe gayā.** Ishvarlal went with Ichhaben.
7 કર્મ કરો ફળની આશા ન રાખો. **karma karo phaḷni āshā na rākho.** Work without hope of reward (saying from the Gita: *lit*. Do your work, do not hope for the fruits).

Map of Gujarat

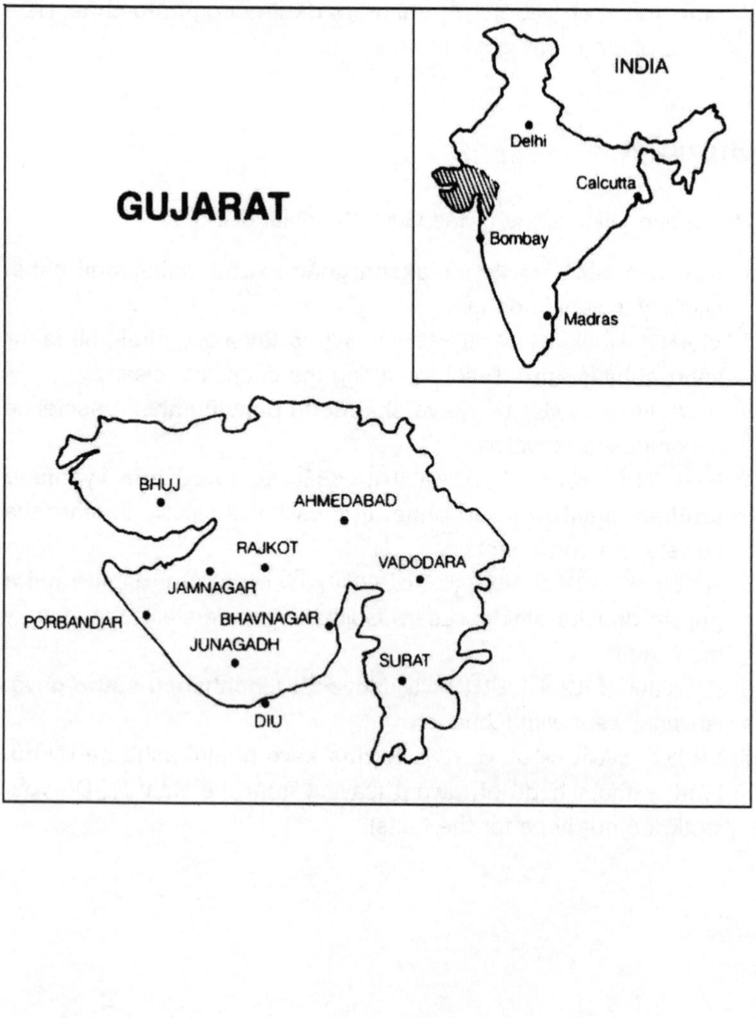

Unit One

કેમ છો? **kem chho?**

How are you?

ગીતાને ઘેર રમેશ **Gitāne gher ramesh**

Ramesh at Gita's home

In this unit you will learn about:

- The use of simple greetings
- The use of personal pronouns (I, you, he/she/it)
- Formation of simple present tense (I am, we are, etc.)
- The use of the honorific plural
- The use of the case suffix **mā̃** (in)

Dialogue 1

કેમ છો? **kem chho?** How are you? **(CD1; 11)**

Two friends, Ramesh Patel and Gita Shah, meet on the road and exchange greetings

રમેશ	નમસ્તે, ગીતાબેન કેમ છો?
ગીતા	નમસ્તે, રમેશભાઈ, મજામાં છું, તમે કેમ છો?
રમેશ	મજામાં, આજકાલ ઠંડી બહુ પડે છે.
ગીતા	હા, તબિયત જાળવજો.

રમેશ તમે પણ જાળવજો, ચાલો ત્યારે આવજો.
ગીતા આવજો.

RAMESH namaste gitāben, kem chho?
GITA namaste rameshbhāi, majāmā̃ chhū̃. tame kem chho?
RAMESH majāmā̃. ājkāl ṭhanḍi bahu paḍe chhe.
GITA hā. tabiyat jāḷavjo.
RAMESH tame paṇ jāḷavjo. chālo tyāre. āvjo.
GITA āvjo.

RAMESH *Hello Gitaben, how are you?*
GITA *Hello Rameshbhai. I'm OK. How are you?*
RAMESH *Fine. It's cold these days.*
GITA *Yes. Please take care.*
RAMESH *You too. OK. Goodbye.*
GITA *Goodbye.*

How to address people

It is customary to address all men as **bhāi** (brother) and all women as **ben** (sister), so **Gitā*ben*** and **Ramesh*bhāi***. This does not apply to close friends or when an elderly person is talking to a boy or girl.

Vocabulary

namaste	hello (*lit.* I bow down to you)
kem	how, why
chho	are
majāmā̃	OK, fine (*lit.* in fun)
chhū̃	am
tame	you (plural, here honorific plural)
ājkāl	nowadays (*lit.* today and tomorrow; **aj** today; **kal** tomorrow *or* yesterday)
ṭhanḍi (*f*)	cold
bahu	very much
paḍe	falls
chhe	is
hā	yes
tabiyat (*f*)	health
jāḷavjo	take care
paṇ	also, but
āvjo	goodbye (*lit.* come again)
chālo tyāre	OK (*lit.* **chālo** walk; **tyāre** then)

Grammatical notes

In sentence formation the verb generally comes last.

Gender

There are three genders in Gujarati: masculine, feminine and neuter:

Masculine: **bāg** garden, **rājā** king
Feminine: **bhī̃t** wall, **rāṇi** queen
Neuter: **bārṇū̃** door, **baḷak** child

Note: every Gujarati noun has a gender.

Unfortunately, there are no rules for memorizing the gender of a word: ear is masculine, eye is feminine and nose is neuter.

However, there are some guidelines:

1 Words ending with **o** are masculine: **chhokro** boy, **bilāḍo** male cat, **kutro** male dog.

2 Words ending with **i** are feminine: **chhokri** girl, **bilāḍi** female cat, **kutri** female dog.

3 Words ending with **ũ** are neuter: **chhokrũ** child, **bilāḍũ** cat, unspecified, **kutrũ** dog, unspecified; used generally when it is not necessary to specify gender.

Countries, mountains and oceans are masculine: Alps, Britain, Pacific, etc. Rivers are feminine: Ganges, Nile, Thames. Cities and lakes are neuter: Bombay, Chicago, Baikal.

In some cases the masculine ending **o** indicates that the subject is larger and the feminine ending **i** that the subject is smaller:

orḍo big room
orḍi small room
chamcho big spoon
chamchi small spoon

Certain words have two genders and in these cases the use of either one is correct:

chā (*m, f*) tea; **savār** (*f, n*) morning; **kharach** (*m, n*) expense; **ghaḍiyāl** (*f, n*) clock, watch

English words imported into Gujarati are given a gender:

Masculine: telephone, coat, camera
Feminine: bus, bank, pencil
Neuter: table, card, station

Number

There are two numbers: singular and plural.

As in English, Gujarati has both a singular and plural form. The suffix attached to a word to form the plural is itself changed according to the ending of that word: **a, ā** and **i** at the end of a word add **o** to form the plural:

māṇas person	**māṇso** persons
rajā holiday	**rajāo** holidays
nadi river	**nadio** rivers

o and **ũ** endings change to **ā** and **ā̃** respectively in the plural form:

ghoḍo horse	**ghoḍā** horses
chhāpũ newspaper	**chhāpā̃** newspapers

Some words can take on an additional **o** after the above changes, e.g. **ghoḍāo** and **chhapāo**. This additional ending is optional.

The words for pulses and grains are always in plural form although they carry no additional suffix:

ghaũ wheat, **chokhā** rice, **mag** moong beans

Other words used only in plural form are: **samāchār** news; **chashmā̃** glasses, spectacles; **mābāp** parents.

Simple present tense (with personal pronouns)

ho to be

Person	*Singular*	*Plural*
I	**hũ chhũ** I am	***ame chhie** we are
II	**tũ chhe** you are	**tame chho** you are
III	**te chhe** he, she, it is	**teo chhe** they are

Note: * Together with **ame** (we), Gujarati has another form **āpṇe** (we all), which includes all those present. English does not have an equivalent word.

Singular	*Plural*
– ũ	**– ie**
– e	**– o**
– e	**– e**

kar to do

I	**hũ karũ chhũ** I do	**ame karie chhie** we do
II	**tũ kare chhe** you do	**tame karo chho** you do
III	**te kare chhe** he/she/it does	**teo kare chhe** they do

bes to sit

I	**hũ besũ chhũ** I sit	**ame besie chhie** we sit
II	**tũ bese chhe** you sit	**tame beso chho** you sit
III	**te bese chhe** he/she/it sits	**teo bese chhe** they sit

The personal pronoun **tame** is also used as an *honorific plural* for a single person: e.g. in the dialogue at the beginning of this lesson, Gita and Ramesh address each other as **tame** (more in Unit 5).

Honorific plural

As a mark of respect the subject, even when in the singular, may take on a plural ending:

Normal: **gāndhi saras māṇas hato**
Gandhi was a good man
Honorific: **gāndhiji saras māṇas hatā**
Gandhiji was a good man

In this example the verb, in the past tense, third person singular **hato** changes to its plural form **hatā**. The suffix **ji** is an additional way of showing respect, after the name.

'Thank you'

'Thank you' is considered very formal in Gujarati and is rarely used in daily conversation. Instead, gestures such as a smile are employed. The word **ābhār** is generally used to thank people on formal occasions in public performances.

Additional vocabulary

garmi (*f*)	hot	**nathi**	is not (as opposed to **chhe** is)
nā	no	**thoḍũ**	little, less

Exercise 1

Fill in the blanks by translating the words in parentheses:

(a) **hũ** _____ (OK) **chhũ.**
(b) **ājkāl** _____ (hot) **bahu paḍe chhe.**
(c) **āj** _____ (cold) **nathi.**

Exercise 2

Translate into Gujarati:

(a) How is she?
(b) She is OK.
(c) It is very cold today.
(d) It is not hot today.
(e) I am working.
(f) She sits.

Exercise 3

Rearrange the following words to make Gujarati sentences:

(a) **chhe āje garmi**
(b) **paḍe bahu ṭhanḍi ājkāl chhe**
(c) **paṇ āvjo tame**
(d) **chhie ame karie**
(e) **bese teo chhe**
(f) **tũ chhe kare**

Dialogue 2

ગીતાને ઘેર રમેશ **Gitāne gher ramesh** Ramesh at Gita's home **(CD1; 16)**

Ramesh goes to Gita's house for the first time

ગીતા નમસ્તે રમેશભાઈ, આવો, બેસો.
રમેશ નમસ્તે ગીતાબેન, ઓહો! તમારું ઘર સરસ છે.
ગીતા હા, આ બેઠક ખંડ છે. બાજુમાં રસોડું છે. ઉપર પણ બે ઓરડાઓ છે.
રમેશ વાહ.
ગીતા આગળ બાગ છે અને પાછળ પણ ખુલ્લી જગા છે. ત્યાં શાકભાજી ઊગે છે.
રમેશ સરસ. તમારી જગા સરસ છે.

GITA namaste rameshbhāi, āvo, beso.
RAMESH namaste gitāben, oho! tamārũ ghar saras chhe.
GITA hā. ā beṭhak khanḍ chhe. bājumã̄ rasoḍũ chhe. upar paṇ be orḍāo chhe.
RAMESH vāh.
GITA āgaḷ bāg chhe ane pāchhaḷ pan khulli jagā chhe. tyā̃ shākbhāji uge chhe.
RAMESH saras. tamāri jagā saras chhe.

GITA *Hello, Rameshbhai. Welcome. Please take a seat.*
RAMESH *Hello, Gitaben. Wow! Your house is beautiful.*
GITA *This is the drawing room. The kitchen is next door. There are two rooms above (on the first floor).*
RAMESH *Lovely!*
GITA *There is a garden at the front and there is an open space at the back (also). The vegetables grow there.*
RAMESH *How nice! Your place is beautiful.*

Vocabulary

āv	come	**tyā̃**	there
bes	sit	**khulli**	open
ghar (*n*)	house	**shākbhāji**	vegetables
khanḍ (*m*)	room	**āgaḷ**	in front of
orḍo (*m*)	room	**pāchhaḷ**	at the back
beṭhak khanḍ (*m*)	sitting room	**upar**	above, up
rasoḍũ (*n*)	kitchen	**niche**	down, below
bāg (*m*)	garden	**bājumā̃**	next to
saras	good, beautiful	**mārũ**	my
be	two	**amārũ**	our
jagā (*f*)	space	**tamārũ**	your
ahī̃	here		

Grammatical notes

mā̃ is a case suffix meaning 'in': e.g. **gharmā̃** in the house.

માં (mā̃) **suffix**

(a) To show 'in':
kuvāmā̃ pāṇi nathi.
There is no water in the well.

(b) To show degree of comparison:
badhā̃ makānomā̃ ā sauthi saras chhe.
This is the best of all the houses.

Infinitive

The infinitive is formed by adding વું **(vũ)** to the root of the verb. The second person singular in the imperative form is always the root of the verb, e.g. આવ (**āv**) come, જો (**jo**) see; so આવવું (**āvvũ**), જોવું **(jovũ)**, ખાવું (**khāvũ**), પીવું (**pivũ**), હસવું (**hasvũ**), etc. are infinitives.

The second person singular of the present tense is the *root of the verb* and, as with English, also forms the imperative:

āvvũ	to come	**āv**	come/you come
besvũ	to sit	**bes**	sit/you sit

Adding **vũ** to the root forms the *infinitive* (see also Unit 6).

Word order and expansion

ā chhe	this is
ā ghar chhe.	This is a house.
ā mārũ ghar chhe.	This is my house.
ā mārũ saras ghar chhe.	This is my beautiful house.

In the above sentences the order is *subject*, *object, verb*.

Personal pronouns **mārũ**, **tāmārũ**, **temnũ**.

The possessive pronouns and adjectives are in agreement with the number and gender of the subject, 'house' (my, your, their).

Exercise 4

Fill in the blanks by translating the words in parentheses:

ā mārũ _____ (house) **chhe.** _____ (next) **rasoḍũ chhe.** _____ (at the back) **bāg chhe.** _____ (above) **orḍo chhe.** _____ (below) **beṭhak khanḍ chhe. bajumā̃** _____ (kitchen) **chhe. mārũ ghar** _____ (good) **chhe.**

Exercise 5

Choose the appropriate form from the square brackets to complete these sentences:

(a) **ā be** _____ (rooms) **chhe** [**orḍo, orḍāo**].
(b) **ā ghar saras** _____ (is not) [**chhe, nathi**].
(c) **gitāben,** _____ (welcome) [**āvjo, āvo**].
(d) **rameshbhai** _____ (goodbye) [**āvo, āvjo**].
(e) **ame kām karie** _____ (are) [**chhe, chhie**].
(f) **tame beso** _____ (are) [**chhe, chho**].

Exercise 6

Correct the mistakes in the following:

(a) **hũ gharmā̃ chhe.**
(b) **tame beṭhak khanḍmā̃ chhie.**
(c) **te pāchhaḷ chhũ.**
(d) **shākbhāji uge chho.**
(e) **tame paṇ jāḷavje.**
(f) **hũ karie chhie.**

Exercise 7

Translate into Gujarati:

(a) Raman is here.
(b) No, this is not the room.
(c) Yes, this is the kitchen.
(d) The garden is in front of the house.
(e) Gita is not in the house.
(f) Ramesh is in the garden.

Exercise 8

Match the following:

hũ	**chhie**
ame	**chho**
tũ	**chhe**
tame	**chhũ**

Exercise 9

Correct these sentences:

(a) **ghar tamārũ chhe saras.**
(b) **chhe upar orḍāo be.**
(c) **shākbhāji chhe uge pāchhaḷ.**
(d) **Ramesh chhe gharmā̃.**
(e) **nathi andar Gitā.**
(f) **shāk chhe tārũ ā.**

Unit Two

પોસ્ટ ઑફિસે **post Ophise**

At the post office

ફળની દુકાનમાં **phaḷni dukānmā̃**

At a fruit shop

In this unit you will learn about:

- More intimate greetings
- Formations in simple future
- Possessive case suffix (English's)
- Days of the week
- Asking and telling time

Dialogue 1

પોસ્ટ ઑફિસે **post Ophise** At the post office

(CD1; 19)

Suresh, an elderly man, meets his friend's teenage daughter, Rekha, at the post office

---

સુરેશ કેમ છે, રેખા?

રેખા ઓહો, સુરેશ કાકા કેમ છો? આ ભારત પાર્સલ મોકલું છું. મિનાને દિવાળીની ભેટ.

સુરેશ	સરસ. આજે મોકલીશ તો મોટે ભાગે દિવાળી સુધીમાં પહોંચી જશે.
રેખા	હા, આજે પાછો શનિવાર છે એટલે ઓફિસ બાર વાગે બંધ થશે.
સુરેશ	કાલે રવિવાર. આરામનો દિવસ.
રેખા	શાનો આરામ. ઘરની સફાઈ કરીશ. બાગકામ કરીશ. ઘણું કામ છે, કાકા.
સુરેશ	ચાલ ત્યારે, રેખા, આવજે.
રેખા	આવજો સુરેશકાકા.

SURESH	kem che, rekha?
REKHA	oho, sureshkākā, kem chho? ā bhārat pārsal moklũ chhũ. minā̃ne divāḷini bheṭ.
SURESH	saras. āje moklish to moṭe bhāge divāḷi sudhimā̃ pahÕchshe.
REKHA	ha! āje pāchho shanivār chhe eṭle Ophis bār vāge bandh thashe.
SURESH	kāle ravivār. ārāmno divas.
REKHA	shāno ārām. gharni saphāi karish. bāgkām karish. ghaṇũ kām che, kākā.
SURESH	chāl tyāre, rekhā, āvje.
REKHA	āvjo sureshkākā.

SURESH	*How are you, Rekha?*
REKHA	*Oh, Sureshkaka, how are you? I am sending this parcel to India. A Divali gift for Mina.*
SURESH	*Good. If you send it today it will probably reach there for Divali.*
REKHA	*Yes. And again, today is Saturday so the office will be closed at 12 noon.*
SURESH	*Tomorrow is Sunday, a day of rest.*
REKHA	*What rest! I will be cleaning the house* [lit. *I will do the cleaning of the house*], *and doing some gardening. There is too much to do, uncle.*
SURESH	*OK, Rekha. Goodbye.*
REKHA	*Goodbye, Sureshkaka.*

More intimate forms of address

Both because he is an elderly man and a friend of Rekha's father, it is customary for Suresh to be addressed by her as 'uncle'. Elderly women are addressed as **kāki** or **māshi**, both translated as 'auntie'.

Vocabulary

bhārat	India
pārsal (*m*)	parcel
moklū̃ chhū̃ (*n*)	am sending (**mokal** send)
divāḷi (*f*)	festival of the lights: an important religious celebration for Hindus, Jains and Sikhs. From Deepavali (Sanskrit), meaning array of lights.
bheṭ (*f*)	gift
saras	good
moṭe bhāge	most probably
sudhimā̃	until
pahÕchshe	will reach
Ophis (*f*)	office
eṭle	therefore
āje	today
kāle	tomorrow
pāchho	again
bār vāge	at 12 o'clock (noon)
bandh	close
ārām (*m*)	rest
divas (*m*)	day
shāno	(of) what
saphāi (*f*)	cleaning
bāgkām (*n*)	gardening
ghaṇū̃	much
kākā (*m*)	uncle (used in honorific plural form)

Grammatical notes

Simple future tense

kar	to do	
Person	*Singular*	*Plural*
I	**karish**	**karishũ/karshũ**
II	**karish**	**karsho**
III	**karshe**	**karshe**

Person	*Singular*	*Plural*
I	r* + **ish**	r + **ishũ/shũ**
II	r + **ish**	r + **sho**
III	r + **she**	r + **she**

Note: *r represents the root of the verb.

	Present	*Past*	*Future*
Habitual action	**te roj khāy chhe.** He eats daily.	**te roj khāto hato.** He ate daily.	**te roj khāshe.** He will eat daily.
Action in progress	**te khāy chhe.** He is eating.	**te khāto hato.** He was eating.	**te khāto hashe.** He will be eating.
Action completed	**teṇe khāi lidhũ chhe.** He has finished eating.	**teṇe khāi lidhũ hatũ.** He had finished eating.	**teṇe khāi lidhũ hashe.** He will have finished eating.
Action to take place	**te khāvāno chhe.** He (still) has to eat.	**te khāvāno hato.** He (still) had to eat.	**te khāvāno hashe.** He will (still) have to eat.

All these are examples of the third person masculine singular. The feminine and neuter forms change only in the past tense.

Case suffixes

The Sanskrit division of eight cases and their suffixes is no longer rigidly adhered to in Gujarati. Depending on the context the same suffix carries different meanings. Again, different suffixes may have the same meaning. Here are the more important case suffixes with their meanings:

Possessive case suffix: no, ni, nũ, nā, nā̃

This case suffix changes according to the number and gender of the object:

divāḷi*no* tahevār	festival (*m sg*)
divāḷi*ni* bheṭ	gift (*f sg*)
divāli*nũ* ghareṇũ	ornament (*n sg*)
divāli*nā* divaso	days (*m pl*)
divāli*nā̃* kāmo	works (*n pl*)

The feminine plural takes the same form as the singular, e.g. **divaḷi*ni* bheṭo.** The use of this case is the equivalent of an apostrophe s ('s) in English, meaning 'of'.

Exercise 1

Translate into Gujarati:

(a) This is a gift.
(b) I do gardening.
(c) He will reach Birmingham tomorrow.
(d) Today is Monday.
(e) Suleman will go to India.
(f) Rekha is in the house.

Exercise 2

Read the dialogue again and match the following:

bheṭ	**rajā**
ravivār	**rāt**
divas	**tahevār**

ghaṇũ	**ārām**
kām	**thoḍũ**
divāḷi	**saras**

Exercise 3

Fill in the blanks by translating the words in parentheses:

(a) **rameshni** ____ (health) **saras chhe**
(b) **chālo tyāre,** ____ (goodbye)
(c) ____ (in the garden) **phool uge chhe**
(d) **ramā** ____ (at eight o'clock) **pahÕchshe**
(e) **ā pārsal** ____ (tomorrow) **karish**
(f) **āj ramzan idni** ____ (holiday) **chhe**

Exercise 4

Correct the mistakes in the following sentences:

(a) **kem chhũ giṭāben?**
(b) **divāḷino bheṭ chho?**
(c) **parsal mokli chhe?**
(d) **saras. tũ āvjũ.**

Exercise 5

Write the verb *khā* (to eat) in the future tense in all three persons, singular and plural.

Exercise 6

Choose the correct words from the parentheses:

(a) **hũ majāmā̃ (chhũ/chhie)**
(b) **(rekhāni/rekhānũ) ghar saras chhe**
(c) **(sureshno/sureshni) ā̃kh bandh chhe**
(d) **ā (shilano/shilani) hāth chhe**
(e) **kāle ravivār (hashe/hashũ)**
(f) **ā Christmas bheṭ minā (no/ni/nũ) hashe**

Exercise 7

Rearrange the following words to make Gujarati sentences:

(a) **thanḍi paḍshe kāle**
(b) **moklũ ā england pārcel hũ chhũ**
(c) **kām chhie karie ame**
(d) **saphāi gharni rām chhe kare**
(e) **chhe kām ghaṇũ divāḷimā̃**
(f) **karish hũ ārām**

Dialogue 2

ફળની દુકાનમાં **phaḷni dukānmā̃** At a fruit shop
(CD1; 22)

Rekha goes to Maganbhai's shop to buy some fruit

રેખા	કેમ મગનભાઇ, શું તાજું છે?
મગનભાઇ	આવો રેખાબેન, આ કેરીઓ આજે જ આવી છે. સફરજન પણ તાજાં જ છે।
રેખા	આ દ્રાક્ષ મીઠી છે?
મગનભાઇ	તદ્દન મીઠી છે જાણે સાકરના કટકા।
રેખા	સાકરના કટકા જેવી તો તમારી જીભ છે. શું ભાવ છે?
મગનભાઇ	કિલોના સો રૂપિયા.
રેખા	બહુ મોંઘી. બીજે તો સસ્તી મળે છે.
મગનભાઇ	તો નેવું આપજો બસ? બે કિલો આપું?
રેખા	નારે એક કિલો બસ. બરાબર જોખશો।
મગનભાઇ	હા, બીજું કાંઈ?
રેખા	ના બીજું બધું તો છે. આવજો.
મગનભાઇ	આવજો.

REKHA	kem maganbhāi, shũ tājũ chhe?
MAGANBHAI	āvo rekhāben, ā kerio ājej āvi chhe. sapharjan paṇ tājā̃j chhe.
REKHA	a drāksh miṭhi chhe?
MAGANBHAI	taddan miṭhi chhe. jā ṇe sākarnā kaṭkā!
REKHA	sākarnā kaṭkā jevi to tamāri jibh chhe. shũ bhāv chhe?

MAGANBHAI pāūḍnā sitter pens.
REKHA bahu mÕghi. bije to sasti maḷe chhe.
MAGANBHAI to sāiṭh āpjo bas? be pāūd āpũ?
REKHA nāre, ek pāūḍ bas. barābar jokhsho.
MAGANBHAI hā. bijũ kāi?
REKHA nā. bijũ badhũ to chhe. āvjo.
MAGANBHAI āvjo.

REKHA *Hello, Maganbhai. Which (fruits) are fresh today?*
MAGANBHAI *Welcome, Rekhaben. These mangoes are fresh* [*have just arrived*]. *The apples are also fresh.*
REKHA *Are these grapes sweet?*
MAGANBHAI *Of course. As sweet as sugar cubes.*
REKHA *Your tongue is like sugar cubes. What's the price?*
MAGANBHAI *Seventy pence a pound.*
REKHA *That's expensive* [lit. *very costly*]. *It's cheaper elsewhere.*
MAGANBHAI *Then pay (give) me sixty pence, OK? Shall I give you two pounds?*
REKHA *Oh, no. One pound is enough. Weigh it correctly.*
MAGANBHAI *Yes. Anything else?*
REKHA *No. I have everything. Goodbye.*
MAGANBHAI *Goodbye.*

Vocabulary

phaḷ	fruit	**sākar**	sugar
kharidi	shopping	**kaṭkā**	pieces
dukān	shop	**bhāv**	rate
keri	mango	**mÕghi**	costly, expensive
sapharjan	apple	**sasti**	cheap
drāksh	grapes	**barābar**	properly, correctly
tājũ	fresh	**jokh**	weigh
miṭhũ	sweet		

Colloquial notes

The dialogues in this unit are more colloquial and informal than those in Unit 1. The customer, Rekha, and the shopkeeper, Magan, know each other quite well. A phrase like **sākarnā kaṭkā** (pieces of sugar, meaning very sweet) has been used to make the dialogue more natural. In normal dialogue the verb is sometimes omitted, e.g. **bahu mÕghi (chhe)** and **ek pāũḍ bas** (**chhe**).

Exercise 8

Pair off the words on the right with the appropriate ones on the left:

phaḷ	**miṭhi**
drāksh	**pāchhaḷ**
bhāv	**garmi**
mÕghi	**sitter pens**
agaḷ	**sasti**
ṭhanḍi	**tāju**

Exercise 9

List the following fruits in order of size (see the glossary for the meaning):

keri **drāksh** **nāḷiyer** **tarbuch**

Exercise 10

Which are the odd words in the following?

(a)	**sapharjan**	**magan**	**rekhā**	**ramesh**
(b)	**ravivār**	**shanivār**	**somvār**	**shākbhāji**
(c)	**bāg**	**ṭhanḍi**	**dukān**	**ghar**

Exercise 11

Read the following passage carefully and answer these questions in Gujarati:

(a) Who is going to Leicester? When?
(b) What will they do in Leicester?
(c) What will they do in Birmingham?

Pestanji ane Vipinbhāi kāle Leicester jashe. Dukānmā̃ jashe ane kharidi karshe. Birmingham paṇ jashe ane Ramaṇbhāine maḷshe.

Exercise 12

(a) **miṭhũ** means 'sweet'. Find out from the glossary the words for salty, bitter, sour, hot.
(b) **keri** means 'mango'. Find out the words for apple, orange, melon, lemon.

Exercise 13

Fill in the blanks using the appropriate verbal form:

hũ kāle savāre ___ (uṭh). nāsto ___ (kar). pachhi bahār ___ (jam). ayeshāben paṇ ___ (āv). ame philm ___ (jo). majā ___ (paḍ).

Asking and telling the time

keṭlā vāgyā chhe?	What time is it?
ek vāgyo chhe	it's one o'clock
be vāgyā chhe	it's two o'clock
traṇ vāgyā chhe	it's three o'clock
. . .	
bār vāgyā chhe	it's twelve o'clock

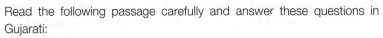

vāgvũ means 'to strike'.

savā means 'quarter past one' but is also used as 'quarter past . . .': e.g. **savābe** quarter past two; **savātraṇ** quarter past three, etc.

sāḍā is used for 'half past . . .': e.g. **sāḍa traṇ** half past three; **sāḍāchār** half past four, etc. (Note: *Do not* use the combination **sāḍā ek** or **sāḍā be**, as Gujarati has the separate words **doḍh**, meaning 'half past one', and **aḍhi** meaning 'half past two'.)

poṇā means 'three-quarters' and is used for 'quarter to . . .': e.g. **poṇā be** quarter to two; **poṇā tran** quarter to three, etc. (Another peculiarity is the use of **poṇo** for 'quarter . . . to one' rather than **poṇā ek**.)

Unit Three

સાથે ખરીદી કરવા **sāthe kharidi karvā**

Planning a shopping trip

ગુજરાતી શાકાહારી રેસ્ટોરંટમાં જમણ **gujrāti̱ shākāhāri resṭoranṭmā̃ jamaṇ**

Eating out in a Gujarati vegetarian restaurant

In this unit you will learn about:
• Negative formations in present and future tenses • Forming questions • Gujarati food

Dialogue 1

સાથે ખરીદી કરવા sāthe kharidi karvā Planning a shopping trip **(CD1; 25)**

Two girls, Rina and Rita, plan a shopping trip followed by dinner at a restaurant

રીના રીટા તું ક્યાં જાય છે?
રીટા શહેરમાં. તું સાથે આવીશ?
રીના હા હા, ચાલ પહેલાં થોડી ક્રિસમસની ખરીદી કરીશું પછી મંદિરમાં જમીશું.
રીટા શું? મંદિરમાં? કોના મંદિરમાં? કયા ધરમનું છે?
રીના રીટા એક સાથે કેટલા સવાલો પૂછીશ? સાંભળ એ નામની શાકાહારી રેસ્ટોરંટ છે. સરસ જમણ આપે છે.
રીટા કેટલું દૂર છે?
રીના અરે સ્ટેશનની પાસે જ છે. ઓક્સ્ફર્ડ સ્ટ્રીટમાં ખરીદી કરીશું ને ત્યાં જમીશું.

RINĀ tũ kyā̃ jāy chhe?
RITĀ shahermā̃. tũ sāthe āvish?
RINĀ hāhā. chāl. pahelā̃ thoḍi kristmasni kharidi karishũ. pachhi mandirmā̃ jamishu.
RITĀ shũ? mandirmā̃? konā mandirmā̃? kayā dharmnũ chhe?
RINĀ ritā, ek sāthe keṭlā savālo puchhish? sā̃bhaḷ. e nāmni shākāhāri resṭoranṭ chhe. saras jaman āpe chhe.
RITĀ dur chhe?
RINĀ are sṭeshanni pāsej chhe. oksphard sṭriṭmā̃ kharidi karishũ ne tyā̃ jamishũ.

RINĀ *Where are you going, Rita?*
RITĀ *To the city. Would you like to come with me?*
RINĀ *Of course! Come on. First we will do some Christmas shopping and then go for a meal at the Mandir.*
RITĀ *What? Mandir? The temple? Which temple?*
RINĀ *Rita, how many questions will you ask at a time? Listen, Mandir is the name of a vegetarian restaurant and they make good food there.*
RITĀ *How far is it?*
RINĀ *Oh, it's just near the station. We will do our shopping in Oxford Street and then go there and eat.*

Vocabulary

chāl	come on (*lit.* walk)	**keṭlā**	how many
shaher (*n*)	city	**savāl** (*m*)	question
sāthe	together	**āp**	give
pahelā̃	first	**dur**	far
thoḍi	a bit	**pāse**	near
pachhi	then	**are!**	oh!
mandir (*n*)	temple	**tyā̃**	there
shũ	what	**jam**	eat
konā	whose	**nām** (*n*)	name
kayā	which	**jamaṇ** (*n*)	meal
dharm (*m*)	religion	**puchh**	ask
kon	who	**sā̃bhaḷ**	listen

Grammatical notes

Asking questions

You can see from the dialogue that there are two ways of asking questions, either by *changing the intonation* as:

ā hāth chhe	This is a hand.
ā hāth chhe?	This is a hand?

Or by using the interrogative pronouns or adjectives. These words fall into two categories, variables and invariables. The variables change according to number and gender. The invariables, as their name indicates, always remain the same.

Variables

(a)	Which	**kayo**	**kai**	**kayũ**	**kayā**	**kayā̃**
		(*m sg*)	(*f sg/pl*)	(*n sg*)	(*m pl*)	(*n pl*)
(b)	What	**sho**	**shi**	**shũ**	**shā**	**shā̃**
		(*m sg*)	(*f sg/pl*)	(*n sg*)	(*m pl*)	(*n pl*)
(c)	How much/many	**ketlo**	**ketli**	**ketlũ**	**ketlā**	**ketlā̃**
		(*m sg*)	(*f sg/pl*)	(*n sg*)	(*m pl*)	(*n pl*)
(d)	What type of	**kevo**	**kevi**	**kevũ**	**kevā**	**kevā̃**
		(*m sg*)	(*f sg/pl*)	(*n sg*)	(*m pl*)	(*n pl*)

Invariables

kyā̃	where
kem	why, how
koṇ	who
kyāre	when

Examples

(a) **ā kayo rasto** (*m sg*) **chhe?**
Which is this road?
ā kai baju (*f sg*) **chhe?**
Which side is this?

ā kayũ kām (*n sg*) **chhe?**
What work is this? (*lit.* Which is this work?)
ā kayā māṇso (*m pl*) **chhe?**
Who are these men? (*lit.* Which are these men?)
ā kayā̃ gharo (*n pl*) **chhe?**
Which are these houses?

(b) **sho bhāv** (*m sg*) **chhe?**
What is the rate?
shi vāt (*f sg*) **chhe?**
What is the story?
Shũ kām (*n sg*) **chhe?**
What is the work?
shā bhāv (*m pl*) **chhe?**
What are the rates?
shā kāmo (*n pl*) **chhe?**
What are the jobs to be done? (*lit.* What works are there?)

(c) **keṭlo lot** (*m sg*) **joie chhe?**
How much flour do you need?
keṭli vār (*f sg*) **thashe?**
How much time will it take?
keṭlũ moṭũ makān (*n sg*) **chhe?**
How big is the house?
keṭlā orḍā (*m pl*) **chhe?**
How many rooms are there?
keṭlā jhāḍo (*n pl*) **chhe?**
How many trees are there?

(d) **kevo māṇas** (*m sg*) **chhe?**
What type of man is he?
kevi banāvaṭni ghaḍiyāḷ (*f sg*) **chhe?**
What type of watch is it?
kevũ kām (*n sg*) **chhe?**
What type of work is it?
kevā rastā (*m pl*) **banāve chhe?**
What type of roads (do) they build?
kevā̃ jhāḍo (*n pl*) **uge chhe?**
What type of trees are growing?

Exercise 1

Pair off the words in column A with those in column B:

A	*B*
saras	**be**
shaher	**dur**
shākāhāri	**gām**
pāse	**kharāb**
savāl	**mā̃sāhāri**
ek	**javāb**

Exercise 2

Which are the odd words out in the following:

(a)	**pahelā̃**	**pachhi**	**sāthe**	**shaher**
(b)	**thoḍū̃**	**ghaṇū̃**	**vadhāre**	**dharm**
(c)	**koṇ**	**sā̃bhaḷ**	**kayā**	**shū̃**

Exercise 3

Translate into Gujarati:

Where are you going, Ramesh? Is it very far? It is just near Victoria. I will do my shopping there.

Exercise 4

Correct the following:

ā kayo ghar chhe? pensilno shi bhāv chhe? ritāno nāk nānū̃ chhe paṇ ā̃kh moṭo chhe. tū̃ āvū̃ chhe?

Exercise 5

Make the appropriate rearrangements of the following words to make Gujarati sentences:

(a) **chhe shahernū̃ kayā?**
(b) **karishū̃ divāḷini kharidi thoḍi**
(c) **ā chhe mandir dharmnū̃ kayā?**
(d) **jaie chāl pahelā̃ shahermā̃.**

Exercise 6

Pose the questions to these answers:

(a) **ahī̃ jamaṇ āpe chhe.**
(b) **ā ritā chhe.**
(c) **prakāsh, gitā ane bhānu sāthe āve chhe.**
(d) **gharthi nishāḷ dur chhe.**

Dialogue 2

ગુજરાતી શાકાહારી રેસ્ટોરંટમાં જમણ **gujrāti shākāhāri resṭoranṭmā̃ jamaṇ** Eating out in a vegetarian restaurant **(CD1; 27)**

Rina and Rita have done their shopping and are now in the restaurant

---

રીના કેમ રીટા કેવી જગા છે?
રીટા સરસ છે. ભારતમાં જ છીએ એમ લાગે છે.
રીના હા, સંગીત પણ ભારતીય છે. રવિશંકરની સિતાર વાગે છે.
રીટા હું એમાં બહુ સમજતી નથી। ઓહો આ તો ઘણું છે. રોટલી, દાળ, ભાત, શાક, કઠોળ, ચટણી, રાઈતું, અથાણું, સમોસા અને મીઠાઈમાં શિખંડ પણ છે.
રીના બરાબર જમ. આખી થાળી જ મગાવી છે. બીજું કાંઈ જોઈએ છે?
રીટા ના રે આ જ વધારે છે. બધું ખૂટશે પણ નહી.

RINĀ kem ritā, kevi jagā chhe?
RITĀ saras chhe. jāṇe bhāratmā̃j chhie em lāge chhe.
RINĀ hā. sangit paṇ bhāratiy chhe. ravishankarni sitār vāge chhe.
RITĀ hũ emā̃ bahu samajti nathi. oho. ā to ghaṇũ chhe. roṭli, dāḷ, bhāt, shāk, kaṭhoḷ, chaṭni, rāitũ, athāṇũ, samosā, ane miṭhāimā̃ shikhanḍ paṇ chhe.
RINĀ barābar jam. ākhi thāḷij magāvi chhe. bijũ kāi joie chhe?
RITĀ nāre. āj vadhāre chhe. badhũ khuṭshe pan nahī̃.

RINĀ *Well, Rita, how do you like the place?*
RITĀ *It's very good. It feels like India.*

RINĀ *Of course. Even the music is Indian. It is Ravishankar's sitar.*

RITĀ *I don't know much about music. Wow! Chapati, lentil soup, rice, vegetables, pulses, chutney, salad, pickles, samosas. And there is even shikhand as a sweet.*

RINĀ *Eat well. I asked for the full Thali. Do you want anything else?*

RITĀ *No. Even this is too much. I can't eat all this.*

Vocabulary

jagā (*f*)	place
jāṇe	as if
bhārtiya	Indian (**Bharat** India)
sitār (*f*)	stringed instrument
vāg	play (musical instrument)
bahu	much

samajti nathi	don't follow
nathi	not
ghaṇū	much
roṭli (*f*)	Indian bread, chapati
dāḷ (*f*)	soup made from lentils
bhāt (*m*)	rice
shāk (*n*)	vegetables
chaṭni (*f*)	spicy hot paste, chutney
rāitū (*n*)	salad with yoghurt
athāṇū (*n*)	pickle
miṭhāi (*f*)	sweet (i.e. any sweet dish)
shikhanḍ (*m*)	a sweet made from yoghurt, sugar and dried fruits
barābar	properly
ākhi	full
magāvi	asked for
bijū kā̃i	anything else (*lit.* second something)
joie	want
vadhāre	much more
khuṭ vū̃	to finish
kaṭhoḷ (*n*)	pulses

Grammatical notes

Negation in present and future tenses

In the *present tense* the negation is shown by changing the verb **chhe** (is) to **nathi** (is not). But the important difference between the two constructions is that **chhe** changes into forms like **chhie, chho**, while **nathi** remains the same.

Person	*Singular*	*Plural*
I	**hū̃ chhū̃**	**ame chhie**
II	**tū̃ chhe**	**tame chho**
III	**te chhe**	**teo chhe**

Person	*Singular*	*Plural*
I	**hũ nathi**	**ame nathi**
II	**tũ nathi**	**tame nathi**
III	**te nathi**	**teo nathi**

In the **future tense** the negation is shown by adding the word **nahi** to the future form.

Person	*Singular*	*Plural*
I	**hũ hoish**	**amehoishũ/hashũ**
II	**tũ hoish/hashe**	**tame hasho**
III	**te hashe**	**teo hashe**

Person	*Singular*	*Plural*
I	**hu hoish nahĩ**	**ame hashũ/hoishũ nahĩ**
II	**tũ hoish/hashe nahĩ**	**tame hasho nahĩ**
III	**te hashe nahĩ**	**teo hashe nahĩ**

Exercise 7

Rearrange the following into four groups of four words connected by meaning:

roṭli	**kyā̃**	**bhāratiya**	**bhāt**
puchhish	**sangit**	**jamish**	**shũ**
sitār	**karish**	**keṭli**	**tablā̃**
dāḷ	**koṇ**	**āvish**	**shāk**

Exercise 8

Fill in the blanks by translating the words in parentheses:

ā sureshnũ ____ (house) **chhe. emā̃** ____ (six) **orḍā chhe. kāle tyā̃ rekha** ____ (will come). **rekhā** ____ (of India) **chhe. banne bahār** ____ (will go) **ane** ____ (shopping) **karshe.**

Exercise 9

Translate into Gujarati:

(a) This is a good house.
(b) Will you come with Rajesh?

(c) I will not go to London.
(d) Where is the room?

Exercise 10

Change the following into negative sentences:

(a) **sulemān paisādār chhe.**
(b) **hũ kāle āvish.**
(c) **rādha gharmā̃ chhe.**
(d) **teo kāle shahermā̃ āvshe.**

Exercise 11

Correct the following passage:

hũ emā̃ samajti nathi chhe. ghaṇi māṇas āvi chhe. kāle koṇ āv sho khabar. āje chhokrā paṇ jaish.

Exercise 12

Write a short dialogue in Gujarati on a visit to a restaurant.

Unit Four

ટેલિફોનમાં વાતચીત **ṭeliphonmā̃ vātchit**

Telephone conversation

કપડાંની દુકાને **kapḍā̃ni dukāne**

At a clothes shop

In this unit you will learn about:

- The simple past tense
- Transitive and intransitive verbs
- **ne** suffix as 'to'
- Adjectives: variable and invariable

Dialogue 1

ટેલિફોનમાં વાતચીત **ṭeliphonmā̃ vātchit**

Telephone conversation **(CD1; 30)**

Navin Patel is having a telephone conversation with his female friend, Naina Shah

નવીન હેલો નૈના, કાલે તું આખો દિવસ ક્યાં હતી?મેં આખો દિવસ ફોન કર્યો પણ જવાબ જ ન મળ્યો.

નૈના હેલો નવીન, ગઈ કાલે હું મામાને ત્યાં હતી. પણ મેં સાંજે તને ફોન કર્યો ત્યારે તું પણ ઘરમાં ન હતો.

નવીન હા. હું પછી બજારમાં ગયો. ખરીદી કરી. બહાર જ જમ્યો ને ઘેર રાતે મોડો આવ્યો.

નૈના ઓહો! શું ખરીદ્યું?

નવીન ખાસ કાંઈ નહીં. બે ખમીસ, બે પાટલૂન, હાથરૂમાલ અને મોજાં લીધાં. સસ્તાં અને સારાં હતાં. હાલમાં બજારમાં મંદી ચાલે છે એટલે બધે સેલ છે.

નૈના વાહ! તો હું પણ જઈશ. આવજે.

નવીન આવજે.

NAVIN hello nainā, kāle tũ ākho divas kyā̃ hati? mẼ ākho divas phon karyā paṇ javābaj na maḷyo.

NAINĀ hello navin. gai kāle hũ māmāne tyā̃ hati. paṇ mẼ sā̃je tane phon karyo tyāre tũ paṇ gharmā̃ na hato.

NAVIN hā. hũ pachhi bajārmā̃ gayo. kharidi kari. bahāraj jamyo ne gher rāte moḍo āvyo.

NAINĀ oho! shũ kharidyũ?

NAVIN khās kāi nahĩ. be khamis, be pāṭḷun, hāthrumāl ane mojā̃ lidhā̃. sastā̃ ane sarā̃ hatā̃. hālmā̃ bajārmā̃ mandi chhe eṭle badhe sel chāle chhe.

NAINĀ vāh! to hũ paṇ jaish. āvje.

NAVIN āvje.

NAVIN *Hello, Naina. Where were you yesterday? I phoned several times but there was no reply.*

NAINĀ *Hello, Navin. I was at* ***mama****'s [maternal uncle's] place yesterday. When I phoned you in the evening you were not at home either.*

NAVIN *Well, I went to the market and did some shopping. I also ate out and got home late.*

NAINĀ *I see. What did you buy?*

NAVIN *Oh, nothing in particular. Two shirts and two pairs of trousers, handkerchiefs and socks. They were good and cheap. With this recession there are sales everywhere.*

NAINĀ *Wow! In that case I'll say goodbye and go shopping myself.*

NAVIN *Goodbye.*

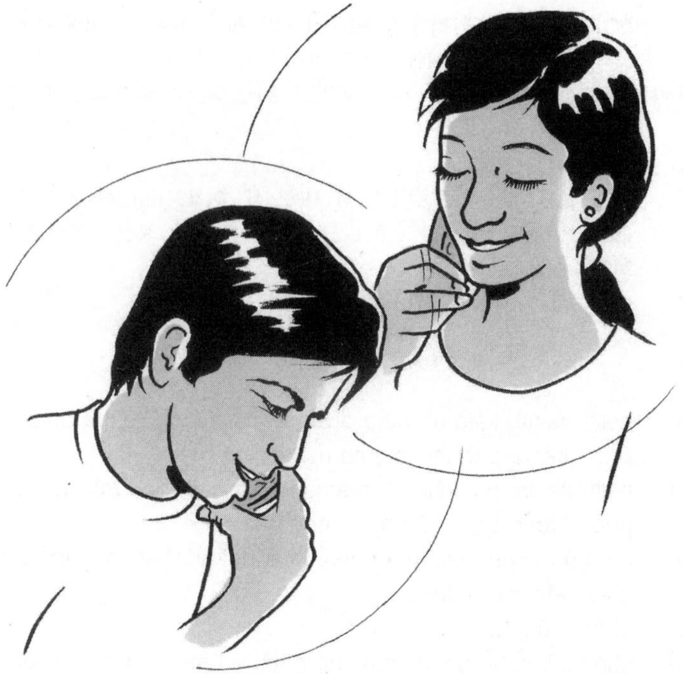

Vocabulary

ākho	whole
divas	day
sā̃j	evening
rāt	night
savāl	question
javāb	answer
māmā	uncle (mother's brother)
tyā̃	at (*lit*. there)
maḷyo	received (**maḷ** also means 'meet')
bajār	market
moḍo	late
khās	special
Kāi	something
nahī̃	not
hamṇā	nowadays, at the moment
khamis	shirt
pāṭlun	trousers
hāthrumāl	handkerchief
mojā̃	socks
hālmā̃	nowadays (same meaning as **hamṇā̃**)
mandi	recession
sel	sale
vāh!	wow!
khās kā̃i nahī̃	nothing in particular

Grammatical notes

Past tense

Unlike the simple present and simple future tenses the verbal forms in the past change according to the gender of the subject.

Intransitive verbs

chāl to walk

Person		*Singular*	*Plural*
I	Masculine	**hũ chālyo**	**ame chālyā**
	Feminine	**hũ chāli**	**ame chālyā̃**
	Neuter	**hũ chālyũ**	**ame chālyā̃**
II		**tũ chālyo** (*m*), **tũ chāli** (*f*), *etc.*	
III		**te chālyo** (*m*), **te chāli** (*f*), *etc.*	

You can see that the plural forms do not change much (except the nasalization at the end) and the forms are the same for all three persons. Compare this with the singular where the masculine forms end with **o** and the feminine and neuter end with **i** and **yũ** respectively.

Intransitive verbs do not require a direct object. Frequently used verbs like **uṭh** (get up), **doḍ** (run), **has** (laugh), **maḷ** (meet), **āv** (come), **shikh** (learn) and **bhaṇ** (study) employ the past tense in a similar way and are all intransitive verbs. The verb **jā** (go) becomes **gayo** in the past tense, i.e. **j** is converted to **g** throughout. Otherwise the same rule applies as with **chāl** above. So this first group of verbs are formed as follows:

Person	*Singular*	*Plural*
I, II, III	Masculine r* + **yo**	r + **yā**
	Feminine r + **i**	r + **yā̃**
	Neuter r + **yũ**	r + **yā̃**

Note: * r represents the root of the verb.

The verb **bes** (to sit) is changed to **beth** in the past tense and only gender suffixes are added, not the usual **y** suffix: **beṭho**, **beṭhi**, **beṭhũ**, etc.

The verb **ho** (to be) changes to **hat**, and again the gender suffixes are added rather than the past tense suffix **y**: **hato**, **hati**, **hatũ**, etc.

The verb **thā** (to become) changes to **tha** and then the past tense suffix **y** *and* the relevant gender suffixes are added: **thayo**, **thai** (and *not* **thayi**), **thayū**, etc.

All these verbs are intransitive, i.e. they do not require a direct object in the sentence.

Transitive verbs

Transitive verbs, which do require a direct object, have an additional feature in the past tense. The subject also undergoes a change in the ending and it is the number and gender of the object that determines the verb, not the subject:

mẼ koṭ (*m*)	**mukyo**	I put the coat
mẼ	**ṭopi** (*f*) **muki**	I put the cap
mẼ	**khamis** (*n*) **mukyũ**	I put the shirt

Changing the subject's gender or number makes no difference in the verb formation.

Transitive verbs also affect the personal pronouns:

Personal pronouns

Person	*Singular*	*Plural*
I	**hũ** becomes **mẼ**	**ame** remains the same
II	**tũ** becomes **tẼ**	**tame** remains the same
III	**te** becomes **teṇe**	**teo** becomes **temṇe/teoe**

Nouns used as subjects in transitive verbs add the suffix **e** in the past tense: e.g.

navine kāgaḷ (*m*) **lakhyo.** Navin wrote a letter.
naināe kāgaḷ (*m*) **vā̃chyo.** Naina read the letter.

Some of the most common transitive verbs are: **khā** (eat), **pi** (drink), **lakh** (write), **vā̃ch** (read), **jo** (see), **kar** (do), **dho** (wash), **muk** (put), **āp** (give), **le** (take).

The verbs **khā** and **pi** take **dh** and not **y** as a suffix in the past tense, *before* the number and gender suffix is added. As these are transitive verbs they agree with the object and not the subject.

mẼ lāḍvo (*m sg*) **khādho.** I ate a laddu.
mẼ lāḍvā (*m pl*) **khādhā.** I ate laddus.
mẼ roṭli (*f sg*) **khādhi.** I ate a chapati.
mẼ roṭlio (*f pl*) **khādhi.** I ate chapatis.
mẼ athāṇũ (*n sg*) **khādhũ.** I ate a pickle.
mẼ athāṇā̃ (*n pl*) **khādhā̃.** I ate pickles.

The verb is not affected if you change the personal pronouns **mẼ** to **tẼ**, **tame**, or proper nouns like **navine** or **naināe**.

The past tense for **pi** is conjugated in the same way: **pidho**, **pidhi**, **pidhũ**, etc.

Exercise 1

Change the following sentences into the past tense:

(a) **hũ āje lanḍanmā̃ chhũ.**
(b) **tũ kāle nishāḷmā̃ āvshe.**
(c) **tamāri pāse paisā chhe.**
(d) **satish latāne gher phon karshe.**
(e) **rehmān ane sakinā sāthe bhaṇe chhe.**

Exercise 2

Fill in the blanks with appropriate words:

āje ravivār (is) ____ **(chhe/chhie). gai kāle** (Saturday) ____ **(budhvār/shanivār) hato. āvti kāle somvār** (will be)____ **(hoishũ/hashe). āje hũ bahār** (will go) ____ **(jasho/jaish) ane bahāraj** (will eat) ____ **(jamshũ/jamish).**

Exercise 3

Translate into Gujarati:

(a) I purchased a pair of socks.
(b) I phoned you yesterday.
(c) William went to Ahmedabad.
(d) Reshma studied Gujarati in India.
(e) She will write a letter.
(f) I ate vegetables and rice.

Exercise 4

Rearrange the following to make Gujarati sentences:

(a) **chhũ hũ karũ kām ghaṇũ.**
(b) **nathi pāse kāgaḷ e tamāri.**
(c) **kāle khādhũ chikan salmāne saras.**
(d) **āvish tyā̃ māre kāle tũ?**
(e) **āvi tyāre surekhā hũ na gharmā̃ hato.**
(f) **jamyo pachhi nokare kapḍā̃ dhoyā̃ te.**

Exercise 5

Pair off the appropriate words in column A with those in column B.

A	*B*
bajār	**sā̃j**
khamis	**kāl**
savār	**pāṭlun**
āj	**kharidi**
gharmā̃	**bahār**

Exercise 6

Invent a simple telephone conversation in Gujarati (about six exchanges) inviting a friend for dinner.

Exercise 7

Correct the following passage:

tame māri sāthe āvti kāle āve chhe? hũ bajārmā̃ jasho. pachhi kharidi kartā ane sāthe jamyā. majā paḍyo.

Dialogue 2

કપડાંની દુકાને **kapḍā̃ni dukāne** At a clothes shop **(CD1; 33)**

Naina goes to a clothes shop.

દુકાનદાર નમસ્તે બેન આવો.

નયના નમસ્તે ભાઈ. હમણાં તો તમારી દુકાનમાં સેલ ચાલે છે, નહી? કંઈ નવું છે?

દુકાનદાર હાજી, આ નવી સાડીઓ છે. સુતરાઉ, રેશમી, ટેરિલિન, ટેરિકોટનમાં બધા રંગોમાં છે. ડિઝાઈન પણ નવી છે.

નયના સરસ. મારે રોજના વપરાશ માટે ટેરિકોટન જોઈએ છે. પણ બહુ મોંઘી નહીં હો.

દુકાનદાર આ જુઓ, કાલે જ માલ આવ્યો. સાવ નવી ડિઝાઈનો છે. રંગ પણ મજાના છે.

નયના હા, પણ આમાં આછા ગુલાબી રંગની નથી? આ તો બધા ઘેરા છે.

દુકાનદાર ઓહો! તમને આછો ગુલાબી રંગ ગમે છે. એમાં તો ઘણી ડિઝાઈન છે. ફૂલ અને પાન કેટલાં સુંદર લાગે છે? પોત પણ સરસ છે.

નયના હા, મને પણ સાડી ગમી. પણ સેલના ભાવમાં આપશોને?

દુકાનદાર અરે બેન આ તો તદ્દન નવો માલ છે. સેલની સાડીઓ તો પેલા વિભાગમાં છે. પણ તમને દસ ટકા વળતર આપીશ| ઘરાકનો સંતોષ એજ અમારો મુદ્રાલેખ છે.

નયના ભલે. આ આપો.

DUKĀNDĀR namaste ben. āvo.

NAINĀ namaste bhāi. hamṇā̃ to tamāri dukānmā̃ sel chhe, nahī̃? kā̃i navũ chhe?

DUKĀNDĀR hāji. ā navi sāḍio chhe. sutrāu, reshmi ṭerilin, ṭerikÕṭanmā̃ badha rangomā̃ chhe. dizāin paṇ navi chhe.

NAINĀ saras. māre rojnā vaprāsh māṭe ṭerikOṭan joie chhe. paṇ bahu mÕghi nahī̃ hõ.

DUKĀNDĀR ā juo. kālej māl āvyo. sāv navi dizāino chhe. rang paṇ majānā chhe.

NAINĀ hā. paṇ āmā̃ āchhā gulābi rangni nathi? āto badhā ghErā chhe.

DUKĀNDĀR oho! tamne āchho gulābi rang game chhe. emā̃ to ghaṇi ḍizāin chhe. phool ane pān keṭlā̃ sundar lāge chhe. pot paṇ saras chhe.

NAINĀ hā! mane paṇ ā sāḍi gami. paṇ selnā bhāvmā̃ āpshone?

DUKĀNDĀR are ben, ā to taddan navo māl chhe. selni sāḍio to pelā vibhāgmā̃ chhe. paṇ tamne das ṭakā vaḷtar āpish. gharākno santosh ej amāro mudrālekh chhe.

NAINĀ bhale. ā āpo.

SHOPKEEPER	*Hello. Welcome.*
NAINA	*Hello. There is a sale on in your shop, isn't there? Have you anything new?*
SHOPKEEPER	*Yes, madam. There are some new sarees. They are available in cotton, silk, terylene and terycotton in all colours. Even the designs are new.*
NAINA	*Excellent. I want something in terycotton for daily use, but not too expensive.*
SHOPKEEPER	*Have a look at these. They have just arrived. The designs are completely new and the colours are lovely.*
NAINA	*Yes, but haven't you got something in light pink? These are very dark colours.*
SHOPKEEPER	*Oh, I see. You like light pink. We have many designs in that colour. This one with flowers and leaves is beautiful. The texture of the cloth is excellent.*
NAINA	*Yes, I prefer this. But I would like it at sale price.*
SHOPKEEPER	*Madam, this is a new line. The sarees on sale are in the other section. But I will give you a 10 per cent discount. Customers' satisfaction is our motto.*
NAINA	*OK. Give me this one.*

Vocabulary

navũ	new
sutrāu	made of cotton (**sutar** cotton)
reshmi	made of silk (**resham** silk)
ṭerilin	terylene
ṭerikoṭan	terycotton
rang	colour
dizāin	design
rojnā vaprāsh maṭe	for daily use
roj	daily
vaprāsh	use
māṭe	for
mÕghi	costly, expensive
māl	goods

āvyo	received (**āv** come)
sāv	completely, totally
majānā	lovely, enchanting
āchhā	light
ghErā	dark
gulābi	pink
phool	flower
pān	leaves
pot	texture
gami	liked (**gam** like)
bhāv	rate
taddan	completely, totally
pelā	that
ṭakā	per cent
vaḷtar	concession
gharāk	customer
santosh	satisfaction
bhale	OK, all right
mudrālekh	motto
oho!	I see!
are!	oh dear!
dukāndār	shopkeeper (**dukān** shop)

Colloquial notes

Notice that the shopkeeper adds **ji** to the word **hā**. This is the polite form and is also used to show respect for the elderly or those who are especially revered:

mā tā ji	mother
pi tā ji	father
rā jā ji	king
si tā ji	the goddess Sita

The suffix **ne** after **āpsho** emphasizes the request. It is colloquial and mainly used in the future tense to make a polite request, as in:

ja sho ne.	Would you please go.
kar sho ne.	Would you please do.
le sho ne.	Will you please take it.

Grammatical notes

However, the **ne** suffix is more frequently used as a case suffix to express the 'to' form:

navinne	to Navin
dukāndārne	to shopkeeper
naināne	to Naina

(ne) suffix

(a) To show the object:

ramesh rāmne jue chhe.
Ramesh sees Ram.

(b) To show the act of giving:

te garibone dān āpe chhe.
He gives alms to the poor.

(c) To express the meaning 'for':

latāne jamvāne bolāvo.
Call Lata for dinner

The adjectives

The adjectives **navo** (new), **mÕgho** (costly), **majāno** (good), **āchho** (light in colour), **ghEro** (dark in colour), **ghaṇo** (much) are all *variable* and the ending changes according to the number and gender of the qualifier:

navo māl (*m sg*)	new goods
navi sāḍi (*f sg*)	new saree

navũ kāpaḍ (*n sg*) new cloth
navā̃ kapḍā̃ (*n pl*) new clothes

Adjectives like **saras** (very good) and **sundar** (beautiful) are *invariables* and so can be used for all numbers and genders without changing.

1 **saras** good, **kharāb** bad, **naram** soft are all invariable.

sundar	**chhokro** good boy	**chhokrāo** good boys
sundar	**chhokri** good girl	**chhokrio** good girls
sundar	**chhokrũ** good child	**chhokrāo** good children

Here the adjective does *not* change with the number and gender of the noun it qualifies.

2 **sāro** good, **moṭo** big, **kāḷo** black are some examples of the *variable* form where the adjective is influenced by number and gender.

sāro chhokro good boy
sāri chhokri good girl
sārũ chhokrũ good child, etc.

They are marked as (v) or (inv) in the glossary at the end of the book.

Exercise 8

Translate into English:

krismasno sel kāle sharu thashe. ghaṇi navi sāḍio paṇ hashe. pachis ṭakā vaḷtar maḷshe. gayā varse paṇ sel hato paṇ temā̃ vaḷtar ochhũ hatũ. to paṇ kharidi vadhu hati. ā varse mandi chhe eṭle loko kharidtā nathi.

Exercise 9

Write six Gujarati sentences about what you will do tomorrow.

Exercise 10

Rearrange the following into four groups of four words connected by meaning:

ahĩ	**reshmi**	**divas**	**upar**
terikOṭan	**āvshe**	**ṭerilin**	**jashe**

sā̃j	**sutrāu**	**savār**	**āvyo**
rāt	**niche**	**gayo**	**tyā̃**

Exercise 11

Change the following as indicated:

(a) **mane ā rang gamto nathi.** (affirmative)
(b) **āje bajārmā̃ sel chhe.** (negative)
(c) **ā naināṇū ghar hatū.** (future)
(d) **gai kāle navin bahār jamyo.** (future)
(e) **ā ramaṇlālni dukān chhe.** (question)
(f) **dukāndār sāḍi vechshe.** (present)

Exercise 12

Write full answers to the questions below after reading the passage which follows:

(a) **vipine kone sāthe lidhi?**
(b) **banne kyā̃ gayā̃?**
(c) **shā māṭe rehmānne tyā̃ gayā̃?**
(d) **temṇe rehmānne shū̃ āpyū̃?**

vipin sā̃je gher gayo. sarlāne sāthe lidhi. banne rehmānne tyā̃ gayā̃. rehmān mā̃do hato. teni khabar puchhi. phaḷ apyā̃. pachhi banne gher āvyā̃.

Unit Five

સ્ટેશન તરફ **sṭeshan taraph**

Towards the station

સ્ટેશન પર **sṭeshan par**

At the station

In this unit you will learn about:

- The three simple tenses (revision)
- Asking and receiving directions
- Duplicative forms
- **ja** for emphasis
- Personal pronouns with suffixes

Dialogue 1

સ્ટેશન તરફ **sṭeshan taraph** Towards the station
(CD1; 36)

Jenny, an American tourist, asks a young woman, Vanita, for directions to the station

---

જેની માફ કરજો બેન, પણ સ્ટેશનનો રસ્તો કયો છે?

વનિતા અહીંથી સીધા જશો એટલે ચાર રસ્તા આવશે. ત્યાં ડાબી બાજુ વળી જશો. પછી થોડું ચાલશો એટલે જમણી બાજુ રમતનું મેદાન

	દેખાશે. એ મેદાન પૂરું થાય એટલે ચાર રસ્તા આવશે. ત્યાં રસ્તો ઓળંગશો અને જમણી બાજુ જશો. સામે જ સ્ટેશન છે.
જેની	બહુ દૂર છે? બસ મળશે?
વનિતા	ના, ના. પાસે જ છે. બસ મળશે પણ વાર લાગશે. એક બસ હમણાં જ ગઈ.
જેની	એમ. તો પહેલાં સીધા,પછી ડાબી બાજુ ને પછી જમણી બાજુ, બરાબર?
વનિતા	હા. તમે બરાબર યાદ રાખ્યું. આવજો.
જેની	આભાર. બેન આવજો.

JENI	māph karjo ben, paṇ sṭeshanno rasto kayo chhe?
VANITĀ	ahĩthi sidhā jasho eṭle chār rastā āvshe. tyā̃ ḍābi bāju vaḷi jasho. pachhi thoḍũ chālsho eṭle jamṇi bāju ramatnũ medān dekhāshe. e medān purũ thāy eṭle pāchhā chār rastā āvshe. tyā̃ rasto oḷangsho ane jamṇi bāju jasho. sāmej sṭeshan chhe.
JENI	bahu dur chhe? bas maḷshe?
VANITĀ	nā, nā. pāsej chhe. bas maḷshe paṇ vār lāgshe. ek bas hamṇā̃j gai.
JENI	Em. to pahelā̃ sidhā, pachhi ḍābi bāju ne pachhi jamṇi bāju, barābar?
VANITĀ	hā. tame barābar yād rākhyũ. āvjo.
JENI	ābhār, ben. āvjo.

JENNY	*Excuse me, but which road do I take for the station?*
VANITĀ	*Go straight ahead until you reach the crossroads then turn left. Walk a little way and you will find a big playground on the right. At the end of the playground you will find another crossroads. Go straight across, and turn right and walk a little further. You will see the station just opposite.*
JENNY	*It is very far? Can I take a bus?*
VANITĀ	*Oh, no. It's quite near. You can get a bus but it will take time. You have just missed one* [lit. *one bus has just left*].
JENNY	*I see. So I first go straight ahead, then take the left and then the right.*
VANITĀ	*Yes, that's right* [lit. *you have remembered correctly*]. *Goodbye.*
JENNY	*Thanks. Goodbye.*

Vocabulary

māph karjo	excuse me	**dekhāshe**	will see
rasto	road	**purũ**	complete
sidhā	straight	**pāchhā**	again
chār rastā	crossroads (*lit.* four roads)	**oḷang**	cross
ḍābi bāju	on the left (*lit.* left side)	**vār lāgshe**	will take time
jamṇi bāju	on the right (*lit.* right side)	**barābar**	OK
ramatnũ medān	playground (**ramat** play)	**yād**	remember
		ābhār	thank you

Grammatical notes

Duplicative forms

Gujarati contains a peculiarity that has to be learned. It is the repetition or addition of words. This odd form sometimes supplements the original meaning, sometimes is used for emphasis and even occasionally changes the meaning altogether. It can be an 'echo' word, or it can be a seemingly meaningless word (although with a similar sound to the original), or even a different word with an extended meaning.

In the dialogue later in this unit you will find the sentence:

ahī̃ shũ shũ joyũ?

Literally: Here what what (you) saw?
Meaning: How many (places) did you see?

In the same dialogue is the sentence **ṭikiṭ kyā̃ maḷshe?** meaning 'Where will I get the ticket?' If you duplicate the word **kyā̃** to form **ṭikiṭ kyā̃ kyā̃ maḷshe** it means 'From how many places will I (be able to) get the ticket?' This is an important feature of Gujarati grammar. The various forms of repetition result in different meanings.

(a) Where the repeated word differs from the original in that the first letter is changed to બ (**b**): e.g. **pāṇibāṇi** meaning 'water *or something like that*'. In this example **bāṇi** in itself is meaningless but by changing the first letter of the preceding word it takes on the meaning of 'something similar' to that word.
(b) Repetition of a different word for emphasis: e.g. **mojmajā** '*great* enjoyment'. Here **moj** has the same meaning as **maja** but joining them together emphasizes the enjoyment.
(c) Where a word which has no individual meaning is added to give the sense of 'etcetera', e.g. **ḍhorḍhā̃khar**: here the word **ḍhor** means 'cattle', **ḍhā̃khar** has no meaning but, combined, the two words carry the sense of 'cattle *and the like*'; and **vāsaṇ kusaṇ**: **vāsaṇ** means 'utensils', **kusaṇ** has no meaning but, joined with **vāsaṇ**, it means 'utensils and things like that'.

ja

Notice the use of **ja** in **pāsej** and **hamnā̃j**. (When attached to a word the final **a** is dropped.) The word **pāse** means 'near' but when **ja** is added it means 'very near' or 'just near'. **hamṇā̃** means 'now' but the addition of **ja** turns it into 'just now'.

hū̃ gharmā̃ chhū̃. I am at home (*lit.* I am in the home).
hū̃ gharmā̃j chhu. I am *definitely* at home.
te gharmā̃ nathij. He is *definitely* not at home.
ā khamis ā dukānmā̃j maḷshe. (You) will find this shirt *only* in this shop.

If you change the position of **ja** in a sentence then the emphasis, and thus the meaning, also changes:

ā rasto kharāb chhe. This is a bad road.
āj rasto kharāb chhe. Only this road is bad (whereas others are good).
ā rastoj kharāb chhe. It is only the road which is bad (implying the *car* is good).
a rasto kharābaj chhe. This road is particularly bad (and others may be better).
a rasto kharāb chhej. This road is undoubtedly bad (whatever has been said to the contrary).

The stress on the above sentences is always on the word to which **ja** is added.

Exercise 1

Pair off the words in column A with the appropriate ones in column B, having regard to gender and number:

A	*B*
moṭũ	**rasto** (*m sg*)
ghaṇi	**phulo** (*n pl*)
nāno	**baheno** (*f pl*)
sārā̃	**sāḍi** (*f sg*)
āchhā	**medān** (*n sg*)
kāḷi	**rango** (*m pl*)

Exercise 2

Someone asks you the way to the shopping centre. Using the following words write five sentences giving him/her directions.

ahī̃ **tyā̃thi** **sidhũ** **ḍabi** **jamṇi** **pachhi**

Exercise 3

Translate into English:

somvāre sā̃je hũ bahār nikḷyo tyāre varsād na hato. ṭhaḍi paṇ bahu na hati. rastāni banne bāju saras jhāḍ hatā̃. hũ ghaṇũ chālyo. pachhi ek jagāe kOphi pidhi. pāchho pharyo tyāre rātnā nav vāgyā hatā.

Exercise 4

Make sense of the following by rearranging the words:

MEGI jashũ bahār banne? āpṇe
JON jarur hā chālo paṇ? jashũ kyā̃
MEGI bāju? rāṇinā jashũ mahel āpṇe
JON paṇ hā loko ghaṇa hashe tyā̃
MEGI jagā to chhe kevi? mandirni voṭphardnā
JON hā chhe saras shānt ane jagā e chālo

Exercise 5

Using the past tense, describe in five sentences your visit to a restaurant.

Exercise 6

Fill in the blanks by translating the words in parentheses:

(a) **ā** ____ (one) **vākyamā̃** ____ (three) **bhulo chhe.**
(b) **tamārā gharthi mandir** ____ (how much) **dur chhe?**
(c) ____ ____ (on the left) **vaḷsho eṭle sṭeshan dekhāshe.**
(d) **ṭikiṭ Ophis** ____ (where) **chhe?**
(e) **lanḍanni bas** ____ (from where) **maḷshe?**

Exercise 7

Correct the mistakes in the following passage:

māri pāse ghar chho. tāri pāse ghar nathi chho. hũ kerini ras pidhũ. sitā sṭeshan gayũ nathi? gāḍi moḍo chhe ne bas vahelũ chhe. ame besish.

Dialogue 2

સ્ટેશન પર **sṭeshan par** At the station **(CD1; 38)**

Jenny reaches the station and asks for further directions

જેની	માફ કરજો ભાઈ, વડોદરાની ટિકિટ કયાં મળશે?
ચિમનલાલ	મને ખબર નથી બેન, પણ આ સામે ટિકિટબારીઓ છે ત્યાં પૂછશો તો વડોદરાની ટિકિટની બારી કોઈ પણ બતાવશે.
જેની	ભલે. આભાર.

[જેની ટિકિટબારીઓ પાસે જાય છે.]

જેની	માફ કરજો બેન, વડોદરાની ટિકિટ કયાં મળશે?
સકિના	ચાર નંબરની બારી પર. તમે પરદેશી છો?
જેની	હા, હું અમેરિકન છું.
સકિના	એમ. સરસ. અહીં શું શું જોયું?
જેની	હું અમેરિકાથી સીધી દિલ્લી આવી. ત્યાંથી આગ્રા, હરદ્વાર. પછી અહીં અમદાવાદ આવી. એક અઠવાડિયું ગુજરાતમાં ફરીશ પછી દક્ષિણ ભારત જઈશ.

સકિના અમારો દેશ સરસ છે. તમને મજા પડશે. પૂર્વ અને પશ્ચિમ ભારત પણ ન ચૂકશો. આવજો.

જેની ચોક્કસ. આભાર. આવજો.

JENI māph karjo bhāi, vaḍodrāni ṭikiṭ kyā̃ maḷshe.

CHIMANLAL mane khabar nathi ben, paṇ ā sāme ṭikiṭbārio chhe tyā̃ puchhsho to vaḍodrāni ṭikiṭni bāri koipaṇ batāvshe.

JENI bhale. ābhār.

[*jeni ṭikiṭbārio pāse jāy chhe*]

māph karjo ben, vaḍodrāni ṭikiṭ kyā̃ maḷshe?

SAKINA chār nambarni bāri par. tame pardeshi chho?

JENI hā. hũ amerikan chhũ.

SAKINA em. saras. ahī̃ shũ shũ joyũ?

JENI hũ amerikāthi sidhi dilli āvi. tyā̃thi āgra, haradvār. pachhi ahī̃ amdāvād āvi. ek aṭhvāḍiyũ gujrātmā̃ pharish pachhi dakshiṇ bhārat jaish.

SAKINA amāro desh saras chhe. tamne majā paḍshe. purva ane pashchim bhārat paṇ na chuksho. āvjo.

JENI chokkas. ābhār. āvjo.

JENNY *Excuse me. Where can I get a ticket for Baroda?*

CHIMANLAL *I don't know, but can you see those ticket windows? Just go and ask. Someone will tell you* [lit. *anyone will show you*].

JENNY *Right. Thanks.*

[Jenny goes to the ticket windows]

Excuse me. Where can I get a ticket for Baroda?

SAKINA *At window 4. Are you a foreigner?*

JENNY *Yes. I'm American.*

SAKINA *Oh, how nice!* [typical Gujarati response] *Where have you been in India?* [lit. *What places have you seen?*]

JENNY *I came straight to Delhi. Then I went to Agra and Haradvar and then came here to Ahmedabad. I will be travelling around Gujarat for a week and then I go south.*

SAKINA *Our country is beautiful. You will enjoy it here. Don't miss the eastern and western parts of India. Goodbye.*

JENNY *Certainly. Thanks. Goodbye.*

Vocabulary

khabar nathi	don't know (**khabar** news)
koi paṇ	anybody
batāv	show
pardeshi	foreigner
aṭhvāḍiyũ	week
phar	move
uttar	north
dakshiṇ	south
purva	east
pashchim	west
desh	country
chuk	miss
chokkas	certainly

Grammatical notes

Pronouns

Gujarati has the same pronouns as are found in English: personal, demonstrative, indefinite, relative, interrogative, reflexive and reciprocal.

All pronouns agree in number, gender and person with the words they qualify.

Personal

The personal pronouns take case suffixes or, as in English, change form completely. Here they are in all three persons and numbers:

hũ I (first person singular)

hũ kām karũ chhũ. I am doing the work.

***mane** to me*

mane kām āpo. Give me work.

***mẼ** I* (used in past tense for transitive verbs; see Unit 4)

mẼ kām karyũ. I did the work.

***māre** by me*

ā kām māre karvānũ chhe? Is this work to be done by me?

***mārāthi** by me* (in passive voice)

mārāthi ā kām thashe nahĩ. The work will not be done by me.

***mārũ** my*

ā mārũ kām chhe. This is my work.

***mārāmā̃** in me*

mārāmā̃ shi khāmi chhe? Does the fault lie in me? (*lit.* what fault is in me?)

ame we (first person plural)

ame is the plural form of **hũ** and all the above follow the same rule: **ame, amne, ame, amāre, amārāthi, amārũ** and **amārāmā̃**.

tũ you (second person singular)

Following the rule the second person singular, **tũ**, becomes **tane, tẼ, tāre, tārāthi, tārũ, tārāmā̃.**

Gujarati maintains the second person singular form **tũ** (thou), which is no longer used in English.

tame *you* (second person plural)

The second person plural, **tame**, follows the same pattern as that for the first person plural: **tamne, tame, tamāre, tamārāthi, tamārũ, tamārāmā̃**.

te *he, she, it* (third person singular)

te kām kare chhe. He/she/it is doing the work.

tene *to him, her, it*
tene kām āpo. Give him/her/it work.

teṇe *he, she, it* (used in the past tense for transitive verbs: see Unit 4)
teṇe kām karyũ. He/she/it did the work.

tenāthi *by him, her, it* (in the passive voice)
tenāthi ā kām thashe nahī̃. The work will not be done by him/her/it.

tenũ *his, hers, its*
a tenũ kām chhe. This work is his/hers (This is its work).

tenāmā̃ *in him, her, it*
tenāmā̃ shi khāmi chhe? What fault lies in him/her/it?

teo *they* (third person plural)

teokām kare chhe. They are doing the work.

temne *to them*
temne kām āpo. Give the work to them.

temṇe *they* (used in past tense for transitive verbs)
temṇe kām karyũ. They did the work.

temnāthi *by them* (in the passive voice)
temnāthi ā kām thashe nahī̃. The work will not be done by them.

temnũ *their*
a temnũ kām chhe. This is their work.

temnāmā̃ *in them*
temnāmā̃ shi khāmi chhe? What fault lies in them?

Demonstrative

ā this
pelo (*m*) that
peli (*f*) that
pelũ (*n*) that
ā these
pelā (*m*) those
peli (*f*) those
pelā̃ (*n*) those

Indefinite

keṭlũk something, **sau** all, **darek** everyone – for all genders and numbers

Relative

je . . . te that, **jevũ . . . tevũ** whichever – for all genders and numbers

Interrogative

koṇ who
kayo (*m sg*)
kai (*f sg*)
kayũ (*n sg*)
kayā(*m pl*)
kai (*f pl*)
kayā̃ (*n pl*) which
shũ what – for all genders and numbers

Reflexive

jāte self, **pote** self

The above reflexive forms remain the same in all numbers and genders and are interchangeable. The meaning of myself, yourself, herself, etc. is understood by the subject:

hũ jāte karũ chhũ. I do it *myself*.
teo jāte kare chhe. They do it *themselves*.

Reciprocal

ekbijā; arasparas; ekmek . . . all meaning 'one another' or 'each other'.

Personal pronouns with suffixes

Singular

I	**hũ** (I)	**mane** (to me)	**mārāthi** (by me)	**māro** (*m*) **māri** (*f*) **mārũ** (*n*) (my)	**mārāmā̃** (in me)	**mẼ** (I) (for transitive verbs in the past tense)
II	**tũ** (you)	**tane** (to you)	**tārāthi** (by you)	**taro** (*m*) **tari** (*f*) **tarũ** (*n*) (your)	**tārāmā̃** (in you)	**tẼ** (you) (for transitive verbs in the past tense)
III (he, she, it)	**te** (to him/her/it)	**tene** (by him/her/it)	**tenāthi** **teni** (*f*)	**teno** (*m*) (in him/her/it) **tenũ** (*n*) (his/hers/its)	**tenāmā̃** (you)	**teṇe** (for transitive verbs in the past tense)

Plural

I	**ame** (we)	**amne** (to us)	**amārāthi** (by us)	**amāro** (*m*) **amāri** (*f*) **amārũ** (*n*) (our)	**amārāmā̃** (in us)	**ame** (we) for transitive verbs in the past tense also (*no* change)

II	**tame** (you)	**tamne** (to you)	**tamārāthi** (by you)	**tamāro** (*m*) **tamāri** (*f*) **tamārũ** (*n*) (your)	**tamārāmā̃** (in you)	**tame** (you) for transitive verbs in the past tense also
					(*no* change)	
III	**teo** (they)	**teone/ temne** (to them)	**teothi/ temnāthi** (by them)	**teono/ temno** (*m*) **teoni/ temni** (*f*) **teonũ/ temnũ** (*n*) (their)	**teomā̃/ temnāmā̃** (in them)	**teoe/ temṇe** (they) (for transitive verbs in the past tense)

Exercise 8

Rearrange the following in four groups of four words connected by meaning:

be	**uttar**	**sidhũ**	**tyā̃**
phar	**purva**	**bes**	**chāl**
sāme	**pā̃ch**	**dakshiṇ**	**ahī̃**
doḍ	**chār**	**pashchim**	**nav**

Exercise 9

Translate into Gujarati:

(a) I don't know whether there is a train today.
(b) Where can I get some good shirts?
(c) I will see beautiful places in this country.

(d) There are good playgrounds in Gujarat.
(e) My food was good but the coffee was very bad.
(f) Do you have much rain here?

Exercise 10

Find the odd word in each group:

(a)	**hāth**	**pag**	**nāk**	**rasto**
(b)	**roṭli**	**divas**	**dāḷ**	**bhāt**
(c)	**kāle**	**māmā**	**mātā**	**pitā**
(d)	**bolyo**	**phuṭbOl**	**bolshe**	**bolish**

Exercise 11

Change the following sentences as indicated:

(a) **medānno rasto kayo hashe?** (past)
(b) **ahī̃thi chār rastā keṭlā dur chhe?** (future)
(c) **āje gāḍio bandh hati.** (present)
(d) **hũ somvāre jamũ chhũ.** (negative)
(e) **rasto oḷangine ḍābi bāju na jasho.** (affirmative)

Exercise 12

Using the simple future tense, describe in five sentences what you would do if you win a jackpot.

Unit Six

હોટેલમાં **hoṭelmā̃**

At the hotel

જોવાલાયક જગ્યાઓ **jovā lāyak jagyāo**

Places worth visiting

In this unit you will learn about:

- Imperative forms (કર **kar**, જો **jo**)
- Use of future forms for polite requests (like કહેશો **kahesho**, જશો **jasho**)
- Auxiliary verbs (like જોઈએ છે **joie chhe**) and infinitives (like કરવું **karvũ**)
- Present, past and future perfect

Dialogue 1

હોટેલમાં **hoṭelmā̃** At the hotel **(CD1; 42)**

Jenny goes to Ahmedabad station, buys a ticket, reaches Baroda and gets a room in a hotel

---

જેની મને વડોદરાની એક ટિકિટ આપશો. કેટલા પૈસા થશે? મારી પાસે પચાસ રૂપિયાની નોટ છે.

ક્લાર્ક પંદર રૂપિયા પચાસ પૈસા. આ લો ટિકિટ અને પરચુરણ. બરાબર ગણી લેશો.

જેની હા. અને ગાડી ક્યા પ્લેટફોર્મ ઉપરથી અને ક્યારે ઊપડશે તે જરા કહેશો?

ક્લાર્ક હા જી. ગાડી ચાર નંબરના પ્લેટફોર્મ પરથી ઊપડશે. તમે જલદી જશો કારણ કે એ પાંચ જ મિનિટમાં ઉપડશે.

જેની આભાર.

[જેની પ્લેટફોર્મ પર જાય છે. ગાડી પકડે છે. વડોદરા પહોંચે છે. રિક્ષામાં બેસે છે. હોટેલમાં જાય છે.]

જેની નમસ્તે. મારું નામ જેનિફર જોન્સ છે. મેં રૂમના રિઝર્વેશન માટે અમદાવાદથી ફોન કર્યો હતો.

ક્લાર્ક નમસ્તે. હા જી. આપનો ૨૭ નંબરનો રૂમ છે. સ્વતંત્ર છે. બાથરૂમ, શાવર વગેરે બધું છે. આ માણસ તમને બધું બતાવશે. તમે કેટલા દિવસ રહેશો?

જેની મોટે ભાગે આજની રાત રહીશ. કદાચ એક રાત વધુ પણ થશે.

ક્લાર્ક કંઈ વાંધો નહી. તમારો બીજો સામાન છે?

જેની ના. આ નાની બેગ જ છે. હું વધુ સામાન સાથે મુસાફરી કરતી નથી.

ક્લાર્ક સરસ. કંઈ તકલીફ હોય તો મને એક નંબર પર ફોન કરશો.

જેની આભાર.

JENNY mane vaḍodrāni ek ṭikiṭ āpsho? keṭlā paisā thashe? māri pāse pachās rupiyāni noṭ chhe.

CLERK pandar rupiyā pachās paisā. ā lo ṭikiṭ ane parchuraṇ barābar gaṇi lesho.

JENNY hā. ane gāḍi kyā pleṭphorm uparthi ane kyāre upaḍshe te jarā kahesho?

CLERK hā ji. gāḍi chār nambernā pleṭphorm parthi upaḍshe. tame jaldi jasho kāraṇ ke te pānch ja miniṭmā̃ upaḍshe.

JENNY ābhār.

[jeni pleṭphorm par jāy chhe. gāḍi pakḍe chhe. vaḍodrā pahõche chhe. rikshạmā̃ bese chhe, hoṭelmā̃ jāy chhe.]

JENNY namste. mārũ nām jennifer jons chhe. mẽ rumnā rizerveshan māṭe amdāvādthi phon karyo hato.

CLERK namste. hā ji. āpno 27 namberno rum chhe. svtantra chhe. bāthrum, shāvar vagere badhũ chhe. ā māṇas tamne badhũ batāvshe. tame keṭlā divas rahesho?

JENNY moṭe bhāge ājni rāt rahish. kadāch ek rāt vadhu paṇ thashe.

CLERK kaĩ vāndho nahĩ. tamāro bijo sāmān chhe?

JENNY nā. ā nāni beg ja chhe. hũ vadhu sāmān sāthe musāphari karti nathi.

CLERK saras. kaĩ takliph hoy to mane ek namber par phon karsho.

JENNY ābhār.

JENNY *Could I have a ticket for Baroda, please? How much does it cost? I have a fifty-rupee note.*

CLERK *Fifteen rupees and fifty paise. Here is your ticket and the change. Please check it* [lit. *please count it properly*].

JENNY *Yes, it's OK. Can you tell me when the train leaves and from which platform?*

CLERK *Yes. The train leaves from platform number four. Please hurry as the train leaves in five minutes.*

JENNY *Thanks.*

[Jenny goes to the platform, catches the train, reaches Baroda, gets a rickshaw and goes to the hotel]

JENNY *Hello. My name is Jennifer Jones. I phoned from Ahmedabad to reserve a room.*

CLERK *Hello. Of course. Your room number is 27. It is a single room* [lit. *independent*], *with bath and shower. This man will show you your room* [lit. *will show you all these things*]. *How long are you staying?*

JENNY *Probably overnight but possibly an extra night.*

CLERK *No problem. Have you got any luggage?*

JENNY *Only this small bag. I travel light*. [lit. *I don't travel with more luggage.*]

CLERK *Good. If you have any problems, just ring me on number one.*

JENNY *Thanks.*

Vocabulary

પરચૂરણ	**parchuraṇ**	change
પકડે છે	**pakḍe che**	catches
પહોંચે છે	**pahÕche che**	reaches
આપનો	**āpno**	yours (honorific singular)
બતાવશે	**batāvashe**	will show

તકલીફ	**takliph**	problem
મોટે ભાગે	**moṭe bhāge**	mostly
કારણ કે	**kāraṇke**	because
મુસાફરી	**musāphari**	journey
રૂપિયા	**rupiā**	rupees
પૈસા	**paisā**	one hundredth of a rupee (also means 'money')
રિક્ષા	**rikshā**	a three-wheeled vehicle

Grammatical notes

The verbal forms આપશો (**āpsho**), જશો (**jasho**), etc. are actually future tense plural but are also used for the singular form. This turns the imperative into a request (without using 'please', which is implied).

The words અને (**ane**), ને (**ne**) 'and', કારણ કે (**kāraṇ ke**) 'because' are conjunctions, which join two sentences.

The word આપ (**āp**) comes from Hindi and is used in place of તમે (**tame**) in formal situations when showing respect, and is treated as honorific plural.

Auxiliary verbs

In Gujarati, certain verbs require the additional supportive verb હો (**ho**) 'to be'. These are known as *auxiliary verbs*, e.g. જોઈએ છે (**joie chhe**), કરે છે (**kare chhe**), બેસે છે (**bese chhe**) ('wants', 'does', 'sits', respectively) where છે (**chhe**) is the auxiliary verb.

કરે છે (**kare chhe**) does, is doing
કરતો હોઈશ (**karto hoish**) will be doing
કરતો હતો (**karto hato**) was doing

They change according to the number, gender and tense.

Perfect tenses

As in English, the perfect tense is formed by using the past in the first person singular, followed by the verb 'to be':

હું ઊઠ્યો છું. (**hũ uṭhyo chhũ**) I have got up (present perfect)
હું ઊઠ્યો હતો. (**hũ uṭhyo hato**) I had got up (past perfect)
હું ઊઠ્યો હોઇશ. (**hũ uṭhyo hoish**) I shall have got up (future perfect)

Transitive verbs need an object to complete the meaning. Intransitive verbs do not have this requirement, e.g.

તે પાણી રેડે છે. (**te paṇi reḍe chhe.**) He/She pours (verb) the water (object).
તે સૂએ છે. (**te sue chhe.**) He/She sleeps.

The verbs સૂ (**su**), ઊઠ (**uṭh**) are intransitive, while રેડ 'pour' is transitive.

The verb કર (**kar**) 'do' is a transitive verb. So હું (**hũ**) changes to મેં (**mẽ**) (see Unit 4).

મેં કર્યું છે. (**mẽ karyũ chhe**.) present perfect
મેં કર્યું હતું. (**mẽ karyũ hatũ**.) past perfect
મેં કર્યું હશે. (**mẽ karyũ hashe**.) future perfect

Exercise 1

Rearrange the following into four groups of four words connected by meaning:

હાથ	પગ	માથું	એકાવન
ઊઠ	એક્સઠ	પૈસા	બેસ
ઈકોતેર	પરચૂરણ	ચાલ	નોટ
રૂપિયા	દોડ	એક્યાશી	કાન

Exercise 2

Pair off the words in A with those appropriate in B:

A	*B*
પંદર	બેગ
ગાડી	કદાચ
પૈસા	પચાસ
સામાન	લેશો
ચોક્કસ	બસ
આપશો	પરચૂરણ

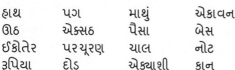

Exercise 3

Translate into English:

આજે રવિવાર હતો. હું સવારમાં મોડો ઊઠ્યો હતો. પછી નાસ્તો કર્યો હતો. ટી.વી. જોયું. પણ ખાસ કંઈ ન હતું. છાપાંની દુકાને ગયો. છાપું ખરીદ્યું. ઘેર પાછો આવ્યો. છાપું વાંચ્યું. ખાસ સમાચાર ન હતા. પછી થોડું બાગકામ કર્યું. સાંજે ગીતા આવશે. તેની સાથે બહાર જઈશ. અમે બહાર જમીશું.

Exercise 4

Find the odd words in each group:

(a)	સસ્તું	મફત	બહેન	કીમતી
(b)	ડુંગર	તળાવ	સરકાર	બાગ
(c)	ડાબી	સોમવાર	જમણી	સીધી
(d)	કયા	આભાર	કેટલા	ક્યારે
(e)	જલદી	ધીમે	બિલાડી	ચાલ

Exercise 5

Here are some answers. What were the questions?

(a) આ ગાડી મુંબઈ જશે.
(b) વડોદરાની ટિકિટના પંદર રૂપિયા પચાસ પૈસા.
(c) આપનો ૨૭ નંબરનો રૂમ છે.
(d) તમારા ખમીસ સાંજે મળશે.
(e) આમ તો ખાવાલાયક ઘણી ચીજો છે.

Exercise 6

Correct the following passage:

હું ભૂખ્યો હતી. હુંને રોટલી ખાધું. શાક ખાતી. દાળભાત ખાધું. પછી પાણી પીધો. કોફી પીધું. થોડો વાર ટીવી જોઈ. નિશાળનો ઘરકામ કરી. પછી સૂતું.

Exercise 7

Your friend has come to your town/city for the first time. In five sentences tell him or her some places to visit, using perfect tenses.

Dialogue 2

જોવાલાયક જગ્યાઓ **jovā lāyak jagyāo** Places worth visiting **(CD1; 44)**

Jenny enquires about places worth visiting in and around Baroda and sets off on her journey

---

જેની નમસ્તે. અહીં વડોદરામાં જોવાલાયક કઈ કઈ જગ્યાઓ છે?
ક્લાર્ક નમસ્તે. આમ તો ઘણું બધું છે પણ કીર્તિ મંદિર, સૂરસાગર તળાવ, મ્યુઝિયમ, કામાટી બાગ, ન્યાયમંદિર વગેરે જગ્યાઓ ખાસ જોવા જેવી છે. નજીકમાં પાવાગઢનો ઊંચો ડુંગર છે તથા ડભોઈનો કિલ્લો પણ છે. આ લો. ગુજરાત સરકારના પ્રવાસ વિભાગની આ સચિત્ર માહિતીપત્રિકા છે. તેમાંથી આપને વધુ વિગતો મળશે.
જેની આભાર. આ બધું તો સરસ છે. હું અત્યારે જ નીકળીશ. બપોરે જમીશ નહીં. બહાર નાસ્તો કરીશ. રાતે પણ મારા મિત્રને ત્યાં જમીશ.
ક્લાર્ક કંઈ વાંધો નહીં. રૂમમાં કોઇ કિંમતી ચીજો નથી ને?
જેની ના ના. કેમેરા ને પર્સ તો મારી પાસે જ છે. હા, ધોબીને કહેશો કે મારાં કપડાં સાંજે આપે.
ક્લાર્ક ચોક્કસ. ચિંતા ના કરશો. હું તેનું ધ્યાન રાખીશ. આવજો. સાચવીને જજો.
જેની આવજો.

JENNY namste. ahĩvaḍodrāmā̃ jovālāyak kai kai jagyāo chhe?
CLERK namste. ām to ghaṇũ badhũ chhe paṇ kirti mandir, sursāgar taḷāv, museum, kāmāṭi bāg, nyāymandir vagere jagyāo khās jovā jevi chhe. najikmā̃ pāvāgaḍhno uncho ḍungar chhe tathā ḍabhoino killo paṇ chhe. ā lo. gujarāt sarkārnā pravās vibhāgni ā sachitra māhitipatrikā chhe. temā̃thi āpne vadhu vigato maḷshe.
JENNY ābhār.ā badhũ to saras chhe. hũ atyāre ja nikḷish. bapore jamish nahĩ. bahār nāsto karish. rāte paṇ mārā mitrane tyā̃ jamish.
CLERK kaĩ vāndho nahĩ. roommā̃ koi kimti chijo nathi ne?
JENNY nā nā. kemerā ne pars to māri pāse ja chhe. hā, dhobine kahesho ke mārā kapḍā̃ sānje āpe.

CLERK chokkas. chintā nā karsho. hũ tenũ dhyān rākhish. āvjo. sāchvine jajo.

JENNY āvjo.

JENNY *Hello. Which places are worth visiting in Baroda?*

CLERK *Actually, there are several places* [*worth visiting*]. *But those of special interest are Kirti Mandir, Sursagar Lake, the Museum, Kamati Bag* [*Park*] *and Nyay Mandir* [*'Temple of Justice'* = *High Court*]. *Nearby there is the mountain Pavagadh and the fort of Dabhoi. Please take this Tourist Board [information] illustrated leaflet for more details.*

JENNY *Thank you. All this is very useful and I will start right now. I will not have lunch. I'll have a snack on my way and also dine at my friend's place in the evening.*

CLERK *Very well. There is nothing valuable in your room?*

JENNY *Oh no. The camera and the purse are with me. And please tell the laundryman to bring my clothes by this evening.*

CLERK *Certainly. Please don't worry. I'll take care of that. Goodbye. Take care.*

JENNY *Goodbye.*

Vocabulary

જોવાલાયક	**jovā lāyak**	worth seeing
જગ્યાઓ	**jagyāo**	places
ઘણું બધું	**ghaṇũ badhũ**	much more (duplicative form)
ખાસ	**khās**	specially
નજીકમાં	**najikamā̃**	nearby
કિલ્લો	**killo**	fort
તળાવ	**taḷāv**	lake
ડુંગર	**ḍungar**	hill
બાગ	**bāg**	park
સરકાર	**sarkār**	government
પ્રવાસ વિભાગ	**pravās vibhāg**	Department of Tourism
સચિત્ર	**sachitra**	with pictures (ચિત્ર picture)
અત્યારે જ	**atyāre ja**	right now
નાસ્તો	**nāsto**	snacks
કંઈ વાંધો નહીં	**kaĩ vāndho nahĩ**	that's all right (*lit.* there is no objection)
કિંમતી	**kĩmati**	costly
ધોબી	**dhobi**	washerman, laundryman
સાચવીને જશો	**sāchvine jasho**	take care
ચિંતા ના કરશો	**chĩtā na karsho**	please don't worry
ધ્યાન રાખીશ	**dhyān rākhish**	will take care of

Grammatical notes

Verbal root

In Gujarati the verbal root is the same as the form of the imperative, second person singular. All other suffixes are added to the root.

Infinitive

The infinitive is formed by adding વું (**vũ**) to the root of the verb. The second person singular in the imperative form is always the root of the verb, e.g. આવ (**āv**) 'come', જો (**jo**) 'see'; so આવવું (**āvvũ**), જોવું (**jovũ**), ખાવું (**khāvũ**), પીવું (**pivũ**), હસવું (**hasvũ**), etc. are infinitives.

The infinitive form is the root + વું (**vũ**). Thus,

કર (**kar**)	do (imperative, also the verbal root)
તું કર (**tũ kar**)	you do (imperative singular)
કરવું (**karvũ**)	to do (infinitive)

Similarly,

ખાવું (**khāvũ**)	to eat
જોવું (**jovũ**)	to see
લેવું (**levũ**)	to take, etc.

From the infinitive જોવું (**jovũ**) we can form:

જોવાલાયક (**jovā lāyak**)	worth seeing (where લાયક (**lāyak**) means 'worth of')

Similarly,

ખાવાલાયક (**khāvālāyak**) worth eating
લેવાલાયક (**levālāyak**) worth taking

You can use જેવી (**jevi**) in place of લાયક (**lāyak**) and the meaning remains the same. Thus,

જોવા જેવી વસ્તુ (**jovā jevi vastu**)	worth seeing thing (i.e. a thing worth seeing)
ખાવા જેવી વસ્તુ (**khāvā jevi vastu**)	worth eating thing
લેવા જેવી વસ્તુ (**levā jevi vastu**)	worth taking thing

The only difference in the usage of લાયક (**lāyak**) and જેવી (**jevi**) is that લાયક (**lāyak**) is invariable. It does not change according to the number and gender of the qualifier, while જેવી (**jevi**) has all the forms જેવો (**jevo**) (*m*), જેવી (**jevi**) (*f*), જેવું (**jevũ**) (*n*) – all singular – and જેવા (**jevā**), જેવાં (**jevā̃**), plural. As usual, જેવી (**jevi**) (*f*) is used for both singular and plural. Thus,

આ કિલ્લો (**ā killo**) (*m sg*) જોવા જેવો છે. (**jovā jevo chhe.**) This fort is worth seeing.

આ કિલ્લાઓ (**ā killāo**) (*m pl*) જોવા જેવા છે. (**jovā jevo chhe.**) These forts are worth seeing.

આ જગ્યા (**ā jagyā**) (*f sg*) જોવા જેવી છે. (**jovā jevi chhe.**) This place is worth seeing.

આ જગ્યાઓ (**ā jagyāo**) (*f pl*) જોવા જેવી છે. (**jovā jevi chhe.**) These places are worth seeing.
આ તળાવ (**ā talāv**) (*n sg*) જોવા જેવું છે. (**jovā jevũ chhe.**) This lake is worth seeing.
આ તળાવો (**ā talāvo**) (*n pl*) જોવા જેવાં છે. (**jovā jevā chhe.**) These lakes are worth seeing.

The imperative forms

As mentioned previously, the imperative forms are also the roots of the verb in the second person singular form. The imperative forms can be used in the present tense or in the future tense but for obvious reasons cannot be used in the past tense. Nor can there be an imperative form in the first person singular or plural. Here are two examples.

કર (kar) do

Present tense

Person	*Singular*	*Plural*
II	તું કર (**tũ kar**)	તમે કરો (**tame karo**)
III	તે કરે (**te kare**)	તેઓ કરે (**teo kare**)

Future tense

II	તું કરીશ/કરશે (**tũ karish/karshe**)	તમે કરશો (**tame karsho**)
III	તે કરશે (**te karshe**)	તેઓ કરશે (**teo karshe**)

પી (pi) drink

Present tense

Person	*Singular*	*Plural*
II	તું પી (**tũ pi**)	તમે પીઓ (**tame pio**)
III	તે પીએ (**te pie**)	તેઓ પીએ (**teo pie**)

Future tense

II	તું પીશ/પીશે (**tũ pish/pishe**)	તમે પીશો (**tame pisho**)
III	તે પીશે (**te pishe**)	તેઓ પીશે (**teo pishe**)

Exercise 8

Translate into Gujarati:

(a) Please give me two apples and some grapes.
(b) What day is it today?
(c) Tomorrow I will be in New York.
(d) Is it a very expensive shirt?
(e) In 1990 I was in India.

Exercise 9

Fill in the blanks with appropriate words:

મારી પાસે ____ (twenty-five) (પચીસ/પચાસ) રૂપિયા છે. ____ (five) (પંદર/પાંચ) રૂપિયા મારી નાની ____ (sister) (ભાઈ/બેન) ને આપીશ. ____ (socks) (મોજાં/હાથમોજાં) ખરીદીશ. પાંચ રૂપિયાના ____ (fruits) (શાકભાજી/ફળો) ખરીદીશ. પછી મારી પાસે પાંચ રૂપિયા ____ (will have) (હશે/થશે). તેને હું ____ (good) (સારા/મારા) કામ માટે વાપરીશ.

Exercise 10

Change the following imperative forms into polite requests and use them in six different sentences:

આપ	બેસ	જમ
લે	પી	જા

Exercise 11

Read the passage below, then write full answers in Gujarati to the questions which follow.

મારા ઘરનું બારણું પૂર્વ દિશામાં છે. સામે રમણલાલ રહે છે. તેમનું બારણું પશ્ચિમ દિશામાં છે. હું રસ્તો ઓળંગીને તેમને ત્યાં ગયો. તેઓ કાલે ભારત જશે. મારો ભાઈ ભારતમાં રહે છે. તેને માટે થોડા ખમીસ રમણલાલ સાથે મોકલીશ. થોડી બદામ પણ મોકલીશ.

(a) મારા ઘરનું બારણું કઈ દિશામાં છે?
(b) રમણલાલ ક્યાં જશે?
(c) તેમની સાથે હું શું મોકલીશ?
(d) કોને માટે મોકલીશ?

Exercise 12

Give the missing directions in Gujarati:

ઉત્તર

(a) ? પૂર્વ

(b) ?

Exercise 13

Make sense of the following dialogue by rearranging the words:

હુસેન: જવાનું આજે આપણે છે ત્યાં મામાને.
સકિના: પણ ખરીદી આપણે માટે. હતું જવાનું.
હુસેન: કરીશું ખરીદી કાલે. હતો ફોન મામાનો.
સકિના: શું છે કાંઈ? ખાસ.
હુસેન: માંદા મામી છે ખૂબ. આવ્યો તાવ.
સકિના: તો. તો પડશે જવું ચોક્કસ.
હુસેન: થા. તૈયાર તું જલદી.

Exercise 14

Copy the following words:

આકૃતિ ઋતુ
પૃથ્વી ક્ષમા
કર્યા ક્રિકેટ
ઈશ્વર ચક્કર

Exercise 15

Join the half letters in column A to the full letters in column B and try to form a word using that conjunct:

A	*B*
સ્	ત
સ્	ટ
ષ્	પ
લ્	પ
મ્	પ

Unit Seven

જૂના મિત્રોની મુલાકાતે **junā mitroni mulākāte**

Meeting old friends

જગ્યાની શોધમાં **jagyāni shodhmā̃**

Looking for accommodation

In this unit you will learn about:

- Pronouns: reflective (પોતે **pote**), interrogative (કોણ **kon**), demonstrative (આ **ā**, પેલું **pelũ**), indefinite (કોણ **kon**)
- More duplicative forms
- Case suffix થી (**thi**)
- Some idiomatic constructions
- Changing the end vowel in some words while adding suffixes

Dialogue 1

જૂના મિત્રોની મુલાકાતે **junā mitroni mulākāte**

Meeting old friends **(CD1; 47)**

Sharad and Nita are husband and wife. Their friends, Ranjan and her husband, Nalin, have come to see them

શરદ	આવો આવો, નલિનભાઈ. ઓહો, આજે તો રંજનબેન પણ સાથે છે! તમે તો હમણાં દેખાતા જ નથી!
નલિન	કેમ છો શરદભાઈ. અમે વિચાર તો ઘણા દિવસથી કરતાં હતાં. પણ છેવટે આજે રંજને જ કહ્યું કે નીતાબહેનને ત્યાં જઈએ.
રંજન	હા. તમે લોકો તો અમારું ઘર ભૂલી જ ગયા છો!
શરદ	એમ નથી. વચ્ચે નીતાને પણ ઠીક ન હતું. હું પોતે પણ માંદો હતો. શરદી, તાવ. નીતા, જો કોણ આવ્યું છે?
નીતા	(રસોડામાંથી આવે છે) ઓહો, રંજન, આજે તું ભૂલી પડી! આવો નલિનભાઈ. શું લેશો? ઠંડું, ગરમ?
નલિન	જે આપશો તે. અમને તો બધું ચાલશે.
શરદ	નીતા, ઠંડી છે એટલે ગરમાગરમ મસાલાની ચા બનાવ.
નીતા	સાથે ભજીયા પણ ચાલશેને?
રંજન	એની તો એ કદી ના જ ન પાડે! ચાલ નીતા, હું અંદર આવું છું. તમે બન્ને વાતો કરો.
શરદ	જોયું નલિન, એમને બંનેને ખાનગી વાતો કરવી છે એટલે કેવો રસ્તો શોધ્યો!
રંજન	એમ કે! તો તમે બંને રસોડામાં જાવ. અમે અહીં બેસીશું.
નીતા	રહેવા દે રંજન! એ પ્રયોગ કરવા જેવો નથી! [સૌ ખડખડાટ હસી પડે છે]

SHARAD	āvo āvo nalinbhāi. oho, āje to ranjanbahen paṇ sāthe chhe, tame to hamṇā dekhātā j nathi.
NALIN	kem chho sharadbhai. ame vichār to ghaṇā divasthi kartā hatā. paṇ chhevṭe āje ranjane j kahyũ ke nitābahenne tyā̃ jaie.
RANJAN	hā tame loko to amārũ ghar bhuli j gayā̃ chho.
SHARAD	em nathi. vacche nitāne paṇ ṭhik na hatũ. hũ pote paṇ māndo hato. shardi, tāv. nitā jo to koṇ āvyũ chhe!
NITĀ	(rasoḍāmā̃thi āve chhe) oho ranjan āje to tũ bhuli paḍi. āvo nalinbhai. shũ lesho? ṭhanḍũ, garam?
NALIN	je āpsho te. amne to badhũ chālshe.
SHARAD	nitā, ṭhandi chhe eṭle garmāgaram masālāni chā banāv.
NITĀ	sāthe bhajiā paṇ chāshe ne?
RANJAN	eni to e kadi nāj na pāḍe. chāl nitā hũ andar āvũ chhũ. tame banne vāto karo.
SHARAD	joyũ nalin, emne bannene khāngi vāto karvi chhe eṭle kevo rasto shodhyo.
RANJAN	em ke. to tame banne rasoḍāmā̃ jāv. ame ahī̃ besishũ.
NITĀ	rahevā de ranjan. e prayog karvā jevo nathi. (sau khaḍkhaḍāt hasi paḍe chhe.)

SHARAD *Welcome, Nalinbhai. Oh, Ranjanben is also with you! We don't see much of you these days!*

NALIN *How are you, Sharadbhai. We were thinking (of coming to see you) for a long time but today Ranjan insisted that we go to see Nitaben.*

RANJAN *Yes. You have forgotten our house completely.*

SHARAD *It's not like that. Nita was not well, nor was I. I've had a cold and fever. Nita, look who is here!*

[Nita comes out of the kitchen]

NITA *Oh, Ranjan! You've come after such a long time* [lit. *you lost your way today*]. *Welcome, Nalinbhai. What would you like? Something hot or cold?*

NALIN *Whatever you like! Anything will be fine.*

SHARAD *Nita, it's cold* (outside). *Prepare some hot tea* [*with spices: Masala tea*].

NITA *And you won't mind* [*having*] *Bhajiyas with that.*

RANJAN *He would never say no to that! Nita, I will come with you* [*to the kitchen*]. *You two can talk here.*

SHARAD *Look at that, Nalin. They want to talk privately and they have found a way!*

RANJAN *Is that so? Then you two can go into the kitchen. We will sit here!*

NITA *Enough! This experiment* [i.e. the men doing the cooking] *is not worth it.*

[All laugh heartily]

Vocabulary

લોકો	**loko**	people (here it is used as 'you two')
ભૂલવું	**bhulvũ**	to forget
ભજિયાં	**bhajiā**	spicy preparation of gram flour mixed with vegetables deep-fried in oil
ચાલશે	**chālshe**	OK, will do (*lit.* walk)
ખાનગી	**khāngi**	private
શોધ્યો	**shodhyo**	found out
ઠંડું	**ṭhandũ**	cold

ગરમ મસાલાની ચા	**garam masālāni chā**	hot tea with special spices
પ્રયોગ	**prayog**	experiment
ખડખડાટ	**khaḍkhaḍāt**	heartily (when used with laugh; *lit.* with sound)
હસી પડે છે		laugh (this is a compound verb, see notes)

Colloquial notes

Some idiomatic constructions

દેખાતાં જ નથી	**dekhātā ja nathi**	have not seen you for ages!
ઘર ભૂલી ગયા છો.	**ghar bhuli gayā chho**	you have come after such a long time (*lit.* you have forgotten this house)
ભૂલી પડી	**bhuli padi**	come after a long time (*lit.* you lost your way). The word પડ (*lit.* fall) always goes with ભૂલ in such phrases. The number and gender suffixes are added: e.g. શરદ ભૂલો પડ્યો. નીતા ભૂલી પડી. etc.
હસી પડે છે	**hasi pade chhe**	breaks into laughter. The verb પડ is used as a compound verb (see Unit 8) with various other verbs and rarely has the original meaning 'fall'.
ના જ ન પાડે	**nā ja na pāde**	will never say no. The verb પાડ literally means 'make it to fall'.

Grammatical notes

Duplicative forms

આવો આવો (**āvo āvo**): the verb આવો (**āvo**) means 'come'. આવો (**āvo**) is an honorific plural. When repeated it implies intimacy.

ગરમાગરમ (**garmāgaram**) 'piping hot': the word ગરમ (**garam**) means 'hot' and when repeated you can say ગરમગરમ (**garamgaram**) or you can use ગરમાગરમ (**garmāgaram**) adding an આ (**ā**) between the two words.

Pronouns

In Unit 5 we studied *personal pronouns* such as હું, તું, તે (**hũ**, **tũ**, **te**), etc. In this dialogue the word પોતે (**pote**) is a *reflexive pronoun* meaning 'self'.

હું પોતે	**hũ pote**	I myself
તું પોતે	**tũ pote**	you yourself
તે પોતે	**te pote**	he/she himself/herself

Another word જાતે (**jāte**) is also used in the same manner: તે જાતે (**te jāte**).

We have already met interrogative pronouns like કોણ (**kon**) 'who', કઈ (**kai**) 'which', શું (**shũ**) 'what' and demonstrative pronouns like આ (**ā**) 'this' (Unit 3). 'This' remains the same in all numbers and genders. પેલું (**pelũ**) 'that' is variable and changes to પેલો (**pelo**), પેલી (**peli**), પેલું (**pelũ**), પેલા (**pelā**), પેલાં (**pelā**), e.g.

પેલો માણસ (**pelo mānas**) (*m sg*)	that person
પેલા માણસો (**pelā mānso**) (*m pl*)	those persons
પેલી છોકરી (**peli chhokari**) (*f sg*)	that girl
પેલી છોકરીઓ (**peli chhokario**) (*f pl*)	those girls
પેલું ઘર (**pelũ ghar**) (*n sg*)	that house
પેલાં ઘરો (**pelā gharo**) (*n pl*)	those houses

The words કોઈ (**koi**) 'some', ઘણું (**ghanũ**) 'much', બધું (**badhũ**) 'all' are the *indefinite pronouns* we used in the previous lessons. ઘણું (**ghanũ**) can join with બધું (**badhũ**) and form a duplicative form ઘણું બધું (**ghanũ badhũ**) meaning 'much more'. This pronoun varies according to the number and gender of the qualifier, while કોઈ (**koi**) is invariable:

કોઈ માણસ (**koi māṇas**) (*m*)	some person
કોઈ છોકરી (**koi chhokari**) (*f*)	some girl
કોઈ ઘર (**koi ghar**) (*n*)	some house
ઘણાબધા માણસો (**ghaṇā badhā māṇso**) (*m pl*)	many people

ઘણીબધી છોકરીઓ (**ghaṇi badhi chhokario**) (*f pl*)	many girls
ઘણાંબધાં ઘરો (**ghaṇā̃ badhā̃ gharo**) (*n pl*)	many houses

The *suffix* થી (**thi**) is known as the ablative case. It shows ablation, i.e. separation:

ઘણા દિવસ*થી* (**ghanā divas*thi***)	since (for) so many days
ચાકૂ*થી* (**chāku*thi***)	cut it (with a knife)
ભારત *થી* બ્રિટન આવ્યો. (**bhārat*thi* britan āvyo**)	came to Britain from India

Exercise 1

Fill in the blanks:

(a) (From Birmingham) ____ લંડન કેટલું દૂર છે?
(b) તે વખતે હું ____ (myself) હાજર હતો.
(c) મારે માટે ચા ____ (will do).
(d) (Those persons) ____ ઘણું કામ કરે છે.
(e) હું લંડન ____ (came) ત્યારે બહુ ગુજરાતીઓ ____ (not) હતા.

Exercise 2

Translate the following passage into English:

હું પોતે ગયા રવિવારે ગ્લાસગો હતો. ત્યાં વરસાદ ન હતો પણ ઠંડી ઘણી હતી. આજે લંડનમાં વરસાદ છે પણ ઠંડી નથી. આજે સાંજે હું નીતિનને ત્યાં જઈશ. એ ગઈ કાલે લુટનથી આવ્યો છે. એ ત્યાં કામ કરે છે. કોઈ વાર જાતે શનિ-રવિ અહીં આવે છે. એ સરસ માણસ છે. અમે સાથે જમીશું.

Exercise 3

Use the following constructions in four different sentences:

(a) ના જ ન પાડે.
(b) આજે તમે જાતે ભૂલા પડ્યા.
(c) ખડખડાટ હસી પડી.
(d) બધું ચાલશે.

Exercise 4

Rearrange the following in four groups of four words connected by meaning:

ચા	કૉફી	ઠંડી	કઈ
બસો	પવન	દૂધ	છસો
કોણ	ચારસો	આ	પાણી
ગરમી	વરસાદ	આઠસો	શું

Exercise 5

Write a short dialogue for the following scenario (using different pronouns):

Meeting a penfriend at the station for the first time.

Exercise 6

Correct the following passage:

આજે હું ઠીક નથી છું. મને તાવ આવ્યું છે. હું ખાધું નથી. દૂધ પીતો છું. સાંજે એક ફળ લેશો. રાતે દવા પીધું ને સૂતું. આવતી કાલે સવારે સારી થશો.

Dialogue 2

જગ્યાની શોધમાં. **jagyāni shodhmā̃** Looking for accommodation **(CD1; 49)**

રામલાલ	આવો ચંપકભાઈ, આવો માશી. બેસો. ચાબા પીશો?
ચંપકલાલ	ના ના રામભાઈ. જરા ઉતાવળ છે. આ તો છગનભાઈ કહેતા હતા કે તમારો ઉપરનો ફ્લેટ ખાલી છે.
રામલાલ	હા, છગનભાઈએ કહ્યું કે ચંપકભાઈ ભારતથી આવ્યા છે અને મકાન શોધે છે.
ચંપકલાલ	હા. ગુજરાતી લત્તામાં હોય તો તમારાં બહેનને ઠીક પડે. એને અંગ્રેજી આવડતું નથી.
રામલાલ	કંઈ વાંધો નહીં. રમા આવી ત્યારે એને પણ આવડતું ન હતું. હવે તો 'થેંક્યુ', 'સોરી' કહે છે! અત્યારે મંદિરે ગઈ છે
મણિબહેન	એમ. જગ્યા ઉપર છે?
રામલાલ	હા, ચાલો ઉપર. આ જુઓ, બેઠકખંડ. આ સૂવાનો ઓરડો. આ રસોડું છે. બાજુમાં નાની ઓરડી છે તેમાં વધારાનો સામાન રહેશે.
મણિબહેન	ભાડું કેટલું છે?
રામલાલ	તમારી પાસેથી વધારે લઈશ નહીં. સો પાઉન્ડ આપજો. લાઈટ, ગેસ, પાણી અને ટેક્સના જુદા થશે.

ચંપકલાલ (મણિબહેનને) એ તો જે વ્યાજબી હશે તે જ લેશે. (રામલાલને) નીચે તમે છો એ જ મોટી વાત છે. ચાલો, પછી તમને ફોન કરીશ.આવજો.

રામલાલ આવજો.

RĀMLĀL āvo champakbhāi, āvo māshi. beso. chābā pisho?

CHAMPAKLĀL nā nā rāmbhāi, jarā utāvaḷ chhe. ā to chhaganbhāi kahetā hatā ke tamāro uparno flat khāli chhe.

RĀMLĀL hā chhaganbhāi e kahyũ ke champakbhāi bhāratthi āvyā chhe ane makān shodhe chhe.

CHAMPAKLĀL hā gujrāti lattāmā hoy to tamarā bahenne ṭhik paḍe. ene angreji āvaḍtũ nathi.

RĀMLĀL kaĩ vāndho nahi, ramā āvi tyāre tene paṇ āvaḍtũ na hatũ. have to 'thank you', 'sorry' kahe chhe. atyāre mandire gai chhe.

MANIBEN em. jagyā upar chhe?

RĀMLĀL hā chālo upar. ā juvo beṭhakkhanḍ. ā suvāno orḍo. ā rasoḍũ chhe. bājumā̃ nāni orḍi chhe temā̃ vadhārāno sāmān raheshe.

MANIBEN bhāḍũ keṭlũ chhe?

RĀMLĀL tamāri pāsethi vadhāre laish nahi. so pāunḍ āpjo. laĩṭe, gas, pāṇi ne ṭex nā judā thashe.

CHAMPAKLĀL (manibahenne) e to je vājbi hashe te j leshe. (rāmlālne) niche tame chho e j moṭi vāt chhe. chālo pachhi tamne phon karish. āvjo.

RĀMLĀL āvjo.

RAMLAL *Welcome Champakbhai. Welcome Mashi. Please take a seat. Would you like to have tea or something?*

CHAMPAKLAL *Oh no, Rambhai. We are in a bit of a hurry. Chhaganbhai told me that your upper flat is vacant.*

RAMLAL *Yes. Chhaganbhai told me that Champakbhai has come from India and needs accommodation.*

CHAMPAKLAL *Yes. We would prefer to have it in a Gujarati area. My wife doesn't speak [know] English.*

RAMLAL *No problem! When Rama came here she knew nothing. Now she can say 'thank you', 'sorry'! She has gone to the temple.*

MANIBEN *I see. Is the flat on the first floor?*

RAMLAL *Yes. Let's go . . . This is the living room. This is the bedroom. This is the kitchen. You can keep your extra things in this boxroom.*

MANIBEN *How much is the rent?*

RAMLAL *I won't charge you much. £100 only. Electricity, water and gas bills and other expenses will be separate.*

CHAMPAKLAL [to Maniben] *Whatever he charges will be reasonable.* [to Ramlal] *The most important thing is that you stay here. (lit. downstairs) OK. I will phone you later. Goodbye.*

RAMLAL *Goodbye.*

Vocabulary

માશી	**māshi**	elderly lady (*lit.* mother's sister. It is customary to say **māshi** to show respect to elderly ladies)
ચાબા	**chābā**	tea and/or something
ઉતાવળ	**utāvaḷ**	hurry
ઉપરનો	**uparno**	upper
ફ્લેટ	**phleṭ**	flat
ખાલી	**khāli**	vacant
જગ્યા	**jagyā shodhe chhe**	place (here, accommodation)
શોધે છે		is searching
લત્તો	**latto**	area
ઠીક	**ṭhik**	OK
આવડતું નથી	**āvaḍtũ nathi**	does not know
નાની ઓરડી	**nāni orḍi**	boxroom (*lit.* small room)
ભાડું	**bhāḍũ**	rent
વાજબી	**vājbi**	reasonable

Colloquial notes

Some idiomatic constructions (CD1; 51)

તમારાં બહેન (**tamārā̃ bahen**) 'my wife' (*lit.* 'your sister'). The older generation would not use the name of wife or husband. They would say તમારાં બહેન (**tamārā̃ bahen**) or તમારા ભાઈ (**tamārā bhāi**) 'your brother' as the case may be.

Grammatical note

ચાબા (**chābā**) This is a duplicative form. The letter બ (**ba**) is repeated after the original word with the same vowel added as that of the preceding letter:

પાણી (**pāni**) 'water' will be પાણીબાણી (**pānibāni**)
કામ (**kām**) 'work' will be કામબામ (**kāmbām**)

The additional meaning it conveys is '. . . or something similar'.

ચા (**chā**) is tea, so ચાબા (**chābā**) would be tea and/or something similar to tea (something like coffee, juice, etc.).
પેનબેન (**penben**) would mean a pen 'or something similar' to write with (e.g. a pencil).

Change while adding a suffix

When adding a suffix the last letter of the word undergoes a change. The general rule is that if the word ends in આ (**ā**) or ઈ (**ei**) no alteration is necessary. But if the word, originally without any suffix, ends in ઉં (**ũ**) or ઓ (**o**) it first changes to આ (**ā**) and then the suffixes are added. Thus:

રાજા (**rājā**) 'king' ends with આ (**ā**) therefore રાજાએ (**rājāe**), etc.
રાણી (**rāni**) 'queen' ends with ઈ (**e**) therefore રાણીને (**rānie**), etc.

But કુતરું (**kutrũ**) 'dog' ends in ઉં (**ũ**) so ઉં (**ũ**) changes to આ (**ā**). Adding the suffixes results in કુતરાએ (**kutrāe**), કુતરામાં (**kutrāmā**), etc. ઘોડો

(**ghodo**) 'horse' ends in ઓ (**o**) so ઓ (**o**) changes to આ (**ā**) and adding the suffixes results in ઘોડામાં (**ghodāmā**), ઘોડાથી (**ghodāthi**), etc.

Exercise 7

Choose the odd word out from each group:

(a)	કૂતરું	તાવ	ઘોડો	બિલાડી
(b)	માણસ	છોકરો	શરદી	છોકરી
(c)	ઓરડી	ઘડો	રસોડું	ઓરડો
(d)	નલિની	શરદ	નીતા	વિચાર
(e)	દૂર	અક્કલ	નજીક	પાસે

Exercise 8

Translate the following sentences into Gujarati:

(a) He would never say no to that.
(b) Would you like to have tea or something similar?
(c) I want some residential accommodation.
(d) I have not seen you for a long time.
(e) Someone is at the door.

Exercise 9

Using duplicative forms, write a short dialogue for the following scenario:

ફળોની દુકાનમાં ખરીદી

Exercise 10

Change the following sentences as indicated:

(a)	મને આ ઘર ગમ્યું નથી.	(affirmative)
(b)	તમારી પાસે પૈસા છે?	(remove question)
(c)	કાલે હું નિશાળે જઈશ.	(present)
(d)	નીતાને ઠીક ન હતું.	(present)
(e)	રામલાલે ઘર બતાવ્યું.	(future)

Exercise 11

Use the following phrases in four different sentences:

(a) એની ચિંતા ન કરશો.
(b) કંઈ વાંધો નહીં.
(c) ચાલો ત્યારે.
(d) રસ્તો શોધ્યો.

Translate your sentences into English.

Unit Eight
નિશાળમાં **nishāḷmā̃**
At school

માંદગી **mā̃dagi**
Sickness

In this unit you will learn about:

- Compound verbs
- Postpositions
- More colloquial expressions
- Gender

Dialogue 1

નિશાળમાં **nishāḷmā̃** At school **(CD1; 52)**

Amit and Meera are students. They are chatting in class before the arrival of their teacher

અમિત આજે શીલાબહેન નથી?

મીરા ના, માંદા પડી ગયાં છે. ત્યાં સુધી ભૂગોળ બિપિનભાઈ શીખવશે.

અમિત એમ. આજે પહેલાં અંગ્રેજી, ગણિત અને વિજ્ઞાન તો છે જ. પણ ઇતિહાસ તથા ચિત્રકામ આજે છે કે કાલે?

મીરા પાછું સમયપત્રક ખોઈ નાંખ્યુંને? લે, મારી પાસે વધારાનું છે. આ સાચવી રાખજે. આજે તો બપોર પછી સંગીત અને રમતગમત છે.

અમિત તો તો મજા પડશે. મિસ સિમ્પ્સન સારાં શિક્ષિકા છે માટે મને સંગીત વિજ્ઞાન જેટલું જ ગમે છે.
મીરા પણ આપણા વિજ્ઞાનશિક્ષક સ્મિથ એવા કડક છે! વળી તેમનું ઘરકામ પણ મેં કર્યું નથી.
અમિત મને વિજ્ઞાન અઘરું લાગતું નથી. ખરી રીતે તો મને વિજ્ઞાન ઘણું ગમે છે.
મીરા મને અંગ્રેજી ગમે છે. મને નવલકથાઓ વાંચવી ગમે છે.
અમિત નવલકથા? છ્ટ. એવો નકામો વખત બગાડવો પોસાય નહીં.
મીરા બહુ સારું, હવે અવાજ નહીં. આપણાં અંગ્રેજી શિક્ષિકા આવી ગયાં છે.

AMIT āje shilāben nathi?
MEERĀ nā mā̃dā paḍi gayā̃ chhe. tyā̃ sudhi bhugoḷ bipinbhāi shikhavshe.
AMIT em āje pahelā̃ angreji, gaṇit ane vignān to chhe j. paṇ itihās tathā chitrakām āje chhe ke kāle?
MEERA pāchhũ samay patrak khoi nākhyũne? le māri pāse vadhārānũ chhe. ā sāchvi rākhje. āje to bapor pachi sangit ane ramatgamat chhe.
AMIT to to majā paḍshe. miss simpson sārā̃ shikshikā chhe māṭe mane sangit vignān jeṭlũ j game chhe.
MEERA paṇ āpṇā vignān shikshak smith to evā kaḍak chhe vaḷi temnũ gharkām paṇ mẼ karyũ nathi.
AMIT mane vignān aghrũ lāgtũ nathi. khari rite to mane vignān ghaṇũ game chhe.
MEERA mane angreji game chhe.mane navalkathāo vā̃chvi game chhe.
AMIT navalkathā? chhaṭ evo nakāmo vakhat bagāḍvo posāy nahi.
MEERA bahu sārũ. have avāj nahĩ. āpṇā angreji shikshikā āvi gayā̃ chhe.

AMIT *Isn't Sheelāben coming today?*
MEERA *No. She's sick. Bipinbhai will be taking us for geography.*
AMIT *I see. Well, we have English, maths and science too, but do you know if we have history and painting today or tomorrow?*
MEERA *It seems you've lost your timetable again. Take this copy. I have a spare one. And keep it safe. We have games and music this afternoon.*
AMIT *That will be nice. Miss Simpson is a good teacher and I like music as much as science.*

MEERA *But the science teacher, Mr Smith, is so strict and I haven't done my homework.*
AMIT *I don't find science difficult. As a matter of fact I like the subject a lot.*
MEERA *English is my subject. I love reading novels.*
AMIT *Novels? Oh no! I don't waste time with novels.*
MEERA *Well, keep quiet. Here comes our English teacher.*

Vocabulary

માંદા	**māndā**	sick
અંગ્રેજી	**angreji**	English
ગણિત	**gaṇit**	mathematics

વિજ્ઞાન	**vignān**	science
ઈતિહાસ	**itiihās**	history
ભૂગોળ	**bhugoḷ**	geography
ચિત્રકામ	**chitrakām**	painting
સંગીત	**sangit**	music
રમતગમત	**ramatgamat**	games
શિક્ષક	**shikshak**	teacher (male)
શિક્ષિકા	**shikshikā**	teacher (female)
અવાજ	**avāj**	noise
સમયપત્રક	**samay patrak**	timetable
વખત બગાડવો	**vakhat**	waste time
ખોઈ નાખ્યું	**khoi nākhyũ**	lost
સાચવી રાખજે	**sāchvi rākhje**	keep it safe
અઘરૂં	**aghrũ**	difficult
વિષય	**vishay**	subject
ઘરકામ	**gharkām**	homework
નવલકથા	**navalkathā**	novel

Grammatical notes

Compound verbs

(a) Gujarati has the peculiarity of combining two verbs which usually form an entirely different third meaning: for example, the verb પડ (**paḍ**) means 'fall' and જા (**jā**) means 'go'. However, the compound verb પડી ગયા (**paḍi gayā**), combined with માંદા (**mā̃dā**) 'sick' means 'is sick'. The closest resemblance is the English 'fallen sick/ill':

શીલાબહેન માંદાં પડી ગયા છે. (**shilāben mā̃dā̃ paḍi gayā chhe.**)
Sheelaben is sick.

(b) The verb ખો (**kho**) means 'lose', નાખ (**nākh**) means 'throw'; but when these two are combined, ખોઈ નાખ્યું (**khoi nākhyũ**) the meaning is 'lost'.

(c) The verb સાચવ (**sāchav**) means 'preserve', રાખ (**rākh**) means 'keep'; but together, સાચવી રાખ, (**sāchvi rākh**) they mean 'keep it safe'.

(d) The verb આવ (**āv**) means 'come'; જા (**jā**) means 'go'. The compound આવી ગયાં (**āvi gayā̃**) (ગયાં (**gayā̃**) is the past tense of જા (**jā**)) means 'came'. Similarly, જા (**jā**) used after verbs like પડ (**paḍ**), ખા (**khā**) (પડી જા (**paḍi jā**), ખાઈ જા (**khāi jā**)) does *not* have the meaning 'go'. It just adds a sense of urgency or immediacy to the meaning of the first verb:

સફરજન ઝટ ખાઈ જા. (**sapharjan jhaṭ khāi jā**.) Eat the apple immediately.
ઘરમાંથી ચાલી જા. (**gharmā̃ṭhi chāli jā**.) Get out of the house.
દવા પી જા. (**davā pi jā**.) Take the medicine.

Note: the first verb in this is generally past tense with **i** ending, e.g. પડી (**paḍi**), ખોઈ (**khoi**), સાચવી (**sācvi**), ખાઈ (**khāi**), etc.

Postpositions

In English, words like 'under', 'before', etc. are prepositions, coming *before* the word they govern, e.g. '*under* the table'. In Gujarati they are called postpositions because they are placed *after* the word they govern, e.g. ટેબલ નીચે. (**ṭebal niche**).

Postpositions follow a noun or pronoun and show its relationship with another word in a sentence:

ટેબલ નીચે ચોપડી છે. (**ṭebal niche chopḍi chhe**.) The book is *under* the table.

These postpositions can be broadly classified according to meaning as given below.

Place and direction

અંદર (**andar**) 'in', બહાર (**bahār**) 'out', પાસે (**pāse**) 'near', ઉપર (**upar**) 'above', નીચે (**niche**) 'below', વચ્ચે (**vachhe**) 'between', etc. denote place or direction:

વર્ગની અંદર શિક્ષક નથી. (**vargni ādar shikshak naṭhi**.) There is no teacher *in* the class.

વિદ્યાર્થીઓ વર્ગની બહાર છે. (**vidyārthio vargni bahār chhe.**) The students are *out* of the classroom.

ગણિત અને વિજ્ઞાન વચ્ચે વિરામ છે. (**gaṇit ane vignān vachhe virām chhe.**) There is a break *between* the maths and science lessons.

Time

પહેલાં (**pahelā̃**) 'before', પછી (**pachhi**) 'after', આગળ (**āgaḷ**) 'before', etc. denote time or sequence:

અમિત પહેલાં મીરા આવી. (**amit pahelā̃ mirā āvi.**) Meera arrived *before* Amit.

ગણિત પછી વિજ્ઞાન છે. (**gaṇit pachhi vignān chhe.**) The science lesson is *after* maths.

Instrumentality

વડે (**vaḍe**) 'by', મારફત (**mārphat**) 'through', etc. denote instrumentality:

અમિતે હાથ વડે લખ્યું. (**amite hāth vaḍe lakhyũ.**) Amit wrote *by* hand.

અરજી મારી મારફત મોકલશો. (**arji māri mārphat mokalsho.**) Send the application *through* me.

Absence

વિના (**vinā**) 'except', વગર (**vagar**), સિવાય (**sivāy**) 'without', etc. denote the absence of a person or thing:

શીલા વગર કોઈ આવશે નહીં. (**shilā vagar koi āvshe nahĩ.**) No one is coming *except* (*lit.* without) Sheela.

Comparison

કરતાં (**kartā̃**) 'compared to', બરાબર (**barābar**) 'equal to', માફક (**māphak**) 'like' show a comparison between people or things:

મીરા કરતાં અમિત મોટો છે. (**mirā kartā̃ amit moṭo chhe.**) Amit is older *than* (*lit.* to) Meera.

કામમાં બંને બરાબર છે. (**kāmmā̃ bāne barābar chhe.**) They are *equal to* each other (i.e. equally good) at the job.

Purpose

માટે (**māṭe**) 'for', ખાતર (**khātar**) 'for', etc. show purpose:

આ દિવાળીની ભેટ તારે માટે છે. (**ā divāḷni bheṭ tāre māṭe chhe**.)
This Divali gift is *for* you.

There are some case suffixes which are used in place of certain postpositions:

લક્ષ્મણથી રામ મોટા છે. (**lakshmaṇthi rām moṭā chhe**.) Ram is older *than* (*lit.* elder to) Laxman.
લક્ષ્મણ કરતાં રામ મોટા છે. (**lakshmaṇ kartā̃ rām motā chhe**.) (Ram is older *than* Laxman.
શીલા ઘરમાં નથી/શીલા ઘરની અંદર નથી. (**shilā gharmā̃ naṭhi/shilā gharni ā̃dar naṭhi**.) Sheela is not *in* the house.

Postpositions are written as a separate word while suffixes become part of the word they influence.

Exercise 1

Translate into Gujarati:

(a) I was sick yesterday.
(b) I like music.
(c) I have lost my pen.
(d) Do it properly.
(e) Meera lost her book.

Exercise 2

Fill in the blanks with appropriate postpositions:

ટેબલ ____ (under) બિલાડી બેઠી હતી. મીરા અને અમિત ઘરની ____ (in) આવ્યાં. બિલાડીને ____ (before) મીરાએ જોઈ. ____ (after) અમિતે જોઈ. મીરા બિલાડી ____ (for) દૂધ લાવી હતી. બિલાડી તરત બંને ____ (near) આવી. મીરાએ તેને પંપાળીને ____ (after) વાટકીની ____ (in) દૂધ આપ્યું. ત્યાં સુધી અમિતે પેન ____ (by) પત્ર લખ્યો.

Exercise 3

Fill in the blanks:

(a) ઈલોના અમેરિકામાં માંદી ____ (was sick)
(b) મેં પાછો હાથરૂમાલ ____ (lost)

(c) અમિતને વિજ્ઞાન ____ (likes)
(d) તારી તબિયત ____ (all right) નથી.
(e) જહોન રવિવારે ફૂટબોલ ____ (will play)

Exercise 4

Correct mistakes where appropriate:

તારો આંખ દુખે છે? આંખમાં દવા નાખ્યો? દવા નથી નાખ્યો છે? દુકાન બંધ હતો? તો બીજી દુકાન ગયો. પૈસા છે? કેટલી પૈસા છે? આ બીજી પૈસા રાખું.

Exercise 5

Translate into English:

(a) મને રમતમાં મજા પડે છે.
(b) આ હેડમાસ્તર કડક નથી.
(c) આ નવલકથા સારી છે.
(d) શનિવારે બપોર પછી અમે ખરીદી કરીશું.
(e) રવિવારે તમારી સાથે વખત ગાળીશ.

Exercise 6

Make sentences using the following compound verbs:

ખોઈ નાખ પડી જા આવી જા

Dialogue 2

માંદગી **mā̃dagi** Sickness **(CD1; 55)**

Amit and Meera are discussing their teacher's sickness

અમિત હજી શીલાબહેન આવતાં નથી. વધુ માંદાં લાગે છે.
મીરા હા. મારી મમ્મી તેમની ખબર કાઢવા આજ સવારે ગઈ હતી. તે કહેતી હતી કે તેમને સખત શરદી થઈ ગઈ છે અને તાવ પણ આવે છે.
અમિત આજકાલ આખા યુરોપમાં ફ્લ્યુના વાયરા છે. ઘણા લોકો તેમાં સપડાઈ ગયા છે.
મીરા તેમાં દર્દીનું શરીર એવું નિચોવાઈ જાય છે! જરાય શક્તિ જ રહેતી નથી.
અમીત આખું શરીર દુખે, માથું દુખે, ને ઉધરસ ખાઈ ખાઈને તો પાંસળાં થાકી જાય.
મીરા ને ડોક્ટરો એસ્પિરિન લઈને આરામ કરવાનું જ કહે છે.

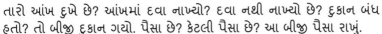

અમિત દરદ મટાડવાને બદલે તેઓ દુઃખ દબાવનારી દવાઓ જ આપે છે.
મીરા સૌને ઝટપટ સાજા થવું હોય છે.
અમિત મારો અમેરિકન મિત્ર ભારત ગયો ત્યારે તેને મેલેરિયા થઈ ગયો હતો. નસીબ સારું તે માંડ માંડ બચ્યો.
મીરા મારી બહેનપણી લીસાને તો તું ઓળખે છે. એ મુંબઈ ગઈ ને સખત ઝાડા થઈ ગયા. દેશ જોવાને બદલે માત્ર હોસ્પીટલ જોઈ!
અમિત મને પણ ગઈકાલથી પેટમાં ખૂબ તકલીફ થાય છે.
મીરા એકાદ-બે ઉપવાસ ખેંચી કાઢ! બધું મટી જશે.

AMIT haji shilāben āvtā nathi. vadhu mā̃ndā lāge chhe.

MEERĀ hā māri mummy temni khabar kāḍhvā āj savāre gai hati. te kaheti hati ke temne sakhat shardi thai gai chhe. ane tāv paṇ āve chhe.

AMIT ājkāl ākhā europmā flunā vāirā chhe. ghaṇā loko temā sapḍai gayā chhe.

MEERĀ temā dardinū sharir evū nichovāi jāy chhe. jarāe shaktij raheti nathi.

AMIT ākhū sharir dukhe, māthū dukhe, ne udhras khāi khāi ne to pā̃sḷā thāki jāy.

MEERĀ ne ḍokṭaro asprin laine ārām karvānū j kahe chhe.

AMIT darad maṭāḍvāne badle teo dukh dabāvnāri davāo j āpe chhe.

MEERĀ saune jhaṭpaṭ sājā thavū hoy chhe.

AMIT māro amerikan mitra Peṭer bhārat gayo tyāre tene malariā thai gayo hato. nasib sārū te mā̃ḍmā̃ḍ bachyo.

MEERĀ māri bahenpaṇi lisāne to tū oḷkhe chhe. e mumbai gai ne sakhat jhāḍā thai gayā. desh jovāne badle mātra hospiṭal joi.

AMIT mane paṇ gai kālthi peṭmā̃ khub taklph thāy chhe.

MEERA ekād be upvās khẽchi kāḍh. badhū maṭi jashe.

AMIT *Sheelaben hasn't arrived yet. She still seems to be sick.*

MEERA *Yes. My mother went to see her this morning and told me she has a heavy cold and a fever.*

AMIT *This flu is everywhere in Europe. A lot of people are suffering with it. It's an epidemic.*

MEERA *When you have flu your body feels drained and you have no strength.*

AMIT *Your body aches, you usually have a bad headache and your ribs hurt from continuous coughing.*

MEERA *And all the doctors do is advise you to take aspirin and rest.*
AMIT *Instead of prescribing a cure, they just give you painkillers.*
MEERA *The problem is that everyone wants instant relief.*
AMIT *I had an American friend who got malaria while travelling in India. He was just lucky to survive.*
MEERA *You know my friend Lisa who went to Bombay? She had acute diarrhoea and instead of seeing the country all she saw was the inside of a hospital!*
AMIT *I've had a lot of trouble with my stomach since yesterday.*
MEERA *Well, just fast for a day or two and you'll be all right!*

Vocabulary

સખત	**sakhat**	heavy
શરદી (*f*)	**shardi**	cold
તાવ (*m*)	**tāv**	fever
નિચોવાઈ જાય છે	**nichovāi jāy chhe**	is drained
પાંસળાં (*n*)	**pā̃salā̃**	ribs
દુઃખ દબાવવાની દવા	**dukh dabāvvāni davā**	painkillers (*lit.* pain suppressors)
ઝટપટ	**jhaṭpaṭ**	instant
માંડ	**mānḍ**	just
ઝાડા	**jhāḍā**	diarrhoea
ઉપવાસ	**upvās**	fast (refrain from eating)
મટી જશે	**maṭi jashe**	will be cured
વાયરા	**vāyarā**	epidemic
તકલીફ	**takliph**	trouble

Grammatical and colloquial notes

ખબર (**khabar**) means 'news'. When it combines with the verb કાઢ (**kāḍh**) 'bring out' it means 'going to see someone who is unwell'.

The verb આવ (**āv**) means 'come', but when used with તાવ (**tāv**) 'fever' it means the person concerned is suffering from fever.

ઉધરસ (**udharas**) is 'coughing', ખા (**khā**) is 'to eat'. Words like cough, sneeze, yawn are always followed by the verb ખા (**khā**):

તે ઉધરસ ખાય છે.	(**te udharas khāy chhe**.) He is coughing.
તે છીંક ખાય છે.	(**te chhĩk khāy chhe**.) He is sneezing.
તે બગાસું ખાય છે.	(**te bagāsũ khāy chhe**.) He is yawning.

The verb ખેંચ (**khẽch**) means 'to pull through', કાઢ (**kāḍh**) means 'to extract'. When used as a compound verb, it implies reluctance and means 'have' or 'pass':

ઉપવાસ ખેંચી કાઢ.	(**upvās khẽchi kāḍh**)	(have a) fast
દિવસો ખેંચી કાઢ.	(**divaso khẽchi kāḍh**)	pass the days (in the sense of 'hanging on' or enduring until better times)

ખેંચી કાઢ (**khẽchi kāḍh**) also has the simple meaning of 'pull out':

દાઢ ખેંચી કાઢી.	(**dāḍh khẽchi kāḍhi**.)	A molar tooth was extracted, pulled.
કાંટો ખેંચી કાઢ્યો.	(**kā̃ṭo khẽchi kāḍhyo**.)	A thorn was pulled out.
મૂળિયું ખેંચી કાઢ્યું.	(**muḷiyũ khẽchi kāḍhyũ**.)	A root was pulled out.

Gender

In Gujarati every noun has a gender. In many words gender is revealed by the end vowel.

Nouns ending in **o** are frequently masculine:

છોકરો (**chhokro**) boy	ઘોડો (**ghoḍo**) horse (*m*)	કૂતરો (**kutaro**) dog (*m*)
તબેલો (**tabelo**) stable	ખભો (**khabho**) shoulder	

Those ending in **i** are frequently feminine:

છોકરી (**chhokari**) girl	ઘોડી (**ghoḍi**) horse (*f*)	કૂતરી (**kutari**) dog (*f*)

આંગળી (**ãngḷi**)	છરી (**chhari**)
finger	knife

Those ending in **ũ** are frequently neuter:

છોકરું	ઘોડું	કૂતરું	બારણું	પીછું
child	horse (unspecified)	dog	door	feather

There are no firm rules with respect to the above: હાથ 'hand' is masculine, જીભ 'tongue' is feminine and કપાળ 'forehead' is neuter, all ending in **a**. However:

Names of rivers are always feminine: ગંગા, નાઈલ, થેમ્સ, મિસિસિપી.

Names of cities and lakes are always neuter: ન્યુ યોર્ક, શિકાગો, મુંબઈ, બાઈકલ, ડાલ.

Names of countries, mountains and oceans are masculine: ભારત, પાકિસ્તાન, હિમાલય, પેસિફિક.

In some cases the suffix is used to show size. The ending **o** indicates 'bigger' and an **i** ending 'smaller': ઓરડો is a big room and ઓરડી a small room; ચમચો is a big spoon and ચમચી a small spoon.

There are some words which are expressed in two genders: ચા 'tea' can be either masculine or feminine; સવાર 'morning' can be feminine or neuter; ખરચ 'expense' can be masculine or neuter.

Words borrowed from English also take on gender, which does not exist in the original: ટેલિફોન is masculine; બસ is feminine; ટેબલ is neuter.

Exercise 7

Which is the odd word in the following columns?

(a) શરીર માથું પાંસળાં વાદળું
(b) મમ્મી મેલેરિયા ભાઈ બહેન
(c) શરદી તાવ અમેરિકા ફ્લ્યુ
(d) યુરોપ ભોજન ઉપવાસ નાસ્તો

Exercise 8

Rearrange the following sentences to make sense:

(a) લોકો વરસાદમાં કાલે ગયા સપડાઈ
(b) નાખ પાણી કાઢી નિચોવી કપડાં
(c) ગયો પડી કેનેડામાં ટોની

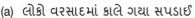

(d) એટલે છે મને તાવ હું લઈશ દવા
(e) તીખાં છે ભજિયા લાગે ભાવે છે પણ

Exercise 9

In five sentences tell your doctor about an illness you have had.

Exercise 10

Change the following sentences as indicated:

(a) મને તો અંગ્રેજી ગમે છે. (negation)
(b) આજે બપોર પછી સંગીત છે. (future)
(c) તને મેલેરિયા થઈ ગયો હતો. (present)
(d) બધું મટી જશે. (past)
(e) વખત ગાળવો મને પોસાય નહીં. (affirmation)

Exercise 11

Pair the opposites:

A	*B*
સાચું	સાજું
સારું	જા
માંદું	ખોટું
આવ	નરમ
કડક	ખરાબ

Exercise 12

Read the passage and answer the questions that follow:

નટુભાઈ માંદા પડી ગયા. હું તેમની ખબર કાઢવા ગઈ. તેમને તાવ આવતો હતો. હું ફળ લઈ ગઈ હતી. તેમને હવે સારું છે. એકાદ અઠવાડિયું આરામ કરશે.

(a) કોણ માંદું પડી ગયું?
(b) તેમને શું થતું હતું?
(c) હવે કેમ છે?
(d) નટુભાઈ કેટલો આરામ કરશે?
(e) મળવા જનાર શું લઈ ગયાં હતાં?

Unit Nine

ગુજરાતી ફિલ્મો **gujarāti philmo**

Gujarati films

શોખ **shokh**

Hobbies

In this unit you will learn about:

- Comparative and superlative degrees
- Some important prefixes and suffixes
- Interjections: words expressing surprise, sorrow, etc.
- Adverbs
- Some more colloquial forms

Dialogue 1

ગુજરાતી ફિલ્મો **gujarāti philmo** Gujarati films

(CD2; 1)

Aman and Barkha are talking about Gujarati films.

અમન ગાંધીજીનું સૌથી પ્રિય ભજન ‘વૈષ્ણવજન તો તેને કહીએ જે પીડ પરાઈ જાણે રે’ તે ગુજરાતી ફિલ્મનું છે?

બરખા હા, પણ તે આપણા આદિ કવિ નરસિંહ મહેતાનું છે. પહેલી ગુજરાતી ફિલ્મ ૧૯૩૨ માં ‘નરસિંહ મહેતા’ નામે બની તેમાં આ ભજન ગવાયું હતું. પછી તો ઘણી ફિલ્મો બની.

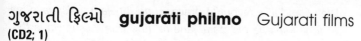

અમન જાણીતી 'સરસ્વતીચંદ્ર' નવલકથાને આધારે તૈયાર થયેલી 'ગુણસુંદરી' ફિલ્મ તો ૧૯૨૭થી ૧૯૪૮ સુધીમાં ત્રણ વાર બની. પહેલી બે કરતાં ત્રીજી સરસ હતી.

બરખા હા, દાદાજી કહેતા હતા કે છેલ્લી ફિલ્મમાં તો જાણીતી કલાકાર નિરુપા રોયે ગુણસુંદરી નું પાત્ર ભજવ્યું હતું. ગુણસુંદરી એટલે સુંદરતા અને પવિત્રતાનું પ્રતિક.

અમન રંગભૂમિનાં નાટકોની ઘણી અસર આ ફિલ્મો પર હતી.

બરખા કેતન મહેતા જેવા નિર્ભય દિગ્દર્શકે ભવની ભવાઈ જેવી પ્રયોગશીલ ફિલ્મો પણ બનાવી. ઘણાં ઈનામો મેળવ્યાં.

અમન હા, ચાલો ત્યારે, ટીવી પર 'ઝાંસીકી રાની' આવવાનો ટાઈમ થઈ ગયો છે.

AMAN gandhijinũ priya bhajan 'vaishṇavajan to tene kahie je piḍ parāi jaṇe re' te gujrāti philmnũ chhe?

BARKHĀ hā, paṇ te āpṇā ādi kavi narsinh mahetānũ chhe. paheli gujrāti philm 1932mā̃ narsinh mahetā nāme bani.

AMAN jāṇiti saraswatichandra navakathāne ādhāre taiyār thayeli gunsundari philm to 1927thi 1948 sudhimā̃ traṇ vār bani hati. paheli be kartā triji saras hati.

BARKHĀ hā, dādāji kahetā hatā ke chhelli philmmā̃ to jāṇiti abhinetri nirupā roye guṇsundarinũ pātra bhajvyũ hatũ. gunsindari eṭle sundartā ane pavitratānũ pratik.

AMAN rangbhuminā nāṭakoni ghaṇi asar ā philmo par hati.

BARKHĀ ketan mahetā jevā kushal digdarshake bhavni bhavāi jevi prayogshil philmo paṇ banāvi. ghaṇā̃ ināmo meḷvyā̃.

AMAN hā, chālo tyāre ṭivi par jhānsi ki rāṇi āvvāno ṭāim thai gayo chhe.

AMAN *Was Gandhiji's favourite prayer song (bhajan) 'vaishnava jan to tene kahie je pid parai jane re' (the true Vaishnava is the one who experiences others' pains) from a Gujarati film?*

BARKHA *Yes, but it is a composition of our first poet Narsinh Mehta. The first Gujarati film in 1932 was made about Narsinh Mehta. This was sung in that film. Then many films were made.*

AMAN *The film Gunsundari based on the well-known novel Saraswatichandra was produced three times from 1927 to 1948. The third was better than the first two.*

BARKHA *Yes, grandpa was saying that in the last film the famous actress Nirupa Roy played Gunsundari. Gunsundari symobolizes beauty and piety.*

AMAN *The stage plays influenced many of these films.*

BARKHA *Fearless directors like Ketan Mehta made experimental films like* Bhavni Bhavai. *Won many prizes.*

AMAN *Oh!* Zansi ki rani *is about to start on the TV.*

Vocabulary

ભજન	**bhajan**	prayer
પીડ પરાઈ	**piḍ parāi**	pain of others
આદિ કવિ	**ādi kavi**	first poet
નવલકથા	**navalkathā**	novel
સરસ્વતીચંદ્ર	**saraswatichandra**	famous Gujarati novel
ગુણસુંદરી	**guṇsundari**	a well-known character of that novel
સુંદરતા અને પવિત્રતાનું પ્રતિક	**sundartā ane pavitratānũ pratik**	a symbol of beauty and piety
રંગભૂમિ	**rangbhumi**	stage
નિર્ભય	**nirbhay**	fearless

ભવાઈ	**bhavāi**	a folk drama
પ્રયોગશીલ	**prayogshil**	experimental
ઝાંસી કી રાની:	**jhānsi ki rāni**	*Queen of Jhansi*, a patriot in Indian freedom. The TV series is most popular.

Grammatical notes

Degrees of comparison

In English, as in Sanskrit, there are *comparative* and *superlative* degrees, expressed by suffixes like 'er' and 'est' (wise, wis*er*, wis*est*) and in Sanskrit **tara** and **tama**.

The literary Gujarati uses more words borrowed from Sanskrit, but in colloquial speech these are rarely used. It is much more common for words like કરતાં and suffixes like માં and થી to be employed:

ગાંધીજીનું સૌથી પ્રિય ભજન વૈષ્ણવ જન છે.
(**gāndhijinũ sauthi priya bhajan vaishṇav jan chhe.**)
Gandhi's most favourite prayer song is 'Vaishnavjan'.

અંગ્રેજીમાં લખનાર શૉ સૌથી સારો નાટકકાર હતો.
(**angrejimā̃ lakhnār shO sauthi sāro nāṭakkār hato.**)
Shaw was the best dramatist writing in English.

ઈબ્સન કરતાં શૉ મને ગમે છે.
(**ibsan kartā̃ shO mane game chhe.**)
I like Shaw better than Ibsen.

ઊંચામાં ઊંચું પૂતળું નેલ્સનનું છે.
(**ũchāmā̃ ũchũ putalũ nelsannũ chhe.**)
Nelson's statue is the highest in London.

Although થી (**thi**) and માં (**mā**) appear in the above examples, they are not used exclusively to show the superlative or comparative:

હું ન્યુ યોર્કથી આજે નીકળીશ.
(**hũ nyu yorkthi āje niklish.**)
I will start from New York today.

હું ઘરમાં છું.
(**hũ gharmā̃ chhũ**.)
I am in the house.

Similarly, in addition to its use as a comparative, કરતાં (**kartā̃**) can also be used as the past tense, feminine or neuter, of **kar** 'to do' and as an adverb:

Comparative: રામ લક્ષ્મણ કરતાં મોટા હતા.
(**rām lakshmaṇ kartā̃ moṭā hatā**.)
Ram was older than Laxman.

Superlative: સૌ કરતાં રામ મોટા હતા.
(**sau kartā̃ rām moṭā hatā**.)
Ram was the eldest brother.

Verb: તેઓ કામ કરતાં.
(**teo kām kartā**.)
They were working.

Adverb: કામ કરતાં કરતાં તે પડી ગયો.
(**kām karatā̃ karatā̃ te paḍi gayo**.)
He fell down while working.

As is seen from the last example, repetition is frequently used for emphasis.

Some important suffixes and prefixes

- તા (**tā**)

  સુંદર (**sundar**) beautiful સુંદરતા (**sundartā**) beauty

  By adding the તા (**tā**) suffix an adjective is converted into a noun.

  પવિત્ર (**pavitra**) pure પવિત્રતા (**pavtratā**) purity
  સ્વતંત્ર (**svatantra**) independent સ્વતંત્રતા (**svatantratā**) independence

- The કાર (**kār**) suffix denotes 'one who does':

  ચિત્રકાર (**chitrakār**) one who paints, a painter (ચિત્ર (**chitra**) painting)

કથાકાર (**kathākār**) one who tells stories, a storyteller (કથા (**kathā**) story, generally religious)

કલાકાર (**kalākār**) one who does art, an artist (કલા (**kalā**) art)

- The અ (**a**) *prefix* expresses negation, absence or lack of:

અવિનય (**avinay**) immodesty (વિનય (**vinay**) modesty)

અછત (**achat**) scarcity (છત (**chat**) abundance)

અયોગ્ય (**ayogya**) improper (યોગ્ય (**yogya**) proper)

- The અપ (**ap**) *prefix* means both 'not' and 'bad':

અપકીર્તિ (**apkirti**) disrepute or bad repute (કીર્તિ (**kirti**) reputation)

અપશુકન (**apshukan**) bad omen (શુકન (**shukan**) omen)

- The નિર (**nir**) *prefix* means 'without':

નિર્જીવ (**nirjiv**) lifeless, dead (જીવ (**jiv**) life)

નિર્ભય (**nirbhay**) fearless (ભય (**bhay**) fear)

Exercise 1

Combine sentences A and B with appropriate conjunctions:

(a) A એ સ્ત્રી સૌથી વધુ જાણીતી હતી.
B એ સ્ત્રી સૌથી વધુ રૂપાળી હતી.

(b) A આજે વરસાદ આવશે.
B આજે વરસાદ ન પણ આવે.

(c) A તેણે કહ્યું.
B મારી પાસે પૈસા નથી.

Exercise 2

Use the following constructions in your own four sentences: e.g. જો માંસાહાર નહી કરું તો નબળો થઈશ.

(a) જો ____ તો ____
(b) જેમ ____ તેમ ____
(c) જ્યારે ____ ત્યારે ____
(d) જ્યાં ____ ત્યાં ____

Exercise 3

Use કશું 'any' in the following sentences, remembering that it changes according to number and gender: e.g. કશો (*m sg*) જવાબ ન આપ્યો.

(a) ____ વાત (*f sg*) ન કરશો.
(b) ____ કામ (*n sg*) કરો.
(c) ____ ખબર (*f pl*) પડે તો ને!
(d) ____ ગોટાળો (*m sg*) થયો લાગે છે.

Exercise 4

Insert the appropriate verb forms in the following paragraph:

મારે ક્યાં ઈંગ્લેન્ડમાં આખો વખત ____ (stay). ભાષણ કરવાનું શીખીને શું ____ (will do)? નાચ શીખીને હું સભ્ય કેમ ____ (become)? હું તો વિદ્યાર્થી ____ (is). મારે વિદ્યા ____ (to get).

Exercise 5

Find the odd word out in each of the following:

(a)	રૂપાળી	રૂપ	સુંદરતા	જવાબ
(b)	સંતાન	પત્ર	બાળક	દીકરો
(c)	નાટક	નટી	પણ	નાટકકાર
(d)	તેણે	બુદ્ધિ	તેને	તેમણે
(e)	છે	રજૂઆત	હતું	હશે

Exercise 6

Pair off opposite words from each column and use them in ten different sentences:

A	*B*
માન	અન્યાય
નીતિ	અસત્ય
સત્ય	નિર્જીવ
જીવ	અનીતિ
ન્યાય	અપમાન

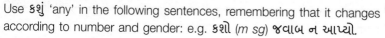

Exercise 7

Describe in five sentences the places worth visiting in your city, using comparative and superlative degrees.

Dialogue 2

શોખ **shokh** Hobbies **(CD2; 3)**

સીતા	નમસ્તે રમેશભાઈ, કેમ છો?
રમેશ	ઓહો, નમસ્તે સીતાબેન, અત્યારમાં ક્યાં ઊપડ્યાં?
સીતા	હું હમણાં સંગીતના વર્ગોમાં જોડાઈ છું. દર શનિવારે સવારે હોય છે. તમે કેમ જોડાતા નથી?
રમેશ	હું અને સંગીત? મારો અવાજ સાંભળીને પડોશીઓ ઘર ખાલી જશે!
સીતા	શી મજાક કરો છો? થોડા દિવસ પહેલાં જ તમને તખ્તા પર ગાતાં જોયા હતા.
રમેશ	એ તો નાટકમાં. તમે જે સાંભળ્યું તે મારો અવાજ ન હતો. એ તો રેકોર્ડિંગ હતું અને હું તો માત્ર અભિનય કરતો હતો.
સીતા	એમ. તમને નાટક ઉપરાંત શેનો શોખ છે?
રમેશ	મને ક્રિકેટ બહુ ગમે છે. તમને?
સીતા	મને રમતનો ખાસ શોખ નથી. હા, કોઈ વાર ટી.વી. પર ફૂટબોલની મેચ જોઈ નાખું ખરી! મેં સાંભળ્યું છે કે તમારી નાની બહેનને ટિકિટો એકઠી કરવાનો શોખ છે.
રમેશ	હા, મીરા તો તેની પાછળ ગાંડી છે. પણ તમારા મોટા ભાઈ ફોટોગ્રાફી પાછળ ગાંડા છે, નહીં?
સીતા	રોહિત હવે માત્ર શોખ તરીકે તે કરતા નથી. હવે તો તે ધંધાદારી બની ગયા છે.
રમેશ	એ એને માટે સારું જ છે. પણ માફ કરજો, હું તો વાતોએ ચડી ગયો. તમારે વર્ગમાં મોડું થશે. આવજો.
સીતા	આવજો.

SITĀ	namaste, rameshbhāi kem chho?
RAMESH	Oho! namaste sitāben, atyārmā̃ kyā̃ upḍyā̃?
SITĀ	hū̃ hamṇā̃ sangitnā vargomā̃ joḍāi chhū̃. dar shanivāre savāre hoy chhe. tame kem joḍātā nathi?
RAMESH	hū̃ ane sangit? māro avāj sāmbhḷine paḍoshio ghar khāli kari jashe!

SITĀ shi majāk karo chho? thoḍā divas pahelā̃j tamne takhtā par gātā̃ joyā hatā.

RAMESH e to nāṭakmā̃. tame je sambhaḷyũ te māro avāj na hato. e to rekorḍing hatũ ane hũ to mātra abhinay karto hato.

SITĀ Em! tamne nāṭak uprā̃t sheno shokh chhe?

RAMESH mane kriketṭ bahu game chhe. tamne?

SITĀ mane ramatono khās shokh nathi. hā, koi vār ṭivi par phuṭbOlni mEch joi nākhũ khari. mẼ sambhaḷyũ chhe ke tamāri nāni bahenne ṭikiṭo ekṭhi karvāno shokh chhe.

RAMESH hā. mirā to teni pāchhaḷ gānḍi chhe. paṇ tamārā moṭābhāi phoṭogrāphi pāchhaḷ gānḍā chhe nahi?

SITĀ rohit have mātra shOkh tarike te kartā nathi. have to te dhandhādāri bani gayā chhe.

RAMESH e ene māṭe sarũ ja chhe. paṇ māph karjo hũ to vātoe chaḍi gayo. tamāre vargmā̃ moḍũ thashe. āvjo.

SITĀ āvjo.

SITA *Hello Rameshbhai. How are you?*

RAMESH *Hello Sitaben. What are you up to so early?*

SITA *I recently started music classes. I go every Saturday morning. Why don't you come?*

RAMESH *Music and I don't get on. The neighbours would leave home if I tried to sing!*

SITA *You're joking. A few days ago I heard you singing on stage.*

RAMESH *That was in a play and what you heard wasn't me. It was a recording and I was just miming to it.*

SITA *What hobbies do you have apart from acting?*

RAMESH *I like cricket very much. What about you?*

SITA *I don't much like sports although I might occasionally watch a football match on television. I hear your younger sister collects postal stamps.*

RAMESH *Yes, Mira is crazy about stamps. But your elder brother is just as mad about photography.*

SITA *Rohit doesn't do it as a hobby any more. He is now a professional.*

RAMESH *Good for him. Anyway, sorry to have talked so much you'll be late for your class. Good bye.*

SITA *OK. Goodbye.*

Vocabulary

શોખ	**shokh**	hobby
સંગીત	**sangit**	music
પડોશી	**paḍoshi**	neighbour
મજાક	**majāk**	joke
ગાંડા	**gānḍā**	mad
અભિનય	**abhinay**	acting
નાટક	**nāṭak**	play
રમત	**ramat**	game
ચોક્કસ	**chokkas**	sure
ખાલી કરવું	**khāli karvũ**	to vacate, empty
જોડાવું	**joḍāvũ**	to join
તખ્તો	**takhto**	stage

Grammatical notes

Interjections

Words like ઓહો (**oho**), અરેરે (**arere**), હાય હાય (**hāy hāy**) express surprise, sorrow, etc.

ઓહો! સીતાબહેન, મેં તમને જોયાં જ નહીં.
(**oho! sitāben, mẽ tamne joyā ja nahĩ.**)
Oh, Sita! Sorry, I didn't see you. (**o-ho** registers mild surprise)

ઓહો! એમ વાત છે?
(**oho! em vāt chhe?**)
Oh, I see! So it's like that!

અરેરે, બિચારો પડી ગયો.
(**arere, bichāro paḍi gayo.**)
Oh God! That poor man has collapsed. (**arere** expresses sympathy and sadness)

હાય હાય, નીલા બહુ બીમાર છે.
(**hāy hāy, nilā bahu bimār chhe.**)
Oh no! Is Neela very ill? (**hāy hāy** is used only by women)

Adverbs

Adverbs denote time, place, manner, degree, cause or purpose, certainty, probability and negation:

આજે શનિવાર છે. (**āje shanivār chhe.**)	*Today* is Saturday.
હમણાં વર્ગ શરૂ થયો. (**hamṇā varg sharu thayo.**)	The class opened *recently*.
અત્યારમાં ક્યાં જાઓ છો? (**atyārmā̃ kyā̃ jāo chho?**)	Where are you going so *early?*
અહીં, પાસે જ છે. (**ahī̃ pāse j chhe.**)	It is *just* round the corner.
તમે કેમ જોડાતા નથી? (**tame kem joḍātā nathi?**)	*Why* don't you join?
હું કોઈ વાર નાટક જોઉં છું. (**hũ koi vār nāṭak joũ chhũ.**)	*Sometimes* I go to a play.
તમે ધીમે ચાલો છો. (**tame dhime chālo chho.**)	You walk *slowly*.
હું ચોક્કસ આવીશ. (**hũ chokkas āvish.**)	I will *certainly* come.
આ કામ કરશો નહીં. (**ā kām karsho nahī̃.**)	*Don't* do this work.

Note: નહીં (**nahī̃**) can also be used to ask 'is it not?':

લેવા કરતાં આપવામાં વધુ આનંદ મળે છે, નહીં?
(**levā kartā̃ āpvāmā̃ vadhu ānand maḷe chhe, nahī̃?**)
It is better to give than to receive, is it not?

Duplicative form

કેટકેટલું: (**keṭkeṭlũ**) the adjective કેટલું (**keṭlũ**) means 'how much', 'how many':

કેટલા માણસ હશે? (**keṭlā māṇas hashe?**)	*How many* people will be there?
મકાન કેટલું મોટું છે? (**makān keṭlũ moṭũ chhe?**)	*How* (*much*) big is the house?

Note, however, that when the duplicative part કેટ (**ket**), formed from the first two letters of કેટલું (**keṭlũ**), is added, it means 'how many varieties of . . .' or 'so many . . .':

કેટકેટલાં મકાનો (**keṭkeṭlā makāno**) so many houses
કેટકેટલી જાતના માણસ (**keṭkeṭli jātnā māṇas**) so many types of people

Colloquial notes

ક્યાં ઊપડ્યાં? (**kyā̃ upaḍyā̃?**) literally means 'where started' but is used in the sense of 'What are you up to?'. When preceded by અત્યારમાં (**atyārmā̃**) (*lit.* just now) it means 'so early'.

ફોટોગ્રાફી પાછળ તો એ ગાંડા છે. (**phoṭogrāphi pāchhal to e gā̃ḍā chhe.**) He's just mad about photography.
સરલા પાછળ તો એ ગાંડો છે. (**sarlā pāchhaḷ to e gā̃ḍo chhe.**) He's mad about Sarla (i.e. in love).

The same phrase is also used in English.

જોઈ નાખું ખરો (**joi nākhũ kharo**) (*m*)/ ખરી (**khari**) (*f*) 'Sometimes I watch/look/see':

કોઈક વાર ટીવી જોઈ નાખું ખરો/(**koik vār ṭivi joi nākhũ kharo**) ખરી. (**khari**) Sometimes I might watch television.

In this example જોવું (**jovũ**) means 'to see/watch/look', નાખ (**nākh**) means 'to throw' and ખરો (**kharo**) means 'right/correct'. When all three appear together the combination means 'might as well see'. હું વાતોએ ચડી ગયો (**hũ vātoe chaḍi gayo**) 'I talked too much': ચડ (**chaḍ**) means 'to climb' and ગયો (**gayo**) means 'went' and વાત (**vāt**) 'talk'; together they mean 'went on talking'.

If કામ (**kām**) 'work' is added to ચડ (**chaḍ**) and જા (**jā**) the compound word takes on the meaning of 'joined':

હું આજથી કામે ચડી ગયો. (**hũ ājthi kāme chaḍi gayo.**) I joined (i.e. started) work today (either for the first time or in the sense of 'resumed').

In colloquial speech the verb is sometimes implied:

એ તો નાટકમાં. (**e to nāṭkmā̃**) (You might have seen me) in the play.
ને મારા મોટાભાઈને ફોટોગ્રાફીનો (**ne mārā moṭābhāine phoṭogrāphino**) My elder brother's (hobby is) photography.
હું ક્રિકેટ રમું છું. તમે? (**hũ kriket ramũ chhũ. tame?**) I play cricket; and you?

Exercise 8

Think of suitable adjectives to fill in the gaps, bearing in mind that there is more than one way of answering:

દાંત	મોઢું	આંખ	નાક
e.g. સફેદ	ગોળ	કાળી	લાંબુ
____	____	____	____
____	____	____	____

Exercise 9

Pair off appropriate words from the two columns:

A	*B*
આજે	પછી
હમણાં	કદાચ
અહીં	ત્યાં
ધીમે	કાલે
ચોક્કસ	ઝડપથી

Exercise 10

Arrange the following in order of size:

હાથી ઘોડો કૂતરો ઉંદર સિંહ કીડી મચ્છર

Exercise 11

Translate into English:

નાટક એ શોખ છે અને ધંધો પણ છે. નાટકકાર નાટક લખે છે. નટનટીઓ નાટક ભજવે છે. લોકો નાટક જુએ છે. કેટલાકને તે ગમે છે. કેટલાકને તે ગમતું નથી.

Exercise 12

Rearrange the following dialogue to make sense:

મીના સંગીતના હું માગું નમસ્તે છું જોડાવા વર્ગમાં:
શિક્ષક શું નમસ્તે તમારે? છે શીખવું
મીના શીખવી મારે છે સિતાર
શિક્ષક છે રૂપિયા પાંચસો, મહિને ફી સિતારની
મીના મળશે ભલે? ક્યાંથી ફોર્મ:

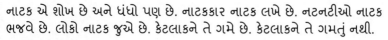

શિક્ષક આપો લો ને સામે આ ભરીને:
મીના વર્ગ છે થાય? શરૂ ક્યારે
શિક્ષક દર સવારે વાગ્યે નવ શનિવારે:

Exercise 13

What are the questions to the following answers?

(a) મને ક્રિકેટનો શોખ છે.
(b) ચોક્કસ આવીશ.
(c) ના, હું સંગીત શીખવાનો નથી.
(d) મારી નાની બહેન ભણે છે.
(e) પડોશીઓ સારા છે.
(f) ગઈ કાલે હું કેપટાઉન હતો.

Exercise 14

Choose the correct verbs from the parentheses.

મારું નામ સુજાતા (હશે/છે/હતું). મારી ઉંમર હાલ ૧૮ વર્ષની (હતી/છે/હશું). હું યુગાન્ડામાં જન્મી (હોઈશ/હતી/છે). હવે હું લંડનમાં રહું (છીએ/હતો/છું). અમે આવતા વરસે અમેરિકા જવાના (હતું/છીએ/હશે).

Unit Ten

હવાઈ મથકનું ઉદ્ઘાટન **havāi mathaknū udghāṭan**

Opening of the airport

માતૃભાષાનો મહિમા **mātrubhāshāno mahimā**

Importance of the mother tongue

In this unit you will learn about:

- Some more compound verbs
- Plurals of English loan words
- Active and passive voice
- Various moods
- Conjuncts (i.e. joining words)
- Participles

Dialogue 1

હવાઈ મથકનું ઉદ્ઘાટન **havāi mathaknū udghātan**

Opening of the airport **(CD2; 6)**

Rekha and Shashi are wife and husband. They talk about the opening of Ahmedabad airport.

રેખા આજના છાપામાં શા સમાચાર છે?

શશી અરે! સરસ સમાચાર છે રેખા. તું સાંભળીને ખુશ ખુશ થઈ જઈશ. બોલ શું હશે?

રેખા લોટરી લાગી છે? તો શીરો બનાવું.

શશી અરે! આ તો આખા ગુજરાતની લોટરી લાગી છે. તેં જાતે આજની ટપાલમાં આવેલું છાપું ખોલ્યું જ નથી?

રેખા આજે ઘરમાં કામ કેટલું હતું? કહી નાખો એટલે ખીચડી મૂકવા જાઉં.

શશી અમદાવાદના નવા એરપોર્ટનું ઉદ્ઘાટન થયું. સાંજ પડી ગઈ હતી. એરપોર્ટ લાઇટોથી દીપી ઊઠ્યું હતું. લોકોએ ફોટા ઝડપી લીધા. ભીડ પણ કેટલી બધી! હવે મોટાં વિમાનો પણ અમદાવાદ ઊતરી શકશે.

રેખા ખરેખર! તે તો આનંદની વાત છે.

શશી હા, ભારત સરકારના ઉડ્ડયન વિભાગના પ્રધાન પ્રફુલ પટેલના હસ્તે થયું.

રેખા નવું એરપોર્ટ તો સરસ થઈ ગયું હશે, નહિ? આપણે લંડન આવ્યા ત્યારે તો કેવી દશા હતી!

શશી હા, ત્રણસો સોળ કરોડના ખર્ચે તૈયાર થયું છે. બધી સગવડ છે. ને એરપોર્ટને સરદાર વલ્લભભાઈ પટેલનું નામ અપાયું છે. એટલે એમનું ભવ્ય પુતળું પણ મૂકાશે.

રેખા સરસ. ચાલો ત્યારે આજે જમવામાં ખીચડીને બદલે શીરો મળશે.

REKHĀ ājnā chhāpāmā̃ shā samāchār chhe?

SHASHI are! saras samāchār chhe rekhā. tū̃ sā̃bhaḷine khush khush thai jaish. bol shū̃ hashe?

REKHĀ loṭri lāgi chhe? to shiro banāvū̃.

SHASHI are! ā to ākhā gujrātni loṭri lāgi chhe. tẽ jāte ājni ṭapālmā̃ āvelū̃ chhāpū̃ kholyū̃ ja nathi?

REKHĀ āje gharmā̃ kām keṭlū̃ hatū̃? kahi nākho eṭle khichḍi mukvā jaū̃.

SHASHI amdāvādnā navā aerporṭnū̃ udghāṭan thayū̃. sā̃j paḍi gai hati. erporṭ laiṭothi dipi uṭhyū̃ hatū̃. lokoe phoṭā jhaḍpi lidhā. bhiḍ paṇ keṭli badhi. have moṭā vimāno paṇ amdāvād utri shakshe.

REKHĀ kharekhar! te to ānandni vāt chhe.

SHASHI bhārat sarakārnā uḍḍyan vibhāgnā pradhān praphul paṭelnā haste thayū̃.

REKHĀ navū̃ aerporṭ to saras thai gayū̃ hashe, nahi? āpṇe lanḍan āvyā tyāre to kevi dashā hati?

SHASHI hā, traṇso soḷ karoḍnā kharche taiyār thayū̃ chhe. badhi sagvaḍo chhe. ne aerporṭne sardār vallabhbhāi paṭelnū̃ nām apāyū̃ chhe. eṭle emnū̃ bhavya putḷū̃ paṇ mukāshe.

REKHĀ chālo tyāre āje jamvāmā̃ khichḍine badle shiro maḷshe.

REKHA *What is the news in today's newspaper?*

SHASHI *Oh! There is good news Rekha. You will be pleased to hear it. Guess what is it?*

REKHA *Won a lottery? Then I will make shiro (sweet dish).*

SHASHI *Oh! This is a lottery for the whole of Gujarat. Haven't you opened the newspaper that arrived by post this morning?*

REKHA *Do you know how much work was at home today? Do tell me so that I can do the cooking.*

SHASHI *New Ahmedbad airport has been opened. It was evening. The airport was illuminated with lights. People snapped shots. (grabbed photos). Lots of crowds were there. Now even big planes will land at the airport.*

REKHA *Really! It is a matter of joy.*

SHASH *Yes, the Aviation Minister of the Government of India, Prafull Patel, opened it.*

REKHA *The new airport must have become nice, hasn't it? It was in such a state when we came to London.*

SHASHI *Yes. It has been built at a cost of three hundred and sixteen million. It has all amenities. The airport has been named Sardar Vallabhbhai Patel, so a grand statue will also be placed there.*

REKHA *Good. There will be shiro today instead of khichdi.*

Vocabulary

છાપું	**chāpū**	newspaper
સમાચાર	**samāchār**	news
શીરો	**shiro**	sweet dish
ટપાલ	**ṭapāl**	mail
ખીચડી	**khichḍi**	lentils mixed with rice and boiled
ઉદ્ઘાટન	**udghāṭan**	opening
વિમાન	**vimān**	aeroplane
ઉડ્ડયન વિભાગ	**uḍḍyan vibhāg**	department
દશા હતી	**dashā hati**	was in (poor) state
સગવડ	**sagvaḍ**	arrangement, convenience
પૂતળું	**putḷū**	statue
દીપી ઊઠ્યું	**dipi uṭhyū**	illuminated
ઝડપી લીધા	**jhaḍpi lidhā**	grabbed
ભીડ	**bhiḍ**	crowd

Grammatical notes

Compound verbs

પડી ગઈ (**paḍi gai**) means 'fallen'; the verb પડ (**paḍ**) means 'fall'. The second verb in this compound is ગઈ (**gai**), the past tense, feminine singular form of જવું (**javū**) 'to go'. In contrast to English, it is not only night that 'falls' in Gujarati, but also morning or evening. This compound can also be joined by the auxiliary verb હતી (**hati**), the past tense feminine of હોવું (**hovū**) 'to be'.

દીપી ઊઠ્યું (**dipi uṭhyū**) means 'came out beautifully': દીપવું (**dipvū**) means 'to appear beautiful' and ઊઠવું (**uṭhvū**) 'to get up'. ઊઠ્યું (**uṭhyū**) is its past tense, third person neuter singular form. This compound is joined by the auxiliary verb હતું (**hatū**), past tense neuter singular form of હોવું (**hovū**). ઝડપી લીધા (**jhaḍpi lidhā**) means 'grabbed': ઝડપવું (**jhaḍpvū**) means 'to take hold of' and લેવું (**levū**) 'to take'. લીધા (**lidhā**) is the past tense masculine plural of લેવું (**levū**). Note that the first verb in the compound verbs is generally in the past tense, ending in **i** (પડી (**paḍi**), દીપી (**dipi**), ઝડપી (**jhaḍpi**), etc.).

Auxiliary verbs

જોવો હતો (**jovo hato**) 'wanted to see', લાગતું હતું (**lāgtũ hatũ**) 'looked like' are all examples of past tense forms of હોવું (**hovũ**) and complete the sense of the main verbs.

Plural of English words used in Gujarati

Generally speaking, the plural formation of English loan words is achieved by the Gujarati suffix ઓ (**o**):

લાઈટ (**laiṭ**) 'light'	લાઈટો (**laiṭo**)
સ્કૂલ (**skul**) 'school'	સ્કૂલો (**skulo**)
ટેબલ (**ṭebal**) 'table'	ટેબલો (**ṭebalo**)
ટ્રેન (**ṭren**) 'train'	ટ્રેનો (**ṭreno**)
ફોટો (**phoṭo**) 'photograph'	ફોટાઓ (**phoṭāo**)

(**o** ending changes to **ā** before the plural suffix is added, just like other **o** ending Gujarati words, e.g. ઘોડો (**ghoḍo**) ઘોડાઓ (**ghoḍāo**).)

The exceptions are words like ફૂટ (**phuṭ**) 'foot' and ઈંચ (**ĩnch**) 'inch', which remain the same in singular and plural:

એ છ ફૂટ લાંબો છે. (**e chh phut lābo chhe.**)	He is 6 feet tall.
આ દોરી દસ ઈંચ કાપો. (**ā dori das ĩnch kāpo.**)	Cut this string 10 inches long.

Active and passive voice

Shashi is eating shiro.
શશી શીરો ખાય છે. (**shashi sheero khāy chhe.**)

Shiro is eaten by Shashi.
શશીથી શીરો ખવાય છે. (**shashithi sheero khāvay chhe.**)

The first sentence is in the active form, where the subject શશી (Shashi) is actively connected to the action of 'eating'. In the second sentence it is the shiro which is important and the subject is passive.

When the passive voice is employed, the verb changes:

Active	*Passive*
નાખે છે. (**nākhe chhe.**)	નખાય છે. (**nakhāy chhe.**)
કરે છે. (**kare chhe.**)	કરાય છે. (**karāy chhe.**)
લખે છે. (**lakhe chhe.**)	લખાય છે. (**lakhāy chhe.**)

Here are some more examples:

તે કામ કરે છે. (**te kām kare chhe.**)	He is doing the work.
તેનાથી કામ કરાય છે. (**tenāthi kām karāy chhe.**)	The work is done by him.
રીટા કાગળ લખે છે. (**riṭā kāgaḷ lakhe chhe.**)	Rita is writing a letter.
રીટાથી કાગળ લખાય છે. (**riṭāthi kāgaḷ lakhāy chhe.**)	A letter is being written by Rita.

In the passive voice:

(a) the suffix થી (**thi**) is added to the subject;

(b) the suffix આય (**āy**) or વાય (**vāy**) is added to the verbal root to form a passive verb;

(c) if the first letter of the verb has an **ā** vowel it changes to **a**: e.g. નાખ (**nākh**), નખાય (**nakhāy**);

(d) similarly a single-letter verb with an **ā** vowel changes to **a**, e.g. આ (**ā**), અવાય (**avāy**), જા (**jā**), જવાય (**javāy**).

Impersonal

There is a third construction in Gujarati which is impersonal and known as **bhāve prayog**:

જનકથી બોલાતું નથી. (**janakthi bolātū nathi.**) Janak is unable to speak (*lit.* Speaking is not possible for Janak).

It is determined by the relation of the impersonal verb to the doer:

પહેલાં મારાથી ખવાતું હતું. (**pahelā̃ mārāthi khavātū hatū.**) I was able to eat before (*lit.* Previously eating was possible by me).

The થી (**thi**) suffix used in the passive voice continues here, but the suffix આતું (**ātũ**) is added to the verbal root, ખવાતું (**khavātũ**), દોડાતું (**doḍātũ**), પીવાતું (**pivātũ**), etc.

Colloquial notes

નહીં ત્યારે! (**nahĩ tyāre!**) The word નહીં (**nahĩ**) means 'not' and ત્યારે (**tyāre!**) means 'then'. Used together, they become the exclamation 'of course'.

In the sentence ભીડ પણ કેટલી બધી! (**bhiḍ paṇ keṭli badhi!**) the last word, હતી (**hati**) (was), would be omitted. The English translation is 'The place was overcrowded'. This construction is used to express proportion, quantity or intensity:

ઊંચો પણ કેટલો બધો! (**ũcho paṇ keṭlo badho!**)	How tall it was!
ઠંડી પણ કેટલી બધી! (**ṭhanḍi paṇ keṭli badhi!**)	It was extremely cold.
પવનનું તોફાન પણ કેટલું બધું! (**pavannũ tophan paṇ keṭlũ badhũ!**)	It was a violent wind.

In these examples the omission of the verbs હતો (**hato**), હતી (**hati**), હતું (**hatũ**), actually emphasizes the degree of the effect.

Exercise 1

Translate the following into English:

(a) હું પેનિસિલ્વેનિયાથી આવું છું.
(b) મારી પાસે આ દેશના સિક્કાઓ નથી.
(c) અહીં રહેવાની સગવડ છે?
(d) દૂરબીનથી દૂરનાં દૃશ્યો સરસ દેખાય છે.
(e) બ્રિટનમાં સૌથી ઊંચો માણસ કોણ છે તે તમે જાણો છો?

Exercise 2

Correct the following passage:

રામલાલભાઈ ઝાડ ઉપર પડી ગયું. તે માથું વાગી ગયું. તેથી બેભાન થઈ ગઈ. શારદાબહેન દોડ આવ્યું ગયાં. ફોન કર્યું. હોસ્પીટલવડે ગાડું આવ્યો. તેને લઈ ગયો

Exercise 3

Find the odd word out in each of the following and then use them in five different sentences:

(a)	ખવાય	પીવાય	જમાય	દોડ
(b)	કર	નખાવું	લખાવું	બોલવું
(c)	સિક્કો	રમત	પૈસો	નાણું
(d)	ધોધ	નદી	ઉંદર	સરોવર
(e)	દૂર	પથ્થર	ઉપર	સામે

Exercise 4

Change as directed:

(a)	મારાથી ભારત જવાશે.	(active voice)
(b)	હું શાકાહારી ખોરાક લઉં છું.	(passive voice)
(c)	અહીં એક ટેબલ છે.	(plural)
(d)	હીરાભાઈથી દોડાતું નથી.	(affirmation)
(e)	ગાય ઘાસ ખાય છે.	(past tense)

Exercise 5

Write a dialogue of six exchanges about a recent holiday.

Exercise 6

Match the words in column A with those in column B:

A	*B*
સારું	અગવડ
ઠંડી	અંધારું
પ્રકાશ	નીચે
ઉપર	ખરાબ
સગવડ	ગરમ

Dialogue 2

માતૃભાષાનો મહિમા **mātrubhāshāno mahima**

Importance of the mother tongue **(CD2; 8)**

પેસ્તનજી નમસ્તે બેન.

મહેરબેન નમસ્તે. આવ બેસ.

પેસ્તનજી બેન, એક સવાલ પૂછું?

મહેરબેન જરૂર.

પેસ્તનજી બેન આપણે ઇંગ્લેંડમાં રહીએ છીએ. બધે જ અંગ્રેજી બોલાય છે. અમારો બધો જ વ્યવહાર અંગ્રેજીમાં ચાલે છે. તો અમારે ગુજરાતી શા માટે શીખવું જોઈએ?

મહેરબેન તારી માતૃભાષા ગુજરાતી છે એ માટે.ભલે ગુજરાતીમાં આખો વ્યવહાર ન પણ ચાલે.માતા, માતૃભાષા અને માતૃભૂમિને ભૂલી જ ન શકાય.ભલે અંગ્રેજીમાં તારો આખો વ્યવહાર અહી ચાલે, પણ ગુજરાત જઈશ ત્યારે શું કરીશ?

પેસ્તનજી પણ સ્કૂલમાં તો મારે કેટલા બધા વિષયો ને ભાષાઓ ભણવાના હોય છે.પછી મગજમાં કેટલું સમાય?

મહેરબેન મગજ એ તો ડોલ નથી કે તે ભરાઈ જાય એટલે બીજું ના માય. મગજ તો બધું જ સમાવી શકે છે. અને સંશોધકો કહે છે કે માતૃભાષાનું જ્ઞાન જો હોય તો બીજી ભાષાઓ અને બીજાં વિષયો શીખવા સહેલા પડે છે. શીખેલી ભાષા નકામી જતી નથી.

પેસ્તનજી આની તો મને ખબર જ ન હતી.

મહેરબેન ફાધર વાલેસ નામના એક પ્રોફેસર હતા.એકડે એકથી ગુજરાતી શીખ્યા.અને અત્યારે ગુજરાતીના જાણીતા લેખક છે, ને કહે છે કે સૌ ગુજરાતી શીખો.

પેસ્તનજી એમ!

મહેરબેન હા, જ્યારે તેમને ખબર પડી કે તેમને ગુજરાતમાં આવીને ગણિત ભણાવવાનું છે ત્યારે નક્કી કર્યું કે ગુજરાતમાં જઈશ તો ગુજરાતી શીખીને જ જઈશ. તે કહે છે કે માતૃભાષા જાય તેની સાથે સંસ્કાર, સંસ્કૃતિ, ધર્મ બધું જ જાય.

પેસ્તનજી તો તો હું હવે ગુજરાતી બરાબર શીખીશ.

PESTANJI namste ben.

MAHERBEN namste āv bes.

PESTANJI ben, ek savāl puchhũ?

MAHERBEN jarur.

PESTANJI ben āpṇe inglanḍmā rahie chhie. badhe ja angreji bolāy chhe. amāro badho ja vyavhār angrejimā chāle chhe. to amāre gujrāti shā māṭe shikhvũ joie?

MAHERBEN tāri matrubhāshā gujarāti chhe e māṭe. bhale gujrātimā ākho vyavhār na chāle. mātā, matrubhāshā ane mātrubhumine bhuli ja na shakāy. bhale angrejimā̃ tāro ākho vyavhār ahi chāle, paṇ gujarāt jaish tyāre shũ karish?

PESTANJI paṇ skulmā̃ to māre keṭlā badhā vishayo ne bhāshāo bhaṇvānā hoy chhe. pacchi magajamā̃ keṭlu samāy?

MAHERBEN magaj e to ḍol nathi ke te bharāi jāy eṭle bijũ nā māy. magaj to badhu ja samāvi shake chhe. ane sanshodhako kahe chhe ke mātrubhāshānu gnān jo hoy to biji bhāshāo ane bijā vishayo shikhvā sahelā paḍe chhe. shikheli bhāshā nakāmi jati nathi.

PESTANJI āni to mane khabar ja na hati.

MAHERBEN phadhar vāles nāmnā ek prophesar hatā. ekḍe ekthi gujarāti shikhyā. ane atyāre gujrātinā jāṇitā lekhak chhe, ne kahe chhe ke sau gujrāti shikho.

PESTANJI em!

MAHERBEN hā, jyāre temne khabar paḍi ke temne gujarātmā̃ āvine gaṇit bhaṇāvvānu chhe tyāre nakki karyũ ke gujrātmā̃ jaish to gujrāti shikhine ja jaish. te kahe chhe ke mātrubhāshā jāy teni sāthe sanskār, sanskruti, dharma, badhu ja jāy.

PESTANJI to to hũ have gujrāti barābar shikhish.

PESTANJI *Hello.*

MAHERBEN *Hello. Come and sit.*

PESTANJI *Miss, can I ask a question?*

MAHERBEN *Certainly.*

PESTANJI *Miss, we live in England. English is spoken everywhere. All our communication is in English, so why should we learn Gujarati?*

MAHERBEN *Your mother tongue is Gujarati, that is why. The whole communication may not be in Gujarati, mother, mother tongue and motherland cannot be forgotten. Let all your communication be in English here, but what will you do when you go to Gujarat?*

PESTANJI *But I have to learn so many subjects and languages in school, then how much more can be stuffed in the brain?*

MAHERBEN *The brain is not like a pail so that once it is filled no more can be added, the brain can accommodate a lot, and researchers say that knowledge of the mother tongue makes it easier to learn other languages and subjects. A language learnt can never be lost.*

PESTANJI *I did not know about this.*

MAHERBEN *A professor called Father Vallace learnt Gujarati from the beginning and is now a well-known author of Gujarati, and says that everyone must learn Gujarati.*

PESTANJI *Is that so?*

MAHERBEN *Yes, when he learnt that he had to teach mathematics in Gujarat, then he decided that he would go to Gujarat only after learning Gujarati. He says that if the mother tongue is lost then culture, civilization, religion everything is lost.*

PESTANJI *Then now I will learn Gujarati properly.*

Vocabulary

સંકલ્પ (*m*)	**sankalp**	decision
વ્યવહાર (*m*)	**vyavahār**	communication
અધ્યાપક (*m*)	**adhyāpak**	lecturer
શુદ્ધ	**shuddh**	pure
મધુર	**madhur**	sweet
માતૃભાષા (*f*)	**mātrubhāshā**	mother tongue
નિશ્ચય (*m*)	**nishchay**	decision
કેળવણી (*f*)	**keḷvani**	education
વ્યક્તિગત	**vyaktigat**	personal
સંપર્ક (*m*)	**sampark**	contact
માર્ગદર્શન (*n*)	**margdarshan**	guidance
મિત્રતા (*f*)	**mitratā**	friendship
દૃઢ	**druḍh**	firm

Grammatical notes

Mood

એ માટે માતૃભાષા જ જોઈએ. (**e māṭe mātrubhāshā j joie.**) 'A mother tongue is needed for that' or 'for which a knowledge of the mother tongue is necessary'. This is a sentence that expresses some duty or obligation. It is in *potential mood*. The verb જોઈએ (**joie**) shows the manner in which the statement is made. Other examples are:

સૌએ સારાં કામ કરવાં જોઈએ. (**saue sārā̃ kām karvā̃ joie.**)
Everyone should do good turns.
ગરીબોને મદદ કરવી જોઈએ. (**garibone madad karvi joie.**)
Poor people should be helped.
સાચું બોલવું જોઈએ. (**sāchū̃ bolvū̃ joie.**) One should speak the truth.

These sentences can be constructed without the auxiliary verb at the end, but its use makes it an *obligatory* form.

Conditional mood

જો ગુજરાતમાં જઈશ તો ગુજરાતી શીખીને જ જઈશ. (**jo gujrātmā̃ jaish to gujrāti shikhine j jaish.**) *lit.* 'If I happen to go in Gujarat, I will go after learning the Gujarati language', meaning 'If I go to Gujarat I will first learn the language.' Here the mood is clearly conditional, governed by 'If . . . then'.

In Gujarati જો (**jo**) (if) is sometimes dropped, the conditional nature of the sentence being understood by the use of તો (**to**) 'then'. Note: in English it is the reverse, with 'if' carrying the import of the sentence and 'then' frequently becoming redundant.

Subjunctive

The subjunctive mood represents doubt, something that may or may not occur.

આખો વ્યવહાર અંગ્રેજીમાં ન પણ ચાલે. (**ākho vyavāhar angrejimā̃ na paṇ chāle.**) The whole dialogue might not be in English.

આજે તડકો ન પણ પડે. (**āje taḍko na paṇ paḍe.**) The sun may not shine today.
કાલે બરફ પડે પણ ખરો. (**kāle baraph paḍe paṇ kharo.**) Tomorrow it might snow.

Imperative

This may be a command or a request:

છોકરાંઓ તોફાન બંધ કરો. (**chokrāo tophān bandh karo.**) Calm down, children.
કાલે પેલી ચોપડી લાવશો? (**kāle peli chopḍi lāvsho.**) Will you please bring that book tomorrow?

Indicative

This involves statements of fact:

સૂર્ય પૂર્વ દિશામાં ઊગે છે. (**surya purva dishāmā̃ uge chhe.**) The sun rises in the east.
ગુજરાત ભારતમાં આવેલું છે. (**gujrāt bhāratmā̃ āvelũ chhe.**) Gujarat is in India.

Adjectives

There are two types of adjectives, variable and invariable. The first group changes according to the number and gender of the qualifier:

આખો (**ākho**) whole, entire	આખો વ્યવહાર (**ākho vyavahār**) (*m sg*)
સાચું (**sāchũ**) real, correct	સાચું કામ (**sāchũ kām**) (*n sg*)

Invariable adjectives, as the name implies, do not change:

શુદ્ધ (**shuddh**) purely, pure	શુદ્ધ અંગ્રેજી (**shuddh angreji**) good/pure English
મધુર (**madhur**) sweet	મધુર ગુજરાતી (**madhur gujrāti**) sweet Gujarati
દૃઢ (**druḍh**) firm	દૃઢ નિશ્ચય (**druḍh nischay**) firm decision

Conjuncts

ત્યારથી (**tyārthi**)	since then
અને (**ane**)	and
છતાં (**chhatā̃**)	even
કે (**ke**)	that
તો (**to**)	then

For example:

એ ખબર પડી ત્યારથી મેં નક્કી કર્યું (**e khabar paḍi tyārthi mẽ nakki karyū̃**) . . . I decided (about it) once I realized that . . .

The two sentences એ ખબર પડી (**e khabar paḍi**) . . . 'I realized/understood that . . .' મેં નક્કી કર્યું (**mẽ nakki karyū̃**) 'I decided' are joined by ત્યારથી (**tyārthi**). The word જ્યારથી (**jyārthi**) 'since then' is implicit.

લડાઈ શરૂ થઈ ત્યારથી ભાવ વધ્યા છે. (**laḍāi sharu thai tyārthi bhāv vadhyā chhe.**) The rates have increased since the outbreak of war.

અધ્યાપકો અને વિદ્યાર્થીઓ અંગ્રેજી બોલતા હતા. (**adhyāpako ane vidyārthio angreji boltā hatā.**) The lecturers and students were (both) speaking in English.

વિદ્યાર્થીઓ સારું અંગ્રેજી જાણતા હતા છતાં વર્ગની બહાર તમિળમાં બોલતા. (**vidyārthio sārū̃ angreji jāṇtā hatā chhatā̃ vargni bahār tamiḷmā̃ boltā.**) The students spoke good English yet used Tamil outside the class.

The sentences વિદ્યાર્થીઓ સારું અંગ્રેજી જાણતા હતા (**vidyārthio sārū̃ angreji jāṇtā hatā**) and વર્ગની બહાર તમિળમાં બોલતા (**vargni bahār tamiḷmā boltā**) are joined by છતાં (**chhatā̃**).

મેં નિશ્ચય કર્યો કે ગુજરાતમાં ગુજરાતી શીખીને જ જઈશ.
(**mẽ nishchay karyo ke gujrātmā gujrāti shikhine j jaish.**)
I decided I would go to Gujarat after learning the language.

The sentences મેં નિશ્ચય કર્યો (**mẽ nishchay karyo**) and ગુજરાતમાં ગુજરાતી શીખીને જ જઈશ (**gujrātmā̃ gujrāti shikhine j jaish**) are joined by કે (**ke**).

ગુજરાતમાં જઈશ તો ગુજરાતી શીખીને જ જઈશ. (**gujrātmā̃ jaish to gujrāti shikhine j jaish**) If I go to Gujarat it will be after learning the language.

The sentences ગુજરાતમાં જઈશ (**gujrātmā̃ jaish**) and ગુજરાતી શીખીને જ જઈશ (**gujrāti shikhine j jaish**) are joined by તો (**to**).

Participles

A participle derives from a verb but functions as an adjective or a noun. In Gujarati it is called **krudant**.

Past participles

કરેલું કામ નકામું જતું નથી. (**karelũ kām nakāmũ jatũ nathi.**)
Work done is never wasted.

Here the suffix એલ (**el**) is added to the root of the verb followed by the number–gender suffixes: કરેલું (**karelũ**) (neuter singular because કામ (**kām**) is neuter):

Root + past participle **el** + number–gender suffix
કર (**kar**) + એલ (**el**) + ઉં (**ũ**) = કરેલું (**karelũ**)

Past participle formations of verbs like ખા (**khā**), પી (**pi**), બેસ (**bes**) take their past tense forms ખાધું (**khādhũ**), પીધું (**pidhũ**), બેઠું (**bethũ**), etc. before the number–gender suffixes:

ખાધેલો ખોરાક (**khādhelo khorāk**)	food that was eaten
પીધેલું પાણી (**pidhelũ pāni**)	water that was drunk
બેઠેલી સ્ત્રી (**beṭheli stri**)	woman who was sitting

Conjunctive participle

This participle denotes an action which has taken place *before* the one expressed by the principal verb, e.g. આવવું (**āvvũ**) (to come) in the following example:

ભારતમાં આવીને હું ગુજરાતી શીખું છું. (**bhāratmā̃ āvine hũ gujrāti shikhũ chhũ.**)
Having *come* to India I am learning Gujarati.

The suffix ઈને (**ine**) is added to the root, i.e. root + **ine**: આવ (**āv**) + ઈને (**ine**) = આવીને (**āvine**). Similarly,

પેરિસ જઈને હું એથન્સ જઈશ. (**periṡ jaine hũ eṭhens jaish.**) After going to Paris I will go to Athens.
ફ્રેન્ચ શીખીને હું ફ્રાન્સ ગયો. (**phrench shikhine hũ phrāns gayo.**) I went to France after learning French.
ઘરકામ કરીને દરરોજ હું વર્ગમાં આવું છું. (**gharkām karine darroj hũ vargmā̃ āvũ chhũ.**) I come to the class each day after doing my homework.

આવીને (**āvine**), જઈને (**jaine**), શીખીને (**shikhine**), કરીને (**karine**) show that the action has already been completed.

Present participle

Here the action is happening in the present.

ગણિતનો અભ્યાસ કરતા ફાધર વાલેસ ગુજરાતી શીખ્યા
gaṇitno abhyās kartā phādhar vāles gujrāti shikhyā.
Father Vallace, who was doing mathematics, studied Gujarati.

The verb કરવું (**karvũ**) is changed into the past participle by root + ત (**ta**) + the number–gender suffix, i.e. કરતા **kartā** (third person honorific form).

Note: the same form can also be in the past tense if used at the end of a word:

ફાધર વાલેસ ગણિતનો અભ્યાસ કરતા.
phādhar vāles gaṇitno abhyās kartā.
Father Vallace was studying mathematics.

Similarly,

ચડતો માણસ	**chaḍto māṇas**	climbing man
તરતી માછલી	**tarti māchhli**	swimming fish
પડતું પાંદડું	**paḍtũ pãdaḍũ**	falling leaf
રમતા છોકરાઓ	**ramtā chhokarao**	playing boys
વાંચતી સ્ત્રીઓ	**vā̃chti strio**	reading women
ભસતા કૂતરાઓ	**bhastā kutrāo**	barking dogs

Note: in Gujarati all the above forms are common although some, namely those connected with people, are not normally used in English.

Future participle

As its name suggests, the action in the future participle has yet to take place:

પરીક્ષા આપનારા વિદ્યાર્થીઓ અહીં બેસશે.
parikshā āpnārā vidyārthio ahī̃ besshe.
Students taking the examination will sit here.

આપવું (**āpvũ**) is 'to give', with the root આપ (**āp**). To form the future participle the નાર (**nār**) suffix is added, followed by the number and gender suffixes: root + નાર (**nār**) + number–gender suffix. Similarly:

દોડનારો ઘોડો	**doḍnāro ghoḍo**	the horse that is going to run
ખાનારી બિલાડી	**khānāri bilāḍi**	the cat that is going to eat
સંતાનારું સસલું	**satānārũ saslũ**	the rabbit that is going to hide
ભાગનારા કાયરો	**bhāgnārā kāyaro**	the cowards who are going to run away
રાંધનારી સ્રીઓ	**rā̃dhnāri strio**	the women who are going to cook
ઊડનારાં પંખીઓ	**uḍnārā̃ pā̃khio**	the birds that are going to fly

Colloquial notes

ખબર પડી (**khabar paḍi**) means 'news'; પડી (**paḍi**) means 'fell'. When combined, they assume the meaning 'got the news'.

Other changes that occur with the usage of પડી (**paḍi**) are

સમજ પડી (**samaj paḍi**) followed, understood (સમજ (**samaj**) understanding)
આવી પડી (**āvi paḍi**) came, i.e. arrived at the wrong place and/or at the wrong time

Here is an example:

હું અહીં ક્યાંથી આવી પડી? **hũ ahī̃ kyā̃thi āvi paḍi?** Why did I (*f*) come here? (to the wrong place)

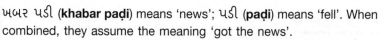

રાત પડી	**rāt paḍi**	night had fallen
રજા પડી	**rajā paḍi**	it was a holiday

પડી (**paḍi**) is the past feminine form of પડવું (**paḍ**) (to fall) and can also be used in its literal sense:

ઝાડ પરથી કેરી પડી. (**jhāḍ parthi keri paḍi.**) A mango fell from the tree.

Exercise 7

Rearrange the following in four groups of four words:

યુરોપ	ભાષા	આગ	વિદ્યાર્થી
અંગ્રેજી	કોલસા	કૉલેજ	એશિયા
ધુમાડો	કેળવણી	અમેરિકા	તમિળ
આફ્રિકા	ગુજરાતી	લાકડાં	વર્ગ

Exercise 8

Which employment matches the individual?

A	*B*
અધ્યાપક	બાંધકામ
વિદ્યાર્થી	બાગકામ
ભોમિયો	બાળઉછેર
માતા	અભ્યાસ
કડિયો	કેળવણી
માળી	માર્ગદર્શન

Exercise 9

Correct the following sentences:

(a) ઘરડાંને મદદ કરવું જો.
(b) આજે પૈસા ન પણ મળીશ.
(c) આખો ઘર બંધ હતો.
(d) હું સાચું નિશ્ચય કરીએ છીએ.
(e) તે ઘેર જા પછી ઑફિસ ગયું
(f) તરતું છોકરી બહાર નીકળ્યો

Exercise 10

Translate into Gujarati:

(a) The flying birds came down.
(b) Barking dogs don't bite.
(c) One should not cheat.
(d) I will not go if it rains.
(e) Personal contact is better than the phone.

Exercise 11

Describe your room using the following vocabulary:

અંદર	બહાર	ઉપર	નીચે	બાજુમાં
સામે	પાસે	આગળ	પાછળ	દૂર

Exercise 12

Fill in the blanks:

જો હું આવીશ તો થાકી ____. એટલે ઘરમાં જ ____. કદાચ વરસાદ પડે પણ ખરો તો છત્રી ____ જશો. મારા ____ ચોપડી લાવ્યા ? અહીં આવ્યો ત્યારથી મેં કશું વાંચ્યું ____. તમે પાછા આવો ત્યાં ____ મારે શું કરવાનું રહેશે?

Exercise 13

Use each of the following words in a different sentence, taking particular care over number and gender.

લેનાર દેનાર ઊઠનાર બેસનાર ખાનાર પીનાર

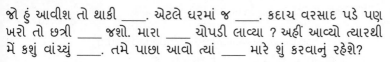

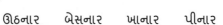

Unit Eleven

થિયેટર તરફ **thieṭar taraph**

Towards the theatre

નાટક જોયા પછી **naṭak joyā pachi**

After the play

In this unit you will learn about:

- More colloquial phrases and compound verbs
- Frequently used English loan words
- Compound words
- The causal form
- The past, present and future continuous

Dialogue 1

થિયેટર તરફ **thieṭar taraph** Towards the theatre
(CD2; 11)

Ilona is a friend of Varsha who is visiting Bombay from London. Varsha and her husband Anant are her hosts

---

વર્ષા કેમ છો ઈલોના, બપોરે શીલાને ત્યાં બરાબર જમ્યા?

ઈલોના હા, આભાર. તમારી શીલાએ ગુજરાતી વાનગી બનાવી હતી. દાળનું સૂપ હતું ને તેમાં કશાકના ખૂબ સ્વાદિષ્ટ ટુકડાઓ નાંખ્યા હતા. મને બહુ જ ભાવ્યું.

વર્ષા ઓહો, એ તો દાળઢોકળી! દાળઢોકળીની વાતમાં શીલાને કોઈ ન પહોંચે! તો હવે સાંજનો શો પ્રોગ્રામ છે? નાટક જોવા જવું છે કે ફિલ્મ?

ઈલોના ફિલ્મો તો લંડનમાં પણ જોઈએ જ છીએને! અહીં તો મારે સારું ગુજરાતી નાટક જોવું છે. બની શકશે?

વર્ષા હા,હા કેમ નહીં? હું હમણાં જ અનંતને ઑફિસમાં ફોન કરી દઉં છું. આપણા સૌ માટે એ ટિકિટો મેળવી લેશે. એ હજી શહેરમાં જ છે.

(થિયેટરમાં)

થિયેટરની બત્તીઓનો પ્રકાશ ધીમે ધીમે ઘટવા લાગ્યો. પડદો ઝળહળી ઊઠ્યો. માઈકમાંથી જાહેર થયું, 'હવે આપની સમક્ષ રજૂ થાય છે, જાણીતું નાટક 'આતમને ઓઝલમાં રાખ મા'. કળાકારો છે. . . .'

VARSHĀ kem chho Ilona, bapore shilāne tyā̃ barābar jamyā̃?

ILONA hā, ābhār. tamāri shilāe gujrāti vāngi banāvi hati. dāḷnũ sup hatũ ne temā̃ kashākhnā khub j svādishṭ ṭukdāo nākhyā hata. mane bahu j bhāvyũ.

VARSHĀ oho, e to dāḷḍhokḷi! dāḷḍhokḷini vātmā̃ shilāne koi na pahõche! to have sā̃jno sho progrām chhe? nāṭak jovā javũ chhe ke philm?

ILONA philmo ṭo *London*mā̃ paṇ joie j chhiene! ahī̃ to māre sārũ gujrāti nāṭak jovũ chhe. bani shakshe?

VARSHĀ hā, hā, kem nahī̃? hũ hamṇā̃ j anantne Ophismā̃ phon kari daũ chhũ. āpṇā sau māṭe e ṭikiṭo meḷvi leshe. e haji shahermā̃ j chhe.

thieṭarni battiono prakāsh dhime dhime ghaṭvā lāgyo. paḍdo jhaḷhaḷi uthyo. māikmā̃thi jāher thayũ, 'have āpni samaksh raju thāy chhe, jāṇitũ nāṭak 'ātamne ojhalmā̃ rākh mā', kalākāro chhe. . . .

VARSHA *How are you, Ilona? Have you had lunch at Sheela's?*

ILONA *Yes, thanks. She made a Gujarati dish – lentil soup with some very tasty pieces in it. I liked it very much.*

VARSHA *Oh, it must be Dal Dhokli. No one can touch Sheela when it comes to Dal Dhokli . . . So what would you like to do this evening? Would you like to go to the theatre or see a film?*

ILONA *I can just as well see films in London. What I would really like to do is go to a good Gujarati play. Is that possible?*

VARSHA *Of course. Why not? I'll phone Anant at his office right now and ask him to get the tickets while he's still in town.*

At the theatre

The hall lights slowly dim. The curtain is illuminated. There is an announcement from the mike. 'Now we present for you the famous play **ātamne ojhalmā̃ rākh mā**. The actors are . . .'

Vocabulary

વાનગી	**vāngi**	dish
દાળ	**dāḷ**	lentil soup
કશાકના	**kashākanā**	of something
ટુકડાઓ	**ṭukḍāo**	pieces
ભાવ્યું	**bhāvyũ**	liked (used only in connection with food)
કોઈ ના પહોંચે	**koi nā pahõche**	no one can touch . . . (*lit.* reach)

બત્તીઓ	**battio**	lamps
પ્રકાશ	**prakāsh**	light
ઘટવા લાગ્યો	**ghaṭvā lāgyo**	got dim
ઝળહળી ઊઠ્યો	**jhaḷhaḷi ooṭhyo**	became illuminated
જાહેર થયું	**jāher thayũ**	was announced
સમક્ષ	**samaksh**	before
રજૂ	**raju**	show, display, present
આતમ	**ātam**	soul (આત્મા)
ઓઝલ	**Ojhal**	cover
રાખ	**rākh**	keep
મા	**mā**	not
આતમને ઓઝલમાં રાખ મા		*lit.* don't keep your soul under cover (i.e. hidden)

Colloquial notes

The phrase કોઈ ના પહોંચે (**koi na pahõche**) is used to show that someone is unsurpassable or incomparable in their field. (પહોંચવું (**pahõchvũ**) means 'to reach'.)

Use of English loan words in Gujarati

Here are some words Gujarati has borrowed from English: પ્રોગ્રામ (**progrām**) 'programme', સૂપ (**sup**) 'soup', ફિલ્મ (**philm**) 'film', ફોન (**phon**) 'phone', ટિકિટો (**ṭikiṭo**) 'tickets' – here the Gujarati plurality suffix (**o**) has been added to the English word 'ticket', થિયેટર (**thieṭar**) 'theatre', માઈક્રોફોન (**maikrophon**) 'microphone'. There are, however, many words which have a Sanskritized Gujarati version which are sometimes found in printed form, e.g. પ્રોગ્રામ (**progrām**) = કાર્યક્રમ (**kāryakram**), ફિલ્મ (**philm**) = ચલચિત્ર (**chalchitra**), ટિકિટ (**ṭikiṭ**) = મૂલ્યપત્રિકા (**mulyapatrikā**), થિયેટર (**thieṭar**) = નાટ્યગૃહ (**nātyahruh**), માઈક (**maik**) = ધ્વનિવર્ધક યંત્ર (**dhvanivardhak yãtra**), etc.

Grammatical notes

Various forms of તો (to)

તો . . . જોઈએ જ છીએને! (**to . . . joie ja chhiene!**) We see it every day.

This phrase shows repetition – and it implies a desire for a change. Similar examples are:

ભાત તો રોજ ખાઈએ જ છીએને! (**bhāt to roj khāie ja chhiene!**) We eat rice every day.
ટીવી તો રોજ જોઈએ જ છીએને! (**ṭivi to roj joie ja chhiene!**) We watch television every day.
ચા તો રોજ પીએ જ છીએને! (**chā to roj pie ja chhiene!**) We drink tea every day.
બસમાં તો રોજ જઈએ જ છીએને! (**basmā̃ to roj jaie ja chhiene!**) We go by bus every day.

In each of these examples the implication is that the speaker wishes that there should be a change in the situation.

Note: તો here has a similar meaning to the English 'as well' and is not part of the જો . . . તો (**jo . . . to**) 'if . . . then' construction.

In the dialogue at the start of this lesson તો changed its meaning in various places according to the context. In ઓહો!, એ તો દાળઢોકળી! (**oho! e to dāḷ dhokḷi!**) 'Oh, it must be Dal Dhokli' it has the meaning 'it was/it must be'. Here is another example:

ઓહ, એ તો નરગીસ. (**oho! e to nargis.**) Oh, that must be the actress Nargis.
તો હવે સાંજનો શો પ્રોગ્રામ છે? (**to have sā̃jno sho progrām chhe?**) *Then* what is the programme in the evening?

Here, તો (**to**) means 'then'. There is no expectation of જો (**jo**) 'if' and again, it is not an 'if . . . then' construction.

અહીં તો મારે સારું ગુજરાતી નાટક જોવું છે. '**ahī̃ to māre sārũ gujrāti nāṭak jovũ chhe.**) Here I want to see a good Gujarati play.

In this example તો is used for emphasis. It is similar to તારે તો આવવું જ પડશે (**tāre to āvvũ ja paḍshe**) 'you will have to come/you must come'.

Some further examples of auxiliary and compound verbs:

Auxiliary verbs: બનાવી હતી (**banāvi hati**), નાખ્યા હતા (**nākhyā hatā**), જોઈએ છીએ (**joie chhie**) are all verbal forms of હોવું (**hovũ**) 'to be'.

Compound verbs: કરી દઉં (**kari daũ**), મેળવી લેશે (**meḷvi leshe**), ઝળહળી ઊઠ્યો (**jhaḷhaḷi uṭhyo**). The roots in the first two verbs are કર (**kar**) 'do' and દે (**de**) 'give', while in the second combination they are મેળવ (**meḷav**) 'obtain' and લે (**le**) 'take' and in the third are ઝળહળ (**jhaḷhaḷ**) 'shine' and ઊઠ (**uṭh**) 'get up'.

To complete the sense or to emphasize the meaning, an auxiliary verb is sometimes added to the compound verb, e.g. કરી દઉં છું (**kari daũ chhũ**).

The use of શક (**shak**) shows doubt and confirmation. As a noun it means 'doubt'. When used as a verb in a question it throws doubt on the previous word:

બની શકશે? (**bani shakshe?**) Will it be possible? (બન (**ban**) literally means 'to happen')

But it carries confirmation when used as a statement:

તેનાથી આ કામ બની શકશે. (**tenāthi ā kām bani shakshe.**) He will do the work (*lit.* the work will be done by him).

If જ (**ja**) follows તેનાથી (**tenāthi**), it gives emphasis, showing that no one but the person concerned could do the work: તેનાથી જ આ કામ બની શકશે. (**tenāthi ja ā kām bani shakshe.**) Similarly, કરી શકશે (**kari shakshe**), થઈ શકશે (**thai shakshe**), જઈ શકશે (**jai shakshe**) can show doubt or affirmation depending on whether the interrogative form is used or not.

By now you are familiar with some of the more important case suffixes. With દાળ<u>નું</u> (**dāḷ<u>nũ</u>**), કશાક<u>ના</u> (**kashāk<u>nā</u>**), ઢોકળી<u>ની</u> (**ḍhokḷ<u>ini</u>**), સાંજ<u>નો</u> (**sãj<u>no</u>**), બત્તીઓ<u>નો</u> (**battio<u>no</u>**), the suffixes નો (**no**), ની (**ni**), ના (**nā**) denote possession and are the equivalent of the English 's.

The suffix માં (**mã**) in તે<u>માં</u> (**mã**), વાત<u>માં</u> (**vātmã**), લંડન<u>માં</u> (**lanḍanmã**), શહેર<u>માં</u> (**shahermã**) carries the meaning 'in'.

Sometimes both માં and થી are used together when the sense changes to 'from', e.g. માઈકમાંથી (**māikmā̃thi**) 'from the microphone'.

The suffix ને (**ne**) in શીલાને (**shilāne**), અનંતને (**anatne**), આતમને (**ātamne**) means 'to'.

શીલાને કોઈ ન પહોંચે. (**shilāne koi na pahõche.**)
આતમને ઓઝલમાં રાખ મા. (**ātamne ojhalmā̃ rākh mā.**)
અનંતને ફોન કરું છું. (**anantne phon karũ chhũ.**)

મા (**mā**) without a nasal vowel is *not* a suffix. It means 'mother' and, in its colloquial form, can also mean 'not'. કર મા (**kar mā**) means 'don't do that' and ઓઝલમાં રાખ મા (**ojhalmā̃ rākh mā**) means 'don't keep in (i.e. wear) the veil'.

Exercise 1

Rearrange the words to make sense of the following dialogue:

દુર્ગેશ છે બહાર? જવું ક્યાં આજે
સુશીલા તો જઈએ છીએ રોજ જ બહાર ને
દુર્ગેશ જોઈએ તો ટીવી આજે
સુશીલા ઓહો છે ફિલ્મ હિંદી સરસ
દુર્ગેશ છે કામ કરે નરગિસ તેમાં સુનીલ દત્ત અને
સુશીલા દિવસે ઘણાં બેસીશું શાંતિથી

Exercise 2

Write a short dialogue directing a stranger to the theatre.

Exercise 3

Choose the correct words from the parentheses:

રસ્તા પર ધીમે ધીમે અંધારું (થયો/થી/થયું). માણસો પણ ઘટવા (લાગ્યો/લાગી/લાગ્યા). એકાએક બત્તીઓ બંધ થઈ (ગયાં/ગયું/ગઈ). શાંતાબહેન ડરી (ગયું/ગઈ) એની પાછળ કોઈ આવતું (હતો/હતી/હતું).તેમને થયું, આમાંથી ભગવાન જ બચાવી (શકશો/શક્શું/શકશે).

Exercise 4

Use an auxiliary verb in the following sentences:

(a) ગઈ કાલે શોભનાએ દાળ સરસ બનાવી ____.
(b) આવતી કાલે હું સાન ફ્રાન્સિકો જવાનો ____.

(c) ગયા વરસે આ ધોધ પાસેના દૂરબીનમાં સુરેશે સિક્કા નાખ્યા ____.
(d) મેં હમણાં જ ખાધું ____ એટલે ભૂખ નથી.
(e) એ આવતી કાલે ત્યાં કામ કરતો ____.
(f) મારે અત્યારે જ પૈસા જોઈએ ____.

Exercise 5

Match the following:

A	*B*
બત્તી	સાંજ
દાળ	ઝડપથી
ફિલ્મ	ભાત
માઈક	પ્રકાશ
ધીમેથી	જાહેરાત
સવાર	નાટક

Exercise 6

Use five words related to the theatre in five different sentences.

Exercise 7

Which adjective matches the person?

A	*B*
ફિલ્મી કળાકાર	તોફાની
પ્રોફેસર	ધૂની
પ્રધાન	સુંદર
ચિત્રકાર	ભૂલકણા
વિદ્યાર્થી	અભિમાની

Exercise 8

Translate into English:

(a) હું બપોરે જમતો નથી.
(b) લીલા રોજ સાંજે ફરવા જાય છે.
(c) જાણીતું નાટક સારું જ હોય તેમ ન પણ બને.
(d) આ લેખ તેનાથી જ લખી શકાશે.
(e) એક કલાકમાં આ કામ કરી દઈશ.

Dialogue 2

નાટક જોયા પછી **naṭak joyā pachhi** After the play **(CD2; 14)**

Varsha, Ilona and Anant discuss the play

વર્ષા કેમ ઈલોના, નાટક કેવું લાગ્યું?

ઈલોના ઘણું સરસ. મને ભાષાની મુશ્કેલી પણ લગભગ ન પડી કારણ પાત્રો અભિનય ઘણો જ સરસ કરતાં હતાં. વળી તમે કથા અગાઉથી સમજાવતાં હતાં.

વર્ષા હા. ને નાટકનો વિષય પણ જકડી રાખે તેવો જ હતો.

અનંત પણ મને અંત બહુ ન ગમ્યો. કૉલેજનો પ્રિન્સિપાલ જેવો માણસ દાણચોરનો નાયક શા માટે બનતો હશે? આ સંપૂર્ણ અવાસ્તવિક લાગતું હતું.

વર્ષા પણ સેટિંગ, ધ્વનિ અને પ્રકાશ આયોજન એટલું બધું વાસ્તવિક લાગતું હતું! છેલ્લા પ્રવેશમાં તો જાણે એમ જ લાગ્યું કે હું મુંબઈના વિમાનમથક પર જ બેઠી છું.

ઈલોના વર્ષા, તમે કહ્યું હતું કે મૂળ નાટક તો મરાઠીમાં લખાયું છે.

વર્ષા હા. મરાઠીમાં એનું નામ 'આંસુ બની ગયા ફૂલ' રાખ્યું હતું.

ઈલોના ખરેખર? ગુજરાતી નામ 'આતમને ઓઝલમાં રાખ મા' કરતાં મૂળ નામ જ વધુ સારું લાગે છે.

VARSHĀ kem Ilona nāṭak kevũ lāgyũ?

ILONA ghaṇũ saras. mane bhāshāni mushkeli paṇ lagbhag na paḍi kārañ pātro abhinay ghaṇoj saras kartā̃ hatā̃. vaḷi tame kathā agāuthi samjāvtā hatā̃.

VARSHĀ hā, ne nāṭakno vishay paṇ jakḍi rākhe tevoj hato.

AÑANT paṇ mane ãt bahu na gamyo. kolejno principāl jevo māṇas dāṇchorono nāyak shā māṭe banto hashe? ā sampurṇa avāstvik lāgtũ hatũ.

VARSHĀ paṇ setting, dhvani ane prakāshāyojan eṭlũ badhũ vāstvik lāgtũ hatũ! chhellā praveshmā̃ to jāṇe emj lāgyũ ke hũ mũbainā vimānmathak paraj beṭhi chhũ.

ILONA varshā, tame kahyũ hatũ ke muḷ nāṭak to marāthimā̃ lakhāyũ chhe.

VARSHĀ hā, marāṭhimā̃ enũ nām 'ā̃su bani gayā phul' rākhyũ hatũ.

ILONA kharekhar? gujarāti nām 'ātamne ojhalmā̃ rākh mā̃' kartā̃ hũ ā nām vadhu pasand karũ, muḷ nāmaj vadhu sārũ lāge chhe.

VARSHA *Ilona, did you like the play?*

ILONA *It was wonderful. The language was not very difficult to follow because the acting was so good and you were already explaining the plot to me.*

VARSHA *The subject was very interesting* [lit. *gripping*].

ANANT *Yes, but I didn't much like the ending. Why should the principal of a college become the boss of a gang of smugglers? It was totally unrealistic.*

VARSHA *But the sets, lighting and sound effects were so realistic. In the final scene I felt I was really at Bombay Airport.*

ILONA *Varsha, you said this play was originally written in Marathi.*

VARSHA *Yes, it was. In Marathi it was called 'The Tears Become Flowers'.*

ILONA *Really? I prefer that to the Gujarati 'Don't Cover Your Soul'. The original sounds much better.*

Vocabulary

મુશ્કેલી	**mushkeli**	difficulty
લગભગ	**lagbhag**	mostly, nearly
અભિનય	**abhinay**	acting
અગાઉથી	**agāuthi**	before
કથા	**kathā**	plot
વિષય	**vishay**	subject
જકડી રાખે એવો	**jakḍi rākhe evo**	gripping
અંત	**ant**	end
દાણચોરો	**dāṇchoro**	smugglers
સંપૂર્ણ	**sãpoorṇa**	totally, completely
ફૂલ	**phul**	flowers
અવાસ્તવિક	**avāstavik**	unrealistic
વાસ્તવિક	**vāstavik**	realistic
ધ્વનિ	**dhvani**	sound
પ્રકાશઆયોજન	**prakāsh āyojan**	light set-up, arrangement of lights
છેલ્લા	**chhellā**	last
પ્રવેશ	**pravesh**	scene

વિમાનમથક	**vimānmathak**	airport
મૂળ	**muḷ**	original, root
નાયક	**nāyak**	leader, hero (in a play)
આંસુ	**ā̃su**	tears
ખરેખર	**kharekhar**	really

Colloquial notes

કેવું લાગ્યું? (**kevũ lāgyũ?**) is very useful in everyday speech. It is used to ask someone's opinion: e.g.

એ માણસ કેવો લાગ્યો? (**e māṇas kevo lāgyo?**) What do you think about the man?
રસીલાની રસોઈ કેવી લાગી? (**rasilāni rasoi kevi lāgi?**) How was Rasila's cooking?
આ કાપડ કેવું લાગે છે? (**ā kāpaḍ kevũ lāge chhe?**) How good is this cloth?
હવે કેમ લાગે છે? (**have kem lāge chhe?**) How do you feel now?

Grammatical notes

Compound words

As with Sanskrit and German, Gujarati conjoins two, or sometimes three, words. They are connected by different types of suffixes, conjuncts, clauses, etc., each of which has a particular name in both Sanskrit and Gujarati. Without going into detail, which is not necessary save in advanced Gujarati, the common name for these compounds is સમાસ (**samās**).

Here are a few of the more frequently used compound words. Two words joined by અને (**ane**):

દાળઢોકળી – દાળ અને ઢોકળી (**dāḷḍhokḷi-dāḷ ane ḍhokḷi**) — lentil soup *and* dhokli
માબાપ – મા અને બાપ (**mābāp-mā ane bāp**) — mother *and* father

ભાઈબહેન – ભાઈ અને બહેન (**bhāibahen-bhāi ane bahen**)	brother *and* sister
ચાપાણી – ચા અને પાણી (**chāpāṇi-chā ane pāṇi**)	tea *and* water
હાથપગ – હાથ અને પગ (**hāthpag-hāth ane pag**)	hand *and* feet
ખરુંખોટું – ખરું અને ખોટું (**kharũkhoṭũ -kharũ ane khoṭũ**)	right *and* wrong

Two words joined by ને (**ne**), થી (**thi**), નો (**no**), ની (**ni**), નું (**nũ**), ના (**nā**), માં (**mā̃**), etc. (case suffixes):

પ્રકાશાયોજન – પ્રકાશનું આયોજન	**prakāshāyojan-prakāshnũ āyojan**	arrangement of lights (*lit.* lights' arrangement)
વિમાનમથક – વિમાનનું મથક	**vimānmathak-vimānnũ mathak**	airport (*lit.* aeroplane's headquarters)
મનગમતું – મનને ગમતું	**mangamtũ-manne gamtũ**	likable (*lit.* pleasing *to* the mind)
વ્યવહારકુશળ – વ્યવહારમાં કુશળ	**vyvahārkushaḷ-vyvahaarmā̃ kushaḷ**	expert *in* social transactions
સ્વાર્થરહિત – સ્વાર્થથી રહિત	**svārthrahit-svārththi rahit**	unselfish (*lit.* free *from* selfishness)

Words joined by જેનું . . . તે: (**jenũ . . . te**)

નકામું – જેનું કામ નથી તે	**nakāmũ-jenũ kām nathi te**	something or someone unnecessary
માથાભારે – જેનું માથું ભારે છે તે	**māthābhāre-jenũ mathũ bhāre chhe te**	stubborn, headstrong (*lit.* one whose head is heavy)
ઘરભંગ – જેનું ઘર ભંગાયું છે તે	**gharbhang-jenũ ghar bhangāyũ chhe te**	widow, widower (*lit.* one whose house is broken)
બહુમાળી – જેને બહુ માળા છે તે	**bahumāḷi-jene bahu māḷā chhe te**	multi-storey building (one which has many storeys)
ત્રિલોચન – જેને ત્રણ આંખ છે તે	**trilochan-jene traṇ ā̃nkh chhe te**	Lord Shiva (*lit.* one who has three eyes)

ચંપાવરણું – જેનો વર્ણ ચંપા જેવો છે તે	**champāvarṇũ-jeno varṇ champā jevo chhe te**	one who has golden-yellow skin

Miscellaneous

આગગાડી – આગ વડે ચાલતી ગાડી	**āggāḍi-āg vaḍe chālti gāḍi**	steam train (*lit.* train which runs with fire)
દાણચોર – દાણ (tax) આપ્યા વગર ચોરીથી જે માલ લાવે છે તે	**dāṇchor-dāṇ** (tax) **āpyā vagarchorithi je māl lāve chhe te**	smuggler (*lit.* an importer who steals by avoiding tax)
દૂધપૌઆ – દૂધમાં બનાવેલા પૌઆ	**dudhpauā-dudhmā̃ banāvelā pauā**	parched rice prepared with milk
દહીંવડાં – દહીંમાં બનાવેલા વડા	**dahī̃vaḍā-dahī̃mā̃ banāvelā vaḍā**	**vaḍās** (spicy dish) made with yoghurt

Causal

In this construction the subject passes on the work to someone else:

અકબર બેસે છે. (**akbar bese chhe.**) Akbar is sitting.
અકબર છોકરાઓને બેસાડે છે. (**akbar chhokrāone besāḍe chhe.**) Akbar makes the children sit.
આદિલ કાગળ લખે છે. (**ādil kāgaḷ lakhe chhe.**) Adil writes a letter.
આદિલ પત્ર લખાવે છે. (**ādil patra lakhāve chhe.**) Adil makes someone write a letter (i.e. dictates).

Here you see that the causal form is made with આડ (**āḍ**) or આવ (**āv**) added to the verbal root *before* other suffixes: બેસ-બેસાડ (**bes-besāḍ**); લખ-લખાવ (**lakh-lakhāv**).

Present continuous

In Gujarati the simple present and present continuous forms are the same, so that તે કામ કરે છે (**te kām kare chhe**) can mean either 'he works' or 'he is working'.

Past continuous

કર (**kar**) do

Person		*Singular*	*Plural*
I		હું કરતો હતો **hũ karto hato**	અમે કરતા હતા **ame kartā hatā**
II		તું કરતો હતો **tũ karto hato**	તમે કરતા હતા **tame kartā hatā**
III	*m*	તે કરતો હતો **te karto hato**	તેઓ કરતા હતા **teo kartā hatā**
	f	તે કરતી હતી **te karti hati**	તેઓ કરતાં હતાં **teo kartā̃ hatā̃**
	n	તે કરતું હતું **te kartũ hatũ**	તેઓ કરતાં હતાં **teo kartā̃ hatā̃**

That is:

I		R + તો હતો	R+ **to hato**	R + -તા હતા	R+ **tā hatā**
II		R + તો હતો	R+ **to hato**	R + -તા હતા	R+ **tā hatā**
III	*m*	R + તો હતો	R+ **to hato**	R + -તા હતા	R+ **tā hatā**
	f	R + તી હતી	R+ **ti hati**	R + -તાં હતા	R+ **tā hatā**
	n	R + તું હતું	R+ **tũ hatũ**	R + -તાં હતા	R+ **tā hatā**

Similarly, પી-પીતો હતો (**pi-pito hato**), લે-લેતો હતો (**le-leto hato**), etc.

Future continuous

Person		*Singular*	*Plural*
I		હું કરતો હોઈશ **hũ karto hoish**	અમે કરતા હોઈશું-હશું **ame kartā hoisũ-hashũ**
II		તું કરતો હોઈશ **tũ karto hoish**	તમે કરતા હશો **tame kartā hasho**
III	*m*	તે કરતો હશે **te karto hashe**	તેઓ કરતા હશે **teo kartā hashe**
	f	તે કરતી હશે **te karti hashe**	તેઓ કરતાં હશે **teo kartā̃ hashe**
	n	તે કરતું હશે **te kartũ hashe**	તેઓ કરતાં હશે **teo kartā̃ hashe**

That is R + the past tense suffix + number–gender suffix followed by the future tense forms of હો (**ho**):

કર + -તો હોઈશ (**kar** + **-to hoish**)
ખા + -તો હોઈશ (**khā** + **-to hoish**)
પી + -તો હોઈશ (**pi** + **-to hoish**)
લે + -તો હોઈશ (**le** + **-to hoish**), etc.

Exercise 9

Rearrange the following in four groups of four words connected by meaning:

આનંદ	ધ્વનિ	ફ્રેંચ	સાઈકલ
અંગ્રેજી	પ્રકાશ	સેટિંગ	શોક
બસ	મરાઠી	ભય	પડદો
ગુસ્સો	વિમાન	ટ્રેન	ગુજરાતી

Exercise 10

Fill in the blanks:

અમે થિયેટરમાં ______ જોવા ગયાં હતાં. અમે _____ અગાઉથી મેળવી લીધી હતી. નાટક ઘણું જાણીતું _______. બધાં જ પાત્રો સરસ _____ કરતાં હતાં. ________ તે ખૂબ ગમ્યું. પછી અમે બહાર _______ ગયાં. જમવાનું ___________ હતું એટલે અમને બહુ _________. પછી અમે ___________ પાછાં આવ્યાં.

Exercise 11

Match the opposite words from the two columns:

A	*B*
ઉપર	જમણી
અંદર	પાસે
આગળ	બહાર
દૂર	નીચે
પહેલાં	પાછળ
ડાબી	પછી

Exercise 12

Add the relevant suffixes to the following:

(a) નાટક____ વિષય સૌ____ ગમે તેવો હતો.
(b) થિયેટર ____ દાખલ થયાં ને બત્તીઓ ____ પ્રકાશ ઘટી ગયો.
(c) શકીલ ____ માઈક ____ બોલેલું બરાબર ન સંભળાયું.
(d) ભારત ____ વડાપ્રધાન હેરો ____ વિદ્યાર્થી હતા.
(e) સરિતા પાસે ____ટિકિટ લઈ દીપક ____ આપ.

Exercise 13

Using the word તો, write five sentences on what you are going to do tomorrow.

Exercise 14

Correct the following sentences:

(a) માથુરથી આ કામ બની શકો.
(b) સાંજની શી પ્રોગ્રામ છે?
(c) હું ને આ નામ ઘણો ગમે છું.
(d) મારો પૈસા ધીમે ધીમે ખલાસ થઈ ગયું.
(e) રજની અને સરોજ બહાર હતો.

Exercise 15

Change the following to the causal form:

(a) ભાનુ રમે છે.
(b) જયા લખે છે
(c) ચંદ્રકાન્ત હસતો હતો
(d) અરજણ ઘાસ કાપશે
(e) જહાંગીર કામ કરે છે

Exercise 16

Change the sentences as directed:

(a) હું આજે નાટક જોવા જાઉં છું. (past continuous)
(b) જહાંગીર અગિયારીમાં જતો હતો. (present continuous)
(c) રવિવારે તમે ઘરની સફાઈનું કામ કરતા હશો. (past continuous)
(d) અમે થિયેટરમાંથી નીકળ્યા ત્યારે સાંજ પડી ગઈ હતી. (future continuous)
(e) નલિની ઑફિસમાંથી છૂટીને દુકાનમાં ચોપડી ખરીદતી હતી. (future continuous)

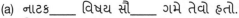

Unit Twelve

પ્રેસ પર **pres par**

At the newspaper office

બોલિવુડ **boliwuḍ**

Bollywood

In this unit you will learn about:

- More active/passive forms
- More causal forms
- More relative pronouns
- More duplicative forms
- The **e** suffix in the cardinals
- Reporting and narrative styles

Dialogue 1

પ્રેસ પર **pres par** At the newspaper office (CD2; 18)

Mr Patel is the editor of a Gujarati weekly. Ms Ami Joshi is the chief reporter. She is asked about a presentation ceremony she covered for the newspaper

---

પટેલ અમી, પછી તમે કાલે યુનિવર્સિટીના પદવીદાન સમારંભમાં ગયાં હતાં? મારાથી તો ન અવાયું.

અમી હા જી. લોગન હોલ ખીચોખીચ ભરાઈ ગયો હતો. SOASની પરીક્ષાઓમાં ઉત્તીર્ણ થનાર સહુને પદવીઓ મળી હતી. સહુ

વિદ્યાર્થીઓ તેમના ખાસ ઝભ્ભાઓમાં હતા. સહુ વિભાગોના અધ્યક્ષો પણ સરઘસ આકારે આવીને તખ્તા પર પોતપોતાની જગ્યાએ ગોઠવાઈ ગયા હતા. તેમણે પણ તેમના પરંપરાગત ઝભ્ભાઓ અને ચોરસ ટોપીઓ પહેરી હતી.

પટેલ એ તો અપેક્ષા હતીજ. પણ કોઈ ખાસ નોંધપાત્ર ઘટના?

અમી હા જી. બે વિદ્વાનોને માનદ ફેલોશિપથી સન્માનવામાં આવ્યા. તેમાંના એક, ડોક્ટર ભાયાણી SOAS દ્વારા આ રીતે સન્માનિત થનારાઓમાં પ્રથમ ગુજરાતી હતા. તેઓ ખૂબજ જાણીતા ભાષાશાસ્ત્રી છે. અને ૬૦ ઉપરાંત પુસ્તકો લખ્યાં છે.

પટેલ ઓહો! એતો આપણે માટે મહત્વના સમાચાર. તમે તેમની મુલાકાત લીધી?

અમી ના જી. તેઓ માંદા હતા, તેથી તેમનાથી આવી શકાયું નહોતું.

પટેલ સભામાં એમના વિષે કોઈ પરિચય અપાયો હતો?

અમી હા જી. SOASના એક સિનિયર પ્રોફેસર રાઇટે એમની સિદ્ધિઓને વિસ્તારથી બિરદાવી હતી. પશ્ચિમના મહાન ભાષાવૈજ્ઞાનિક ડોક્ટર ટર્નર સાથે તેમની તુલના કરવામાં આવી હતી. એ આખા વ્યાખ્યાનની નકલ મેં મેળવી લીધી છે.

પટેલ સરસ. એનો અહેવાલ જેમ બને તેમ જલદી તૈયાર કરી નાખો. ને તેમનો ફોટો પણ મેળવી લો. કાલના અંકમાં હું તેને લઇ લેવા માંગુ છું.

PATEL ami pachhi tame kāle universiṭinā padvidān samārambhmā̃ gayā̃ hatā̃? marāthi to na avāyũ.

AMI hāji. Logan Hall khichokhich bharāi gayo hato.soasni parikshāmā̃ uttirṇa thanār saune padvio maḷi hati. sau vidyārthio temnā khās jhhabbaomā̃ hatā. Sau vibhagonā adhyaksho paṇ sarghasākāre āvine takhtā upar potpotāni jagyāe goṭhvāi gayā hatā. temṇe paṇ temnā parāparāgat jhhabbāo ane choras ṭopio paheri hati.

PATEL e to apekshā hati ja. paṇ koi khās nondhpātra ghaṭnā?

AMI hāji. be vidvānone mānad pheloshipthi sanmānvāmā̃ āvyā. temānā ek ḍo. Bhāyāni, soas dvārā ā rite sanmānit thanārāomā̃ pratham gujrāti hatā. teo khub ja jāṇitā bhāshāshāstri chhe ane 60 uprā̃t pustako lakhyā̃ chhe.

PATEL oho! e to āpṇā māṭe mahtvnā samāchār. tame temni mulākāt lidhi?

AMI nāji. teo māndā hatā tethi temnāthi āvi shakāyũ nahotũ.

PATEL sabhāmā̃ emnā vishe koi parichay apāyo hato?

AMI hāji. soasnā ek senior prophesar riṭe emni siddhione vistārthi birdāvi hati. pashchimnā mahān bhāshāvaignānik ḍokṭar Ṭarnar sāthe emni tulnā karavāmā̃ āvi hati. e ākhā vyākhyānni nakal mẼ meḷvi lidhi chhe.

PATEL saras. eno ahevāl jem bane tem jaldi taiyār kari nākho ne temno phoṭo paṇ melṿi lo. Kālnā ākmā̃ hũ tene lai levā māgũ chhũ.

PATEL *Ami, did you go to the presentation at the university yesterday? I could not.*

AMI *Yes, sir. The hall was full to capacity. All the successful graduate and postgraduate students collected their degrees. They were all dressed in gowns and the heads of department arrived in procession to take their seats on the dais. They too had traditional robes and mortarboards on their heads.*

PATEL *That's to be expected. Was there anything particularly notable?*

AMI *Yes, sir. Two scholars were awarded honorary fellowships. One of them, Dr Bhayani, is the first Gujarati to be honoured in this way by the School of Oriental and African Studies (SOAS). He is a well-known linguist who has written more than sixty books.*

PATEL *That's an important story for us. Did you interview him?*

AMI *No, sir. Dr Bhayani could not come because he is ill.*

PATEL *Did anyone say anything about him?*

AMI *Yes. Professor Wright, a senior professor at SOAS, praised his achievements at some length, comparing him to Dr Turner, the most famous Western linguist. I got hold of a copy of his speech.*

PATEL *Good. Write your report as quickly as possible and get a photograph of Dr Bhayani. I want to carry the story in tomorrow's paper.*

Vocabulary

પદવીદાન (*n*)	**padvidān**	convocation
સમારંભ (*m*)	**samārambh**	ceremony
ખીચોખીચ	**khichokhich**	packed to capacity
ઉત્તીર્ણ	**utitirṇa**	pass (in examination)
ખાસ	**khās**	typical
વિભાગોના અધ્યક્ષો (*m*)	**vibhāgonā adhyaksho**	heads of department
ઝભ્ભા (*m*)	**jhabhhā**	gowns, robes
સરઘસાકારે (*N*)	**sarghasākāre**	in procession
પરંપરાગત (*inv*)	**paȓparāgat**	in traditional manner
નોંધપાત્ર (*inv*)	**nõdhpātra**	noteworthy
વિદ્વાનો (*m*)	**vidvāno**	scholars
સન્માનવું	**sanmānvũ**	to honour
મુલાકાત (*f*)	**mulākāt**	interview
ગેરહાજરી (*f*)	**gerhājri**	absence
ભાષાશાસ્ત્રી	**bhāshāshāstri**	linguist
તુલના (*f*)	**tulnā**	comparison
વ્યાખ્યાન (*n*)	**vyākhyān**	lecture
અહેવાલ (*m*)	**ahevāl**	report
ઉપરાંત	**uparā̃t**	over and above
સંશોધન (*n*)	**sanshodhan**	research
પરિચય (*m*)	**parichay**	introduction
બિરદાવી	**birdāvi**	appreciated
સિદ્ધિઓ (*f*)	**siddhio**	achievements

Grammatical notes

More active and passive forms

(a) મારાથી ન અવાયું. (**mārāthi na avāyũ**) It was not possible (for me) to come. (passive)

હું ન આવી શક્યો. (**hũ na āvi shakyo.**) I could not come. (active)

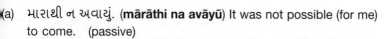

(b) તેમનાથી એ કામ હંમેશ મુજબ કરાયું હશે. (**temnāthi e kām hãmesh mujab karāyũ hashe.**) The work might have been done (by them). (passive)

તેમણે એ કામ હંમેશ મુજબ કર્યું હશે. (**temṇe e kām hãmesh mujab karyũ hashe**.) They might have done the work. (active)

(c) ડોક્ટરથી આવી શકાયું ન હતું. (**ḍokṭarthi āvi shakāyũ na hatũ.**) It was not possible for the doctor to come. (passive)

ડોક્ટર આવ્યા ન હતા. (**ḍokṭar āvyā na hatā**.) The doctor could not come. (active)

(d) તમારાથી તૈયાર કરાશે? (**tamārāthi taiyār karāshe?**) Will the work be prepared (by you)? (passive)

તમે તૈયાર કરશો? (**tame taiyār karsho?**) Will you prepare the work? (active)

In the active voice the subject plays the main role in a sentence while in the passive voice it is the object which has primacy.

હેમા ચોપડી વાંચે છે. (**hemā chopḍi vãche chhe.**) Hema is reading a book.

In the above sentence the subject, હેમા (**hemā**), is actively associated with the verb, વાંચે છે (**vãche chhe**).

હેમાથી ચોપડી વંચાય છે. (**hemāthi chopḍi vanchāy chhe.**)
The book is read by Hema.

Here the object, ચોપડી (**chopḍi**), is the focus while the verb and subject are passive. The થી (**thi**) suffix is added to the subject in this type of construct while the verb વાંચ (**vãch**) changes to વંચાય (**vanchāy**). Similarly, ખાય (**khāy**) changes to ખવાય (**khavāy**), જાય (**jāy**) to જવાય (**javāy**), બેસ (**bes**) to બેસાય (**besāy**), etc.

bhāve prayog

There is a third formation in Gujarati, ભાવે પ્રયોગ (**bhāve prayog**) where the construction is impersonal and determined by the relation of impersonal verb to agent:

એનાથી ચલાતું નથી.
enāthi chalātũ nathi.
Walking is not possible by him (i.e. he is unable to walk).

More causal forms

(a) ત્યાં વિદ્યાર્થીઓને બેસાડયા હતા. **tyā̃ vidyārthione besāḍyā hatā.** The students were made to sit there. (causal)

ત્યાં વિદ્યાર્થીઓ બેઠા હતા. **tyā̃ vidyārthio beṭhā hatā.** The students were sitting there.

(b) તમે ફોટો કોઇની પાસે કઢાવી લો. **tame photo koini pāse kaḍhāvi lo.** Get someone to print the photograph. (causal)

તમે ફોટો કાઢો. **tame photo kādho.** Print the photograph. (yourself).

(c) હું ટાઈપિસ્ટ પાસે તૈયાર કરાવું છું. **hũ ṭāipist pāse taiyār karāvũ chhũ.** I will have it typed by the secretary. (causal)

હું ટાઈપ કરું છું. **hũ ṭaip karũ chhũ.** I will type it myself.

This construction carries the meaning 'to get (someone) to do'

Simple હું કામ કરું છું. **hũ kām karũ chhũ.** I am doing the work.
Causal હું કામ કરાવું છું. **hũ kām karāvũ chhũ.** I am getting someone to do the work.
Simple તું બેસે છે. **tũ bese chhe.** You are sitting.
Causal તું બેસાડે છે. **tũ besāḍe chhe.** You make someone sit.

The causal suffix આવ (**āv**) or આડ (**āḍ**) is added to the verb.

Although the suffixes are not always interchangeable, there are no absolute rules about which one to use, e.g. you cannot say કરાડું (**karāḍũ**) or બેસાવું (**besāvũ**).

However, if the root of the verb ends with **ā**, **i**, **u** or **o**, you place a **v** before the causal suffix: e.g. ખા (**khā**) 'eat', પી (**pi**) 'drink', સૂ (**su**) 'sleep', જો (**jo**) 'see', will become ખવાડ પિવાડ સુવાડ જોવાડ (**khavāḍ, pivāḍ, suvāḍ, jovāḍ**):

હું ખાઉં છું. **hũ khāũ chhũ.** I am eating.
હું ખવાડું છું. **hũ khavāḍũ chhũ.** I am making someone eat.

Similarly, પીવાડું (**pivāḍũ**), સુવાડું (**suvāḍũ**), etc. You can also use root + **va** + **ḍ** + **āv** as an alternative, e.g. પીવડાવ (**pivḍāv**), ખવડાવ (**khavḍāv**), સુવડાવ (**suvḍāv**), etc.

Compound verbs

ભરાઈ ગયો, ગોઠવાઈ ગયા, મેળવી લો, કરી નાખો.

Sometimes two verbs are used together to form an extended meaning. For example, ફેંક (**phẼk**) 'throw' + દે (**de**) 'give', combine to form ફેંકી દે (**phẼki de**) 'throw away', meaning 'immediately'. Though the verb **de** means 'give', the combination gives a different meaning, that of immediacy.

એણે પેન ફેંકી. **eṇe pen phẼki.** He threw the pen.
એણે પેન ફેંકી દીધી. **eṇe pen phẼki didhi.** He threw away the pen. (immediately)

Sentences with verbs implied

(a) પણ કોઈ ખાસ નોંધપાત્ર ઘટના (બની હતી)?
But was there anything noteworthy?

The verb બની હતી 'happened' is implied.

(b) આપણા માટે મહત્વના સમાચાર (છે).
These are (this is) important news for us.

The verb (are) is implied.
Note: unlike English, 'news' is plural in Gujarati.

Exercise 1

Translate the following sentences into Gujarati:

(a) Did you go to Athens yesterday?
(b) Your description is very clear.
(c) How can we achieve the real objectives of education?
(d) Give me your notes immediately.
(e) I am sorry I could not come to your party.
(f) I recently got my degree.

Exercise 2

Write in Gujarati in five sentences about the degree/diploma/certificate you might have received.

Exercise 3

Match the following:

A	*B*
પદવીદાન	ટોપી
પ્રોફેસર	ઉત્તીર્ણ
પરીક્ષા	તબિયત
નાદુરસ્ત	ગેરહાજરી
હાજરી	વિદ્વાન
ઝબ્બો	સમારંભ

Exercise 4

Fill in the appropriate participles:

ભસ ____ કૂતરો	(barking dog)
વાંચ ____ છોકરી	(reading girl)
પડ ____ ફળ	(falling fruit)
પડ ____ મકાન	(the building that was going to fall)
ચૂંટા ____ પક્ષ	(the party is going to be elected)
કરે ____ કામ	(the work done)

Exercise 5

Using the vocabulary from the dialogue, describe a concert or a play you have been to.

Exercise 6

Find the odd words in each of the following:

(a)	ખીચોખીચ	ખાલીખમ	ભરાયો	ફળ
(b)	તરત જ	મગજ	હમણાં જ	અત્યારે જ
(c)	બિલાડું	પાંદડું	ઘોડું	સસલું
(d)	વિદ્યાર્થીઓ	પદવીઓ	ઝભ્ભાઓ	ગધેડાઓ
(e)	હસતું	જંતુ	ખાતું	પીતું

Dialogue 2

બોલીવુડ **boliwuḍ** Bollywood (CD2; 22)

Aman and Barkha are discussing Bollywood (the Indian film industry)

અમન આ બોલીવુડ શું છે? જ્યાં જુઓ ત્યાં તેનું જ નામ બધેય સંભળાય છે. હોલીવુડનું નામ તો સાંભળ્યું હતું.

બરખા એ હોલીવુડ પરથી જ બોલીવુડ થયું છે. અમેરિકામાં તો હોલીવુડ નામની જે જગ્યા છે. તે આખા વિશાળ વિસ્તારને હોલીવુડ કહે છે. જ્યારે આ તો મુંબઈમાં રજૂ થતી હિન્દી ભાષાની ફિલ્મો માટે વપરાતો શબ્દ છે. અને હવે તે ભારતના ફિલ્મજગત માટે પણ વપરાય છે.

અમન પણ મારા બંગાળી મિત્ર તો એમ કહે છે કે ટોલીવુડ પરથી બોલીવુડ થયું. પશ્ચિમ બંગાળમાં ટોલિગંજ વિસ્તારમાં ફિલ્મો બનતી તેને લીધે ટોલીવુડ નામ આવ્યું.

બરખા ગમે તે હોય. ભારતીય ફિલ્મો માટે જાણીતો થઈ ગયેલો શબ્દ દુનિયાભરમાં બધે વપરાય છે. બોલીવુડ ડાન્સ તો હવે એક પ્રકાર તરીકે તેને કેટલાક લોકો સ્વીકારતા થયા છે.

અમન પણ ભારતના શાસ્ત્રીય નૃત્યના પ્રેમીઓ તેને સ્વીકારવા તૈયાર નથી હો. તેમને તો ભરત નાટ્યમ, કથક, મણિપુરી જેવાં નૃત્યો જોઈને તેમની આંખો ઠરે છે.

બરખા હિંદી ફિલ્મોની વાત કરીએ તો રાજકપૂર, નરગીસ, મીનાકુમારી, અમિતાભ બચ્ચન, શાહરૂખખાન જેવા અનેક કલાકારોએ બોલિવૂડનું ગૌરવ વધાર્યું.

અમન હા, 'લગાન' ફિલ્મ તો આંતરરાષ્ટ્રીય સ્તરે જાણીતી થઈ ગઈ.

બરખા નિરૂપારોય, સંજીવ કુમાર, પરેશ રાવળ, આશા પારેખ, અરૂણા ઈરાની જેવા ગુજરાતી કલાકારો હિંદી ફિલ્મોમાં પણ જાણીતા હતા.

અમન અને લંડનના ગુજરાતી કલાકાર દેવ પટેલે તો 'સ્લમડોગ મિલિયોનર' માં અદ્દભૂત પ્રતિષ્ઠા મેળવી છે.

AMAN ā bolywooḍ shũ chhe? jyā̃ juo tyā̃ tenũ ja nām badheya sambhḷāy chhe. holywooḍnũ nām to sambhaḷyũ hatũ.

BARKHĀ e hollywooḍ parthi ja bolywooḍ thayũ chhe. amerikāmā̃ to holywooḍ nāmni je jagyā chhe. te ākhā vishāḷ vistārne hollywood kahe chhe. jyāre ā to mumbaimā̃ raju thati hindi bhāshāni philmo māṭe vaprāto shabda chhe. ane have te bhāratnā philmjagat māṭe paṇ vaprāy chhe.

AMAN paṇ mārā bangāḷi mitra to em kahe chhe ke ṭollywooḍ parthi bollywooḍ thayũ. pashchim bangāḷmā̃ ṭolyganj vistārmā̃ philmo banti tene lidhe tolywooḍ nām āvyũ.

BARKHĀ game te hoy bhārtiya philmo māṭe jaṇito thai gayelo shabd duniyābharmā̃ badhe vaprāy chhe. bollywooḍ dā̃s to have ek prakār tarike tene keṭlāk loko svikārtā thayā chhe.

AMAN paṇ bhāratmā̃ shāshtriya nrutyanā premio tene svikārvā taiyār nathi ho. temne to bharat nāṭyam, kathak, maṇipuri jevā nrutyo joine temni ānkho ṭhare chhe.

BARKHĀ hindi philmoni vāt karie to rājkapur, nargis, minākumāri, amitābh bachhan, shāhrukhkhān jevā anek kaḷkāroe bolivuḍnū̃ gaurav vadhāryū̃.

AMAN hā, 'lagān' philm to antarrashṭriy stare jaṇiti thai gai.

BARKHĀ nirupā roy, sanjiv kumār, paresh rāvaḷ, āshā pārekh, aruṇā irāni jevā gujrāti kalākāro hindi philmomā̃ jāṇitā hatā.

AMAN ane lanḍannā gujrāti kalākār dev paṭele to 'slumḍog miliyonar' mā̃ adbhut pratishthā meḷvi che.

AMAN *What is this Bollywood? Wherever you go, it is heard everywhere. I have heard the name Hollywood.*

BARKHA *Bollywood came from that name. There is a place called Hollywood in America. That whole vast area is called Hollywood. Whereas this is used for Hindi films produced in Mumbai. And now this has become famous worldwide for the Indian film world.*

AMAN *But my Bengali friend says that Bollywood comes from Tollywood. Tollywood came from films made in western Bengal's Tollyganj area.*

BARKHA *Whatever it is, the word that has become famous for Indian films is used widely in the world. Some of the people now accept Bollywood dance as a form of dance.*

AMAN *But the lovers of Indian classical dance are not willing to accept it. They like Bharat Natyam, Kathak, Manipuri type of dances.*

BARKHA *Talking of Hindi films, stars like Raj Kapoor, Nargis, Meena Kumari, Amitabh Bachhan, Shahrookh Khan and others have added to the prestige of Bollywood.*

AMAN *Yes, the film* Lagan *has become internationally famous.*

BARKHA *Gujarati stars like Nirupa Roy, Sanjeev Kumar, Paresh Raval, Asha Parekh, Aruna Irani also became famous in Hindi films.*

AMAN *The London resident Gujarati actor, Dev Patel, has achieved fame.*

Vocabulary

વિશાળ	**vishāḷ**	big, extensive
પ્રતિષ્ઠા	**pratishṭhā**	prestige
ગમે તે હોય	**game te hoy**	whatever it may be
જાણીતો	**jāṇito**	well known
મોટાભાગના	**moṭābhāgnā**	most of
સ્વીકારવું	**svikārvũ**	to accept
ભરતનાટ્યમ	**bhārat natyam**	South Indian classical dance form
કથક	**kathak**	North Indian classical dance form
મણિપુરી	**maṇipuri**	classical dance from Manipur, India
આરંભ	**ārambh**	beginning
દુનિયાભરમાં	**duniabharmā̃**	all around the world
પ્રસિદ્ધ	**prassiddh**	known (also means published)
જાણીતી અભિનેત્રી	**jāṇiti abhinetri**	famous actress

Grammatical notes

Relative pronoun: જે . . . ત (je . . . te)

The relative pronoun જે (**je**) is used for both persons and things and does not change with number and gender.

જે વાવશે તે લણશે. (**je vāvshe te laṇshe.**) Whatever (you) sow, (that) (you) will reap.
મેં જે સુંદર ગાયો જોઈ તે તંદુરસ્ત હતી. (**mẽ je sundar gāyo joi te tandurast hati.**) can also be used as an adjective.

The beautiful films (which) I saw were lengthy. મેં જે સુંદર ફિલ્મો જોઈ તે લાંબી હતી. (**mẽ je sundar philmo joi te lā̃bi hati.**)

The case suffixes ને (**ne**), થી (**thi**), માં (**mā̃**), etc. can also be used with these pronouns:

મેં જે સુંદર ફિલ્મો જોઈ તેથી જિજ્ઞાસા વધી. (**mẽ je sundar philmo joi tethi jignāsā vadhi.**) The beautiful films (which) I saw, increased my curiosity (*lit.* my curiosity was increased *because of that*).

The duplicative forms જે જે (**je je**) . . . તે તે (**te te**):

જે જે આ ફિલ્મો જુએ તે તે ખુશ થાય છે. (**je je ā philmo jue te te khush thay chhe.**) Whoever sees these films is happy.

The repetition of જે (**je**) changes the meaning from 'who' to 'whoever'.

Conjunctive participle

The text in this lesson contains the following examples of the conjunctive participle:

નૃત્યો જોઇને આંખો ઠરે છે. (**nrutyo joine ā̃nkho ṭhare chhe.**) It is good to see the dances. (*lit.* The eyes are satisfied after seeing the dances.)

બોલિવુડ ડાન્સ જોઈને એક પ્રકાર તરીકે તેને સ્વીકારે છે. (**boliwuḍ ḍā̃s joine ek prakār tarike tene svikāre chhe.**) (*lit.* After watching Bollywood dances, they accept it as a type of dance.)

The e suffix in cardinal numbers

When an **e** suffix is added to a cardinal number it carries the meaning 'all the':

ત્રણે ફિલ્મો જોઈને . . . (**traṇe philmo joine** . . .) After watching *all the* three films . . .

તમે દસે ચોપડી વાંચી લીધી? (**tame dase chopḍi vā̃nchi lidhi?**) Have you finished *all the* ten books?

Colloquial notes

આંખો ઠરે છે. (**ā̃nkho ṭhare chhe.**) means 'the eyes cool down' and indicates something pleasant to see:

સરસ નૃત્યો જોઇને તેમની આંખો ઠરે છે. (**saras nrutyo joine temni ā̃nkho ṭhare chhe.**) One is pleased to see the beautiful dances.

એનો હોશિયાર દીકરો જોઈને મારી આંખ ઠરી. (**eno hoshiyār dikro joine mari ā̃nkh ṭhari.**) I was happy to see his intelligent son.

It is, of course, also used in its normal sense of 'cooling down':

ગરમ પાણી તરત ઠરી ગયું. (**garam pāṇi tarat ṭhari gayũ.**) The hot water quickly cooled.

Exercise 7

Use the verb ઠરવું in two sentences, each with a different meaning.

Exercise 8

Fill in the following columns with suitable adjectives:

ફિલ્મ	નૃત્ય	પ્રોફેસર	પત્રકાર	તંત્રી
e.g. સારી	સુંદર	વિદ્વાન	ચાલાક	કુશળ
____	____	____	____	____
____	____	____	____	____
____	____	____	____	____
____	____	____	____	____

Note: there is more than one answer.

Exercise 9

What are the opposites of:

A	*B*
તંદુરસ્ત	____
સુંદર	____
વ્યવસ્થા	____
વિશાળ	____
સામાન્ય	____

Exercise 10

Describe your present job/studies and compare it with work you have done in the past.

Exercise 11

Change the sentences as directed:

(a)	કાલે મારી પાસે મકાન હશે.	(negation)
(b)	કરેલું કામ નકામું જતું નથી.	(affirmation)
(c)	હું યુરોપ જઈશ. હું અમેરિકા જઈશ.	(make into a single sentence)
(d)	ગઈ કાલે મને પેટમાં દુખતું હતું.	(future continuous)
(e)	મને મોસ્કોમાં ગમે છે પણ ન્યુ યોર્કમાં ગમશે?	(remove the doubt)
(f)	શીલાને કાનમાં સખત દુખાવો છે.	(past continuous)

Unit Thirteen

ગાંધીજીની સંસ્થાઓમાં **gāndhijini sansthāomā̃**

At Gandhiji's institutions

સવારમાં ફરવા **savārmā̃ pharvā**

Morning walk

In this unit you will be revising:

- Auxiliary verbs
- Omission of a verb
- Omission of જો in the 'if . . . then' construction
- Duplicatives
- Case suffixes
- Conjuncts
- Compound words
- Participles – past, present, future
- Honorific plural
- Degrees of comparison

Dialogue 1

ગાંધીજીની સંસ્થાઓમાં **gāndhijini sansthāomā̃**

At Gandhiji's institutions **(CD2; 23)**

Malisa is a visitor from France. Balvant is in Ahmedabad and takes his guest to Gandhian Institutes.

માલિઝા આજે ક્યાં લઈ જવાના છો બળવંતભાઈ ?

બળવંત આજે બીજી ઓકટોબર છે. ભારતને આઝાદી અપાવનાર મહાત્મા ગાંધીનો જન્મદિવસ. એટલે તમે કહો તો તેમણે સ્થાપેલા ગુજરાત વિદ્યાપીઠ અને સાબરમતી આશ્રમ જોવા જઈએ.

માલિઝા હા, સરસ. ફ્રાંસમાં મેં તેમની ગાંધી ફિલ્મ પણ જોઈ હતી. સત્ય અને અહિંસાને જીવનમાં ઉતારનાર એ મહાન વ્યક્તિની સંસ્થાઓને જોવાનું મને ખૂબ જ ગમશે.

બળવંત ચાલો.

(બંને આશ્રમ રોડ પર આવેલી ગુજરાત વિદ્યાપીઠમાં પહોંચે છે.)

બળવંત ગાંધીજીએ ગુજરાતનાં ગામડાંઓનાં વિકાસને કેન્દ્રમાં રાખી આ ગ્રામવિદ્યાપીઠ શરૂ કરી. બીજી યુનિવર્સિટીઓ કરતાં તદ્દન જુદી જ ભાત પાડતી આ વિદ્યાપીઠ છે. માતૃભાષામાં જ પ્રાથમિકથી માંડીને પીએચડી સુધીનું સમાજસેવાલક્ષી શિક્ષણ અહીં અપાય છે.

માલિઝા અંદર તો વિશાળ ઉપવન જેવું જ લાગે છે. મોર પણ ફરતા દેખાય છે. અને વૃક્ષો પણ કેટલાં બધાં! પણ અહીં ફકત ગ્રામસેવાનું જ શિક્ષણ અપાય છે?

બળવંત ના. ભારતીય ભાષાઓ શીખવવાનું પણ સંસ્થાનું કેન્દ્ર છે. જાતજાતનાં વિષયોનાં પુસ્તકો ધરાવતું વિશાળ ગ્રંથાલય પણ છે. જૈન ધર્મનો તો ખાસ વિભાગ છે. દેખીતી રીતે ગાંધીજીના તો બધા જ ગ્રંથો અહીં હોય જ; તેમણે લખેલા તથા તેમના ઉપર લખાયેલા.

માલિઝા ઓહો, અહીં તો કમ્પ્યૂટરનો અભ્યાસ પણ થતો લાગે છે.

બળવંત હા, આધુનિક યુગ સાથે તો રહેવું જ જોઈએ. પત્રકારત્વ અને સમૂહમાધ્યમોમાં પણ પીએચડી સુધીનો અભ્યાસ કરી શકાય છે. હવે ગાંધી આશ્રમે જઈશું?

(બંને સાબરમતીના કિનારે આવેલા ગાંધીઆશ્રમમાં જાય છે.)

બળવંત ગાંધીજી પોતે દક્ષિણ આફ્રિકા હતા ત્યારે ફિનિક્સમાં પહેલો આશ્રમ ૧૯૦૪માં સ્થાપ્યો. પછી ટોલસ્ટોય ફાર્મ. ભારત પાછા આવી અમદાવાદમાં પહેલાં કોચરબમાં અને પછી આ આશ્રમ. સ્વતંત્રતાની મોટા ભાગની લડત અહીંથી જ થઈ.

માલિઝા આ એમનો ખંડ છે, નહિ? કેટલો સાદો છે. જમીન પર બેઠક અને નાનું ટેબલ. અને બાજુમાં ચરખો. પેલી બાજુ ગોશાળા લાગે છે. ગાયો પણ છે છતાં સ્વચ્છતા પણ કેટલી બધી. આશ્રમવાસીઓ પોતે જ બધું સાફ રાખતા હશે.

બળવંત હા, ગાંધીજીને ગંદકી જરાય ગમતી ન હતી. દરેક પોતપોતાની જગ્યા ચોખ્ખી રાખે, તો બધું ચોખ્ખું રહે. હવે અહીં આશ્રમનો ઈતિહાસ રજૂ કરતો પ્રકાશ અને ધ્વનિનો કાર્યક્રમ રજૂ થશે તે જોઈશું.

માલિઝા જરૂર. આભાર.

MALIZĀ āje kyā̃ lai javānā chho baḷvant bhai?

BALVANT āje biji okṭober chhe. bhāratne āzādi apāvnār mahātmā gādhino janmadivas. eṭle temṇe sthāpelā gujrāt vidyāpiṭh ane sābarmati āshram jovā jaie.

MALIZĀ hā, saras. fransmā̃ mẽ temni gāndhi philm paṇ joi hati. satya ane ahinsāne jivanmā̃ utārnār e mahān vyaktini sanshthāone jovānũ mane khub ja gamshe.

BALVANT chālo.

(banne āshram roḍ par āveli gujrāt vidyāpiṭhmā̃ pahõche chhe.)

BALVANT gāndhijie gujrātnā gāmḍāonā vikāsne kendramā̃ rākhi ā grāmvidyāpiṭh sharu kari. biji universiṭio kartā̃ taddan judi bhāt pāḍti ā vidyāpiṭh chhe. mātrubhāshāmā̃ ja prāthmikthi mānḍine piechḍi sudhinũ samājsevālakshi shikshan ahĩ apāy chhe.

MALIZĀ andar to vishāḷ upvan jevũ ja lāge chhe. mor paṇ phartā dekhāy chhe. ane vruksho paṇ keṭlā badhā chhe. paṇ ahĩ fakta grāmsevānũ ja shikshaṇ apāy chhe?

BALVANT nā. bhārtiya bhāshāo shikhvānũ paṇ sansthānũ Kendra chhe. jātjānā vishayonā pustako dharāvtũ vishāḷ granthālay paṇ chhe. jain dharmano to khās vibhāg chhe. dekhiti rite gāndhijinā to badhā ja grantho ahĩ hoy ja. temṇe lakhelā tathā temnā upar lakhāyelā.

MALIZĀ oho, ahĩ to kampuṭerno abhyās paṇ thato lāge chhe.

BALVANT hā, ādhunik yug sāthe to rahevũ ja joie. patrakāratva ane samoohmādhyamomā̃ piechdi sudhino abhyās kari shakāy chhe. have gāndhi āshrame jaishũ?

(banne sābarmatinā kināre āvelā gāndhiāshrammā̃ jāy chhe.)

BALVANT gāndhiji pote daxin āfrikā hatā tyāre phinixmā̃ pahelo āshram 1904mā̃ sthāpyo. pachhi ṭolstoy phārm. bhārat pāchā āvi amdāvādmā̃ pahelā kochrabmā̃ ane pachhi ā āshram. svatantratāni moṭā bhāgni laḍat ahī̃thi ja thai.

MALIZĀ a emno khanḍ chhe, nahī̃? keṭlo sādo chhe. jamin par beṭhak ane nānũ ṭebal. ane bājumā̃ charkho. peli bāju goshāḷā lāge chhe. gāyo paṇ chhe chhatā̃ svachchhtā paṇ keṭli badhi. ashramvāsio potej badhũ sāph rākhtā hashe.

BALVANT hā, gāndhijine gandki jarāye gamti na hati. darek pot potāni jagyā chokkhi rākhe to badhũ chokkhũ rahe. have ahī̃ āshramno itihās raju karto prakāsh ane dhvanino kāryakram raju thashe te joishũ.

MALIZĀ jarur. ābhār.

MALIZA *Where are you taking me today, Balvantbhai?*

BALVANT *Today it is 2nd October, the birthday of Mahatma Gandhi who was instrumental in getting freedom for India. So we go to see the Gujarat Vidyapith and Sabarmati Ashram established by him.*

MALIZA *Yes. Fine. I also saw his Gandhi movie in France. I will really enjoy seeing the institutes established by that great person who practised truth and non-violence.*

BALVANT *Let us go.*

[Both reach the Gujarat Vidyapith situated on Ashram Road.]

BALVANT *Gandhiji started this rural university bearing in mind the progress of villages of Gujarat. This is a university which creates a different pattern from other universities. Social education is imparted from beginning to PhD level in the mother tongue.*

MALIZA *It looks like a large park. Peacocks are seen moving about. And there are many trees. Only social education relating to villages is given here?*

BALVANT *No. There is a Centre for learning Indian languages. There is also a vast library of books on various subjects. There is a special department for Jain religion. Naturally all books on Gandhiji are here. Books written by him and about him.*

MALIZA *Oh! Computers are also studied here.*

BALVANT *Yes, one must stay with modern times. One can also do a PhD in Journalism and mass media studies. Now shall we go to Gandhi Ashram?*

[Both go to Gandhi Ashram which is situated on the banks of River Sabarmati.]

BALVANT *In 1904, when Gandhiji was in South Africa, he established the first ashram in Phoenix. Then Tolstoy Farm. Upon returning to India, first in Kochrab which is in Ahmedabad, and then this ashram. A large part of the independence fight took place from here.*

MALIZA *This is his room, isn't it? So simple. A seat on the floor and a small table. And a spinning wheel next to it. On that side there seems to be a cowshed. Those cows are there yet there is a lot of cleanliness. Ashramites are themselves keeping it clean, I think, so everyone keeps one's place clean, everything is clean.*

BALVANT *Yes. Gandhiji did not like filth. If everyone keeps one's place clean everything is clean. Now we will watch a sound and light presentation on the history of the ashram.*

MALIZA *Certainly. Thank you.*

Vocabulary

આઝાદી	**āzādi**	independence
જન્મદિવસ	**janma divas**	birthday
સત્ય	**satya**	truth
અહિંસા	**ahĩsā**	non-violence
મહાન	**mahān**	great
ગામડું	**gāmḍũ**	village
વિકાસ	**vikās**	development
માતૃભાષા	**mātrubhāshā**	mother tongue
સમાજસેવાલક્ષી	**samājsevālakshi**	related to social service
ઉપવન	**upvan**	park
વિશાળ	**vishāḷ**	big
મોર	**mor**	peacock
વૃક્ષ	**vruksh**	tree
ગ્રંથ	**granth**	book
ગ્રંથાલય	**granthālay**	library

આધુનિક	**ādhunik**	modern
પત્રકારત્વ	**patrakārtva**	journalism
સમૂહમાધ્યમ	**samuh mādhyam**	mass media
ચરખો	**charkho**	spinning wheel
સ્વચ્છતા	**svachhtā**	cleanliness
ગંદકી	**gādaki**	dirt
પ્રકાશ અને ધ્વનિનો કાર્યક્રમ	**prakāsh ane dhvanino kāryakram**	light and sound show

Revision

Note the various forms of the verbal root હો (**ho**):

ગ્રંથો અહીં <u>હોય</u> (**grantho ahī̃ <u>hoy</u>**), સાફ રાખતા <u>હશે</u> (**sāph rākhtā <u>hashe</u>**), દક્ષિણ આફ્રિકા <u>હતા</u> (**dakshiṇ āphrikā hatā**).

Note the omission of the verb in the following sentences.

અને વૃક્ષો પણ કેટલાં બધાં! (છે) **ane vruksho paṇ keṭlā̃ badhā̃ chhe! (chhe)**
પછી ટોલ્સ્ટોય ફાર્મ આશ્રમ (સ્થાપ્યો) **pachhi ṭolstoy phārm āshram (sthāpyo)**.
નાનું ટેબલ ને બાજુમાં ચરખો (છે) **nānũ ṭeble ne bājumā̃ charkho (chhe)**.
સ્વચ્છતા પણ કેટલી બધી (છે) **svachhtā paṇ keṭli badhi (chhe)**.

Note the omission of the word જો (**jo**) 'if' in the 'if . . . then' construction.

(જો) દરેક પોતપોતાની જગ્યા ચોખ્ખી રાખે તો બધુ ચોખ્ખું રહે. (**jo**) **darek potpotāni jagyā chhokkhi rākhe to badhũ chokhkhũ rahe.**

Note the use of the reflexive pronouns in these sentences:

દરેક <u>પોતપોતાની</u> જગ્યા ચોખ્ખી રાખે. **darek <u>potpotāni</u> jagyā chhokkhi rākhe.**
ગાંધીજી <u>પોતે</u> દક્ષિણ આફ્રિકા હતા. **gāndhiji <u>pote</u> dakshiṇ āphrikā hatā.**

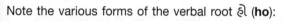

In the first sentence પોતાનાં (**potānā̃**) has a *duplicative* form: પોતપોતાનાં (**potpotānā̃**). This is a style used for emphasis both in colloquial speech and writing.

જાતજાતનાં (**jātjātnā̃**) is another 'duplicative' form meaning 'of various types'. જાત (**jāt**) meaning 'type'. When repeated it gives the sense of 'variety':

જાતજાતનાં વિષયોનાં પુસ્તકો . . . (**jātjatnā̃ vishayonā̃ pustako . . .**)

Note the case relations with suffixes like ગુજરાતનાં (**gujrātnā̃**), માતૃભાષામાં (**mātrubhāshāmā̃**), ધર્મનો, ગાંધીજીને (**gāndhijine**), etc.

Also note the use of prepositions like બાજુમાં (**bājumā̃**), સુધીનો (**sudhino**), etc.

Note the use of conjuncts like તથા (**tathā**) છતાં (**chhatā̃**):

તેમણે લખેલા તથા તેમના ઉપર લખાયેલા. (**temṇe lakhelā tathā temnā upar lakhayelā.**)
ગાયો પણ છે છતાં સ્વચ્છતા પણ કેટલી બધી. (**gāyo paṇ chhe chhatā̃ svachhtā paṇ keṭli badhi.**)

Exercise 1

Translate the following sentences into Gujarati:

(a) Jane's house is on the hill.
(b) Suleman was going to the airport.
(c) I paid quite a large amount for this car.
(d) There was recently a big conference of industrialists in Delhi.
(e) Which is the best and most healthy exercise?
(f) I like to watch the rising sun on the seashore at Somnath.

Exercise 2

Rearrange the following into four groups connected by meaning:

હરવું	મોટાં	બાગ	પંખી
નાના	ફરવું	જંતુ	ખેતર
પ્રાણી	વાડી	મધ્યમ	ચઢવું
બગીચો	પક્ષી	ઊતરવું	વિશાળ

Exercise 3

Complete the following with appropriate adjectives (there can be more than one answer):

ખેડૂત	વકીલ	ડૉક્ટર	સ્વામી	ઉદ્યોગપતિ	ડ્રાઈવર
____	____	____	____	____	____
____	____	____	____	____	____
____	____	____	____	____	____

Exercise 4

Correct any mistakes in the following paragraph:

હું મુંબઈના વિમાની મથક ઊતર્યું ત્યારે સવાર પડ્યો હતો. આકાશમાં સૂરજ દેખાતી ન હતું ને વરસાદ પડતી હતું. મેં એક ટેક્સી મગાવ્યો ને ડ્રાઈવરને કહ્યો કે ચર્ચગેટ જવી છે. કેટલી પૈસો? તે કહ્યું ભાઈસાહેબ, મીટર પ્રમાણું આપજી. હું સામાન મૂકી, ડ્રાઈવર ગાડી ચાલ.

Exercise 5

Change the following into the future tense:

ઇંગ્લેન્ડમાં ગાંધીજી વકીલાતનું ભણવા આવ્યા હતા. તેઓ સાદાઈથી રહેતા. એક રૂમમાં રહેતા. સવારે ઓટમીલની પોરીજ બનાવતા. સાંજે કોકો બનાવીબ્રેડ સાથે ખાતા. બપોરે બહાર જમતા. કામની જગાએ ચાલીને જતા.

Dialogue 2

સવારમાં ફરવા **savārmā̃ pharvā** Morning walk
(CD2; 24)

જગદીશ ઊઠો ભાનુભાઇ, ફરવા જવું છે ને?
ભાનુભાઈ અત્યારમાં?
જગદીશ હા. ઊગતા સૂર્યને જોવો છે ને? આબુમાં આવ્યા છીએ! ફરવા, સૂવા નહીં!
ભાનુભાઈ હા, પણ અત્યારમાં જનારા માણસો કેટલા?
જગદીશ ઘણાં હશે. ઊઠો. ઊગતો સૂર્ય તમારું સ્વાગત કરવા તૈયાર છે.
(ભાનુભાઈ ઊઠીને પાછા સૂઈ જાય છે!)
જગદીશ ભાનુભાઇ પાછા સૂઈ ગયા. સાત વાગ્યા. ઊઠો.

ભાનુભાઈ હેં! હા. મને ચાલવું બહુ ગમતું નથી. કારની ટેવ છે ને.
જગદીશ ચાલો ચાલવાની કસરત સૌથી સહેલી ને સારી છે.
ભાનુભાઈ હા પણ આ કમરનો દુખાવો બહુ હેરાન કરે છે.
જગદીશ આ હિલસ્ટેશનની હવામાં બધું મટી જશે. તમે ચાલો તો ખરા! એટલી સ્ફૂર્તિ આવશે કે કાલે તમે જ મને ઊઠાડશો. કરેલી મહેનત નકામી નહીં જાય.
ભાનુભાઈ ચાલો ત્યારે. સવારની હવા પણ સૌથી શુદ્ધ હોય છે, નહીં?
જગદીશ હા. તેને ફેફસામાં ભરી લો. શહેરોમાં તો ક્યાં ચોખ્ખી હવા પણ મળે છે!
(બંને આબુના સનરાઈઝ પોઈન્ટ પર જાય છે.)

JAGDISH uṭho bhāubhāi, pharvā javũ chhe ne?
BHĀNUBHAI atyārmā̃?
JAGDISH hā. ugtā suryane jovo chhe ne? ābumā̃ āvyā chhie. pharvā, suvā nahī̃.
BHĀNUBHAI hā. paṇ atyārmā̃ janārā māṇso keṭlā?
JAGDISH ghaṇā hashe. uṭho. ugto surya tamārũ svāgat karvā taiyār chhe.
(bhānubhai uṭhine pāchhā sui jāy chhe.)
JAGDISH Bhānubhāi pāchā sui gayā. sāt vāgyā. uṭho.
BHĀNUBHAI hẽ! hā. mane chālvũ bahu gamtũ nathi. kārni ṭev chhe ne.
JAGDISH chālo chālvāni kasrat sauthi saheli ne sāri chhe.
BHĀNUBHAI hā. paṇ ā kamarno dukhāvo bahu herān kare chhe.
JAGDISH ā hilsṭeshanni havāmā̃ badhũ maṭi jashe. tame chālo to kharā. eṭli sphurti ā̃vshe ke kāle tame ja mane uṭhāḍsho. kareli mahenat nakāmi nahī̃ jāy.
BHĀNUBHAI chālo tyāre, savārni havā paṇ sauthi shuddh hoy chhe, nahī̃?
JAGDISH hā, tene phephsāmā̃ bhari lo. shaeromā̃ to kyā̃ chokkhi havā paṇ maḷe chhe?
(banne ābunā sunrise poinṭ par jāy chhe.)

JAGDISH *Wake up Bhanubhai, going for a walk, aren't you?*
BHANUBHAI *At this time?*
JAGDISH *Yes. Want to see the rising sun? We have come to Abu! To walk, not to sleep.*
BHANUBEN *Yes. But how many go at this time?*
JAGDISH *Maybe many. Wake up.The rising sun is ready to welcome you.*

[Bhanubhai goes to sleep again after waking up.]

JAGDISH *Bhanubhai sleeping again. It is seven in the morning. Wake up.*

BHANUBHAI *Oh, yes. I don't like walking. I'm used to a car.*

JAGDISH *OK, walking exercise is the easiest and best of all.*

BHANUBHAI *Yes. But this backache troubles me a lot.*

JAGDISH *Everything will be cured in this hill station climate. Make an effort to walk! You'll feel so energetic that you will wake me up tomorrow. Labour done is not lost.*

BHANUBHAI *Let's go. The morning air is the cleanest, isn't it?*

JAGDISH *Yes, fill it in your lungs. Fresh air is not available in the cities.*

[Both go to Abu's Sunrise Point.]

Vocabulary

ઊગતો	**ugto**	rising
સ્ફૂર્તિ	**sphurti**	energy
ગમતું	**gamtũ**	like
કસરત	**kasrat**	exercise
શુદ્ધ	**shuddh**	pure
કમર	**kamar**	waist
મટી જશે	**maṭi jashe**	will be cured

Grammatical notes

Present participle

ઊગતો સૂર્ય (**ugto surya**), ચાલતી સ્ત્રી (**chālti stri**),
ઊડતું પંખી (**uḍtũ pankhi**)

The words underlined are the present participles. They are actually the past tense verbs of ઊગ, ચાલ, ઊડ, but when used before the noun serve as adjectives and show action in the present.

Past participle

ગયેલા દિવસો (**gayelā divaso**), કરેલી મહેનત (**kareli mahenat**), પીધેલું પાણી (**pidhelũ pāṇi**)

The underlined words are past participles and show action already completed.

Future participle

જનારા માણસો (**janārā maṇso**), તરનારી છોકરીઓ (**tarnāri chhokario**), કૂદનારું વાંદરું (**kudnārũ vãndrũ**)

The underlined words are future participles which express action which is yet to occur.

Conjunctive participle

ઊઠીને (**uṭhine**), ફરીને (**pharine**), જઈને (**jaine**)

Here an action has already taken place before that of the verb.

General participle

This participle does not refer to any particular tense.

મને ફરવું બહુ ગમતું નથી. (**mane *pharvũ* bahu gamtũ nathi.**)
I don't much like walking.
અમને છૂટા પડવું ગમતું નથી. (**amne *chuṭā paḍvũ* gamtũ nathi.**)
We don't like to be separated.

Honorific plural

Throughout the passage the honorific plural form તમે (**tame**) is used. Accordingly, the verbs are also in the plural form.

Conjuncts

Note the use of conjuncts like પણ (**paṇ**), કે (**ke**) in the following sentences:

તમે આનંદ અનુભવી શકશો, <u>પણ</u> આવા જનારા કેટલા?
(**tame ānand anubhavi shaksho, *<u>paṇ</u>* āvā janārā keṭlā?**)
(*lit.*) You will enjoy, but how many of us do that?

એટલી સ્ફૂર્તિ આવશે <u>કે</u> રોજ જવાનું નક્કી કરશો.
(**eṭli sphurti āvshe *<u>ke</u>* roj javānũ nakki karsho**.)
You will feel so energetic that you will want to go every day.

Superlatives

ફરવાની કસરત *સૌથી* સહેલી અને સારી છે. (**pharvāni kasrat *sauthi* saheli ane sāri chhe**.) Walking is the best exercise of all.

સવારની હવા તો *સૌથી* શુદ્ધ હોય છે. (**savārni havā to *sauthi* shuddh hoy chhe**.) The morning air is the purest of all.

As mentioned previously there are no specific suffixes to show comparatives or superlatives. The suffix થી (**thi**) is added to the word સૌ (**sau**) 'all', thereby meaning 'amongst all'. Note that the suffix થી (**thi**) is not used exclusively to show the superlative.

Exercise 6

Rearrange the words to make sense of the following dialogue:

હોટેલવાળો	છો શું કરો? સાહેબ
સ્વામી	છું ધાર્મિક આપું વ્યાખ્યાનો હું
હોટેલવાળો	રસ સરસ છે ધર્મમાં પણ મને સાહેબ
સ્વામી	છે સારું રસ છે તમને એવો એમ તે
હોટેલવાળો	વાંચ્યું મેં છે ફક્ત હજી બાઈબલ જ
સ્વામી	આચરણ તેમાનું છે તો ખરું
હોટેલવાળો	કહી સાચી તદ્દન આપે વાત
સ્વામી	આનંદ કરીને તમારી વાત થયો સાથે

Exercise 7

Translate into English:

(a) વકીલો હંમેશાં ખોટું જ બોલે છે તે સાચું નથી.
(b) આ મકાનની કિંમત લગભગ મારા મકાન જેટલી જ છે.
(c) નવાઈની વાત તો એ છે કે એ કદી અમદાવાદની બહાર ગયો જ નથી.
(d) મને કુદરતના દ્રશ્યો જોવાં બહુ જ ગમે છે.
(e) કરેલું કામ કદી નકામું જતું નથી.
(f) ઘરની બહાર નીકળીને તેમણે મારું સ્વાગત કર્યું

Exercise 8

Write down five things you were going to do yesterday.

Exercise 9

Arrange the following in order of size:

વિમાન સાઈકલ ગાડું કાર ખટારો

Exercise 10

Match the words in each column:

A	*B*
સરસ	આનંદ
ખુશી	કીર્તિ
યશ	શુદ્ધ
દરિયો	સારું
વહાણ	સમુદ્ર
ચોખ્ખું	જહાજ

Exercise 11

Write a short dialogue on directing a stranger from the railway station to a hill station.

Exercise 12

Describe a morning walk using the following words:

અંદર બહાર ઉપર નીચે આગળ પાછળ આજે કાલે સામે

Unit Fourteen

પત્રલેખન **patralekhan**

Letter writing

In this unit you will learn about:

- Personal letters
- Official letters
- Governmental letters
- Invitations

Personal letter

૧૮ એલ્મ ગાર્ડન્સ,
હેમ્પસ્ટેડ,
લંડન,
તા: ૨૬.૦૪.૨૦૧૧

પ્રિય બહેન કુસુમ,

ઘણા દિવસથી તારો કોઈ પત્ર નથી. વચ્ચે નવીનભાઈ અને નીતાભાભી આવ્યાં હતાં ત્યારે સૌના કુશળ સમાચાર આપ્યા હતા. પણ તમે બધાં એવાં તે ક્યાં કામમાં રોકાઈ ગયાં છો કે બે લીટી લખવાનીય ફુરસદ ન મળે!

એટલે જ એમ થયું કે ચાલો જાતે જ જઈ આવું! આ દિવાળીની રજાઓમાં ત્યાં આવવા વિચાર છે. ભારત છોડયાને આજકાલ કરતાં દસ વરસ થઈ ગયા! સાચું લાગતું નથી! હજી જાણે હમણાં જ તો મુંબઈના સહાર એરપોર્ટ પરથી તમે મને વળાવ્યો હતો! સમય કેવો ઝડપથી પસાર થઈ જાય છે!

ત્યાં આવીશ એટલે મુંબઈમાં પ્રતાપભાઈ અને ભાભીને મળાશે. પ્રદ્યુમનભાઈનું કલાપ્રદર્શન પણ જહાંગીર આર્ટ્સ ગેલેરીમાં ચાલતું હશે તે જોવાશે. પૂનામાં રંજન અને તેની વહુ પલ્લવીને ત્યાં પણ જવું છે. તેમના બાળકો પરાગ અને

પ્રણવને કેટલાય વખતથી જોયાં નથી. હવે તો મોટા થઈ ગયા હશે! રાજકોટમાં ચંદાની તબિયત નરમગરમ રહે છે. ભાઈબીજને દિવસે ત્યાં પહોંચવાની ગણતરી છે. એ તો રાજીનારેડ થઈ જશે! તમારી સૌની સાથે વડોદરાનો વિકાસ પણ જોવો છે.

તમારા માટે શું શું લાવું તેની યાદી બનાવી તરત મોકલશોને? સૌને યાદ.

લિ.જતીનના સ્નેહસ્મરણ

18 Elm Gardens
Hampstead
London NW3 2BJ
31 October 2010

My dear Kusum,

I've not heard from you for ages. A few days ago I saw Navin and Nita, who tell me you are well. What keeps you so busy that you cannot write even a few lines! So I am now thinking of coming to India for Diwali and hope to see you then. I can't believe that it is already ten years since I left for England. It seems like yesterday that I took off from Sahar Airport, Mumbai. Time flies!

I will be seeing Pratapbhai and Bhabhi in Bombay and am hoping to make time in order to see Pradumna's exhibition of paintings at the Jehangir Art Gallery. I would also like to see Ranjan and his wife, Pallavi, in Poona. I haven't seen their sons, Parag and Pranav, for such a long time. They must be quite grown up by now.

I will be making a special trip to Rajkot on Bhaibeej to see my sister, Chanda, whose health these days is only so-so. I know she will be surprised and very pleased to see me.

I will, of course, be seeing you in Baroda. Please let me know what I can bring you from London.

Love,
Jatin

Vocabulary

કુશળ સમાચાર	**kushaḷ samāchār**	news (of well-being), OK
ફુરસદ	**phursad**	to make time
વળાવ્યો	**vaḷāvyo**	bade goodbye
નરમગરમ	**naramgaram**	so-so (*lit.* soft and warm)
રાજીનારેડ	**rājināred**	very happy
ભાઈબીજ	**bhāibij**	the second day of the new year according to the Hindu calendar. It means Brother's Day (ભાઈ = brother, બીજ = second day)
ગણતરી	**gaṇatri**	hope to (*lit.* counting)

Notes

(a) As with letters in English the address goes at the top right-hand side and is followed by the date.

(b) The word પ્રિય is equivalent to 'Dear' but the name of the person to whom the letter is written is preceded by ભાઈ (for a man) or બહેન (for a woman).

(c) If you are writing to an older person add પૂજ્ય before the name instead of પ્રિય (પૂજ્ય 'revered').

(d) If the letter is semi-formal (i.e. the person is known to you but the relationship is distant) address the recipient as સ્નેહી ભાઈશ્રી/બહેન as the case may be.

(e) When you end the letter use લિ., which is a short form of the word લિખિતંગ, which denotes the writer.

(f) After લિ. you can either write આપનો (*m*), આપની (*f*) or just your name: e.g.

લિ. આપનો જગદીશ
લિ. આપની ચંદા
or લિ. જગદીશ/ચંદા

(g) After the name there is a variety of endings:

પ્રણામ or વંદન or નમસ્કાર (*lit*. bow down)	for elderly people
સ્નેહસ્મરણ (happy memories)	for people of the same age group
જય ભારત or જય જય (*lit*. victory to India, or victory)	a general form of address
સલામ આલેકૂમ (peace to you)	used by Muslims

(h) Older people writing to younger use ચિ. (a short form of ચિરંજીવ) instead of પ્રિય, meaning 'may you live long'.

(i) He/she will end the letter by writing આશીર્વાદ, literally: blessing. Muslims will end with the Arabic equivalent: દુઆ.

Exercise 1

Write a letter to your grandmother in India enquiring about her health.

Professional letters

An example of a professional letter is given here with a woman from New York asking a publisher about a book.

પુષ્પા અમીન
૧ સ્ટુઅર્ટ પ્લેસ
વ્હાઈટ પ્લેન્સ
ન્યુ યોર્ક
તા. ૩૧.૧૦.૨૦૧૦

પ્રતિ
વ્યવસ્થાપકશ્રી
રટલેજ
૧૧ ન્યુ ફેટર લેન
લંડન

વિષય: આપના ગુજરાતી પુસ્તક અંગે

શ્રીમાન

સવિનય જણાવવાનું કે આપના તરફથી તાજેતરમાં ગુજરાતી ભાષા સહેલી રીતે અંગ્રેજી મારફત શીખવવાનું પુસ્તક પ્રગટ થયું છે એમ જાણવા મળ્યું છે. મારી બહેનપણી સરોજે એ પુસ્તક જોયું છે. એના કહેવા પ્રમાણે સૌ સહેલાઈથી ગુજરાતી શીખી જાય એવી સરળતાથી એ લખાયું છે.

મારી દીકરી અહી જ જન્મીને મોટી થઈ છે. તેને ગુજરાતી લખતાંવાંચતા આવડે તેવી મારી ઈચ્છા છે. તે માટે મારે આ પુસ્તકની જરૂર છે. તો તેની કિંમત, ટપાલ તથા રવાનગી ખર્ચ અંગે મને વળતી ટપાલે જણાવશો? જો અહીં જ એ મળતું હોય તો પુસ્તકવિક્રેતાનું સરનામું મોકલશો. આપના આ જાતનાં અન્ય પ્રકાશનોની યાદી પણ મોકલવા કૃપા કરશો.

આભાર
આપની વિશ્વાસુ
પુષ્પા અમીન

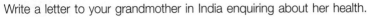

Pushpa Amin
1 Stuart Place
White Plains
New York 10689
31.10.2010

The Manager
Routledge
11 New Fetter Lane
London EC4P 4EE

Subject: Your book on Gujarati

Dear Sir,

I understand you have recently published a book on learning Gujarati through English. My friend Saroj who has seen it tells me it is written in such a way everyone can learn Gujarati easily.

My daughter was born and brought up here. I would very much like her to read and write Gujarati. I want this book for that (reason).

Please let me know by return of post the cost of the book, including postage and packing charges. Please let me know if it is available here and the address of the bookseller. I would also be very grateful if you could send me a list of any other Gujarati publications.

Thanking you,
Yours faithfully,
Pushpa Amin

Vocabulary

વ્યવસ્થાપક	**vyavashthāpak**	manager
તાજેતરમાં	**ṭājetarmā̃**	recently
મારફત	**mārphat**	through
જન્મીને મોટી થઈ	**janmine moti thay**	born and brought up
રવાનગી ખર્ચ	**ravāngi kharch**	delivery charges (post and packing)
વળતી ટપાલે	**vaḷṭi tapāle**	by return of post
પુસ્તકવિક્રેતા	**pustakvikretā**	bookseller
અન્ય પ્રકાશનો	**anya prakāshano**	other publications

Notes

(a) Formal letters are addressed શ્રીમાન (*m*), શ્રીમતી (*f*), the equivalent of 'Dear Sir/Madam'.

(b) સવિનય જણાવવાનું કે is the formal beginning of a letter. It means 'I respectfully inform you that . . .'

(c) આપનો/ની વિશ્વાસુ is equivalent to 'Yours faithfully'.

Exercise 2

Write a letter, as a manager, replying to a query about a book.

Invitation to a wedding

Such invitations used to be very formal and stylized but this is changing. A current invitation may read as follows:

સ્નેહીશ્રી,
અમારી દીકરી
ચિ. શર્વરી
ચિ. નિહાલ
ભાનુબેન મહેન્દ્રભાઈ દેસાઈના સુપુત્ર
સાથે
સપ્તપદીમાં પગલાં પાડશે.
આનંદના એ અવસરે સહભોજનમાં
સહભાગી થવા સ્નેહભર્યું નિમંત્રણ

જયેન્દ્રવ્યાસ	રજની વ્યાસ
શૈલા વ્યાસ	સરોજ વ્યાસ
હરેન્દ્ર વ્યાસ	અનિલા વ્યાસ
કારતક વદ ૧૧	ચંદરવો પાર્ટી પ્લોટ
તા. ૨૩.ઓક્ટોબર, ૨૦૧૧	જલતરંગ કલબ
રવિવારે બપોરે ૧૨.૦૦	ધરણીધર દેરાસર થઈને અમદાવાદ ૩૮૦ ૦૦૭

Dear
Our daughter SHARVARI will marry (with) NIHAL
(son of Bhanuben and Mahendrabhai Desai)
On such a happy occasion we cordially invite you to join us for dinner

Jayendra Vyas	*Rajni Vyas*
Shaila Vyas	*Saroj Vyas*

Harendra Vyas   Anila Vyas
Chandarvo Party Plot
Jaltarang Club
Ahmedabad 380007

Vocabulary

સુપુત્ર	**suputra**	son (*lit.* good son: સુ good, પુત્ર son)
અવસર	**avsar**	occasion (generally a happy one)
સહભોજન	**sahbhojan**	dining together
સહભાગી	**sahbhāgi**	partake
નિમંત્રણ	**nimãtraṇ**	invitation
કારતક વદ ૧૧	**kārtak vad 11**	reading of the Hindu calendar: the eleventh day of the second half of the first month, i.e. **Kartak**.
સપ્તપદીમાં પગલાં પાડશે	**Saptapadimā̃ paglā̃ pādshe**	will marry (*lit.* walking seven steps). In the marriage ritual bride and groom take seven steps together, at each point stopping and swearing an oath of fidelity to each other. સપ્ત means 'seven' and પદ means 'steps'.

Governmental letters

Correspondence to or from government agencies takes on a particular form, unlike that of other official letters.

નં

નાણાંવિભાગ સચિવાલય ____
ગાંધીનગર ____
તા.

પ્રતિ
શ્રી નાયબ સચિવ
બાંધકામ વિભાગ
સચિવાલય
ગાંધીનગર ____

વિષય: નાણાંકીય મંજૂરી

ઉપર્યુક્ત વિષય પરત્વે આપના તા. .... પત્ર નં. ના ઉત્તરમાં સવિનય જણાવવાનું કે ઉક્ત કેસના કાગળો આ વિભાગમાં નથી. આ વિભાગના તા.

.....ના પત્ર નં. અનુસાર તે કેસ બાંધકામ વિભાગને પાછો મોકલાઈ ગયો હોઈ, આપના વિભાગમાં તપાસ કરવા વિનંતી છે.

નાયબ સચિવ
નાણાં વિભાગ
ગુજરાત સરકાર

No.

Finance Department
Sachivalaya
Gandhinagar
Dated:

To:
The Deputy Secretary
Public Works Department
Sachivalaya
Gandhinagar

Subject: Financial Sanction

In reply to your letter No. ____ dated ____, on the subject mentioned above, I have the honour to state that the papers concerning the said case are not with this Department. Since the case has already been returned to the Public Works Department under this Department letter No. ____ dated ____ you are requested to look for it in your own Department.

Deputy Secretary to the Government of Gujarat.
Finance Department

Vocabulary

નાણાં વિભાગ	**nāṇā̃ vibhāg**	Finance Department
સચિવાલય	**sachivālay**	Office of the Secretary of State
ગાંધીનગર	**gā̃dhinagar**	Capital of Gujarat State
નાયબ સચિવ	**nāyab sachiv**	Deputy Secretary
બાંધકામ વિભાગ	**bā̃dhkām vibhāg**	Public Works Department
નાણાંકીય મંજૂરી	**nāṇā̃kiya mā̃juri**	Financial Sanction
ઉપર્યુક્ત	**uparvyukt**	above-mentioned
ઉક્ત	**ukta**	said

Unit Fifteen

ભાષાંતર **bhāshāntar**

Translation

In this unit you will:

- Develop the ability to translate English into Gujarati and vice versa
- Be introduced to literary styles
- Have glimpses into aspects of Gujarat

Exercise 1 **(CD2; 26)**

Translate into Gujarati:

My life in London

I decided to take rooms on my own account instead of living any longer in a family. I also decided to move from place to place according to the work I had to do. The rooms were so selected as to enable me to reach the place of business on foot in half an hour. This saved fares and gave me walks of eight to ten miles a day. This habit kept me practically free from illness throughout my stay in England and gave me a fairly strong body.

(Mahatma Gandhi)

Vocabulary

selected	**pasād kari**	પસંદ કરી
enable	**shakya**	શક્ય
business	**kām**	કામ
fares	**bhādā̃**	ભાડાં
habit	**tev**	ટેવ
practically	**lagbhag**	લગભગ
fairly	**ṭhikṭhik**	ઠીકઠીક

Exercise 2

Translate into Gujarati:

Gujaratis have migrated throughout the world and increasing numbers, both younger-generation Gujarati and non-Gujarati, want to learn the language. Gujarati is one of the most widely spoken languages of India and is the official language of Gujarat State, which itself has nearly 40 million inhabitants. Gujaratis form a large proportion of the 15 million Indians living overseas, with 600,000 in the UK, not just from India but from Britain's many former colonies.

Vocabulary

migrated	**sṭhaḷānter**	સ્થળાંતર
throughout the world	**duniābharmā̃**	દુનિયાભરમાં
generation	**pedhi**	પેઢી
official	**sarkāri**	સરકારી
inhabitants	**vasvāt karnārā, rahevāsi**	વસવાટ કરનારા, રહેવાસી
proportion	**Bhāg, pramān**	ભાગ, પ્રમાણ
overseas	**dariāpār**	દરિયાપાર

Exercise 3

Translate into Gujarati:

The first generation of Gujarati speakers in the UK use the same range of Gujarati as is found in the home country. Their vocabulary, however, is worthy of comment. Because of the long period of British rule in India, many English words such as 'station', 'ticket', 'pen', 'court' and 'coat' were a part of their everyday speech. These loan words have continued with the addition of words like 'video', 'tube', 'computer' and 'rocket'. Gujaratis formerly settled in East Africa also use certain Swahili words such as 'jugu' (peanuts), 'kisu' (penknife), 'bakudi' (bowl) and 'maramoja' (quick).

Vocabulary

worthy of comment	**nÕdhpatra**	નોંધપાત્ર
range	**kakshā**	કક્ષા
vocabulary	**shabdabhandoḷ**	શબ્દભંડોળ
loan	**uchhinā**	ઉછીના

Exercise 4

Translate into Gujarati:

How many languages are there in the world? What languages do they speak in India? What languages have the most speakers? What languages were spoken in Australia or in California before European immigration? When did Latin cease to be spoken and when did French start? How did English become such an important world language? These and similar questions are asked often by the interested layman. As regards the first question one can say that some 4,000 languages are spoken today. Laymen are often surprised that the figure should be so high.

(Bernard Comrie)

Vocabulary

speakers	**bolnārā**	બોલનારા
immigration	**pardeshthi āvi vasvāt karvo**	પરદેશથી આવી વસવાટ કરવો
layman/men	**sāmānya mānas**	સામાન્ય માણસ
surprised	**navāi pāme chhe**	નવાઈ પામે છે

Exercise 5

Translate into English:

ભારતના નકશા ઉપરનો આપણો ભૂવિભાગ બહુ લાંબો પહોળો નથી, પણ એની એક ખાસિયત ઊડીને આંખે વળગે છે. એને ભારતના બીજા કોઈ રાજ્યને નથી એવડો વિસ્તૃત, હજાર માઈલનો, દરિયાકિનારો છે. બીજી ખાસિયત એ છે કે જમીન ફળદ્રુપ છે અને ત્રીજી એ છે કે ચારે બાજુથી અનેક પ્રજાસમૂહો અહી

આવીને વસ્યા છે, જેમાં દરિયાઈ માર્ગે "પવિત્ર અગ્નિ" સાથે પધારેલા અને દૂધમાં સાકરની જેમ ગુજરાતની વસ્તીમાં ભળી ગયેલા પારસીઓ ખાસ ધ્યાન ખેંચે છે. મહાભારતમાં ઉલ્લેખ છે કે અર્બુદગિરિ (આબુ) અને સમુદ્ર વચ્ચેનો આ પ્રદેશ ગાયના દૂધભર્યા આંચળ જેવો છે. દ્વારકા, ભરૂચ, ખંભાત, સુરત બંદરો જુદા જુદા સમયમાં વિકસ્યાં. બહોળા દરિયાકિનારાએ, ધરતીની ફળદ્રુપતાએ, અનેક જાતિસમૂહોના સંગમે ગુજરાતની પ્રજાના સ્વભાવઘડતરમાં ફાળો આપ્યો છે, અમદાવાદની બજારનો મજાનો મંત્ર રહ્યો છે- કડદો/-બાંધછોડ, compromise. વ્યવહારુ ઉકેલ,. આ વ્યવહારુપણું ઘણા નિરર્થક ક્લેશ, સંઘર્ષ, વેરઝેર મિટાવવામાં મદદરૂપ બને છે.

(ઉમાશંકર જોશી)

Vocabulary

નક્શો	**naksho**	map
ભૂવિભાગ	**bhuvibhāg**	land (*lit.* ભૂ land, વિભાગ section)
ખાસિયત	**khāsiyat**	peculiarity
ઊડીને આંખે વળગે	**udine ā̃nkhe valge**	eye-catching (*lit.* flies and clings to the eye)
વિસ્તૃત	**vistruṭ**	extensive
ફળદ્રુપ	**phaḷdrup**	fertile
પ્રજાસમૂહ	**prajāsamuh**	groups of people
દરિયાઈ માર્ગે	**dariāi mārge**	by the sea
પવિત્ર અગ્નિ	**pavitra agni**	holy fire (as worshipped by the Parsis)
ધ્યાન ખેંચે છે	**dhyān khẽche chhe**	draws attention
આંચળ	**ā̃nchaḷ**	udder
બહોળા	**bahoḷā**	extensive
સંગમ	**sā̃gam**	union (*lit.* mixing of people)
કડદો	**kaḍdo**	compromise
વ્યવહારુ ઉકેલ	**vyavāhru ukel**	practical solution
નિરર્થક	**nirarthak**	unnecessary
ક્લેશ	**klesh**	agony
સંઘર્ષ	**sā̃gharsh**	conflict
વેરઝેર	**verjher**	animosities
મિટાવવામાં	**mitāvvāmā̃**	in removing, eradicating

Exercise 6

Translate into English:

ગુજરાત એક રમણીય ભૂમિ છે. એ રસાળ છે, સુંદર છે, સમૃદ્ધ છે. નદીઓ અને સરોવરો, વાડીઓ અને ખેતરો, ગામડાં અને નગરો, ઉદ્યોગો અને બજારો, મંદિરો અને મહાલયોથી ગુજરાતની ધરતી સભર છે. એનો ઈતિહાસ પણ તેવો જ ગૌરવભર્યો છે.અનેક ઐતિહાસિક સ્મારકો, ધાર્મિક સ્થાનો, ઔદ્યોગિક મથકો અને કુદરતી સૌંદર્ય સ્થળો ગુજરાતની સાંસ્કૃતિક ચેતનાનો પરિચય કરાવે છે. આ પ્રદેશોમાં ફરતા ફરતા ભગવાન કૃષ્ણથી મહાત્મા ગાંધીજી સુધીની અનેક વિરલ વિભૂતિઓનાં સ્મરણો જાગે છે. ગુજરાતની હજારો વર્ષથી જળવાયેલી અસ્મિતા આપણે તેમાં જોઈ શકીએ છીએ.

(રજની વ્યાસ)

Vocabulary

રમણીય	**ramniya**	beautiful
ભૂમિ	**bhumi**	land
રસાળ	**rasāḷ**	fertile
સમૃદ્ધ	**samruddha**	prosperous
નદીઓ	**nadio**	rivers
સરોવરો	**sarovaro**	lakes
વાડીઓ	**vādio**	orchards
ખેતરો	**khetaro**	farms
ગામડાં	**gāmdā̃**	villages
નગરો	**nagaro**	cities
ઉદ્યોગો	**uddyogo**	industries
બજારો	**bajāro**	markets
મહાલયો	**mahālayo**	palatial buildings
ધરતી	**dharti**	land
સભર	**sabhar**	full of
ઈતિહાસ	**itihās**	history
ગૌરવભર્યો	**gauravbharyo**	glorious
ઐતિહાસિક	**aitihasik**	historical
સ્મારકો	**smārako**	monuments
ઔદ્યોગિક	**audyogik**	industrial
મથકો	**mathako**	centres

કુદરતી	**kudrati**	natural
સૌંદર્યસ્થળો	**saundaryasthalo**	beauty spots
સાંસ્કૃતિક	**sā̃skrutik**	cultural
ચેતના	**chetnā**	consciousness
વિરલ	**viral**	rare
વિભૂતિઓ	**vibhutio**	personalities
સ્મરણો	**smaraṇo**	reminiscences
અસ્મિતા	**asmitā**	identity

Exercise 7 **(CD2; 28)**

Translate into English:

સામાજિક જીવનમાં શિક્ષણને જેટલું મહત્વ છે એટલું બીજી કોઈ વસ્તુને નથી. શિક્ષણ દ્વારા આપણે જ્ઞાન મેળવીએ છીએ. સમાજને ઉપયોગી થઈએ છીએ. શિક્ષણના સ્વરૂપ પર સમાજનું સ્વરૂપ આધાર રાખે છે. સારું શિક્ષણ મળે તો આપણે આપણા દોષ જોઈ શકીએ છીએ. પ્રગતિ કરી શકીએ છીએ. આથી સમાજનો પણ વિકાસ થાય છે. શિક્ષણ અનેક રીતે મળી શકે છે. બાળકનો જન્મ થાય ત્યારથી જ એ શરૂ થાય છે. એ શિક્ષણ અનુભવમાંથી મળે. નિશાળના ભણતરમાંથી મળે. વડીલોના માર્ગદર્શનથી મળે. વાંચનમાંથી મળે.

(ડો. કાલેલકર)

Vocabulary

સામાજિક	**sāmājik**	social
શિક્ષણ	**shikshaṇ**	education
મહત્વ	**mahattva**	importance
જ્ઞાન	**gnān**	knowledge
ઉપયોગી	**upyogi**	useful
સ્વરૂપ	**svarup**	type
દોષ	**dosh**	faults
પ્રગતિ	**pragati**	progress
વિકાસ	**vikās**	development
જન્મ	**janma**	birth
અનુભવ	**anubhav**	experience
ભણતર	**bhaṇtar**	study
માર્ગદર્શન	**mārgdarshan**	guidance

Exercise 8

Translate into English:

ગુજરાત તો ભારતનું નંદનવન છે. તાપી કે નર્મદા જેવી મહાસાગર જેવી નદીઓ જુઓ. પાલિતાણાનાં જૈન દહેરાંઓ જુઓ. અમદાવાદની મસ્જિદોનાં સ્થાપત્ય અને કોતરકામ જુઓ. મોઢેરાનું પ્રાચીન સૂર્યમંદિર જુઓ. પુરાતન સંસ્કૃતિના અવશેષો જ્યાં છે તે લોથલ જુઓ. ઊંચો ગઢ ગિરનાર ચઢો કે સમુદ્રકિનારે આવેલું સોમનાથનું ભવ્ય મંદિર જુઓ. બધે જ કુદરતની કૃપા અને મનુષ્યના સર્જનનો સુમેળ દેખાશે.

Vocabulary

નંદનવન	**nā̃danvan**	garden of paradise
મહાસાગર	**mahāsāgar**	great ocean
દહેરાં	**daherā̃**	temples
મસ્જિદો	**masjido**	mosques
સ્થાપત્ય	**sthāpatya**	architecture
પ્રાચીન	**prāchin**	ancient
પુરાતન	**puratan**	ancient
અવશેષો	**avshesho**	monuments
ભવ્ય	**bhavya**	glorious
કૃપા	**krupā**	blessings
સર્જન	**sarjan**	creation
સુમેળ	**sumeḷ**	harmony
કોતરકામ	**kotarkām**	carving

Exercise 9

Translate into English:

ગુજરાતને ભારતના કુલ ૩૫૦૦ માઈલના સાગરકાંઠામાંથી ૧૦૦૦ માઈલનો કાંઠો મળ્યો છે. જૂના જમાનામાં દ્વારકા, ખંભાત, સુરત જેવાં બંદરો મારફતે દેશપરદેશ સાથે વેપાર ચાલતો. ગુજરાતીઓ સાગરખેડુઓ તો હતા જ, ને હજીય છે. અનેક જાતની પ્રજાઓ સાથે તે હળતાભળતા. સાહસ એનું બીજું નામ જ ગુજરાતી. દુનિયાનો કોઈ ખૂણો એવો નહી હોય જ્યાં ગુજરાતી જઈને વસ્યો ન હોય! કરાંચી કે કલકત્તા, લંડન કે પેરિસ, ન્યુ યોર્ક કે ટોકિયો, બધે

એ હોય જ. આનાથી ગુજરાતીના ચારિત્ર્યનો મોટો ભાગ ઘડાયો છે. વેપાર એના લોહીમાં છે. એ પૈસો કમાઈ જાણે છે ને વાપરી પણ જાણે છે.

(રજની વ્યાસ)

Vocabulary

સાગરકાંઠો	**sāgarkā̃tho**	sea coast
બંદર	**bā̃dar**	port
વેપાર	**vepār**	trade
સાગરખેડુઓ	**sāgarkheduo**	voyagers
હળતાભળતા	**haḷtābhaḷtā**	mixed
સાહસ	**sāhas**	courage
ચારિત્ર્ય	**chāritrya**	character
લોહીમાં	**lohimā̃**	in the blood

Exercise 10 **(CD2; 31)**

Translate into English:

મુંબઈ એક એવું મહાનગર છે જ્યાં આળસુ માણસને પણ પરસેવાના રેલા ઊતરતા રહે છે. અહીં તદ્દન નવરો માણસ પણ કાયમ ઉતાવળમાં હોય છે. કોઈ શહેર મહાનગર બની જાય એની ખબર શી રીતે પડે? એ માટે બે લક્ષણો ધ્યાનમાં રાખવા પડે. જ્યારે ધૂળ ઘટતી જાય અને ધુમાડો વધતો જાય ત્યારે જાણવું કે નગર હવે મહાનગર બની ચૂક્યું છે, વળી વૃક્ષનાં થડની સંખ્યા ઘટતી જાય અને બત્તીના થાંભલાની સંખ્યા વધતી જાય ત્યારે તો ચોક્કસ જાણવું કે મહાનગર વિકસી રહ્યું છે.

(ગુણવંત શાહ)

Vocabulary

મહાનગર	**mahānagar**	metropolis
આળસુ	**āḷsu**	idler
પરસેવો	**parsevo**	perspiration
તદ્દન	**taddan**	totally, completely
નવરો	**navro**	unemployed or having free time
કાયમ	**kāyam**	always

ઉતાવળમાં	**utāvaḷmā̃**	in a hurry
લક્ષણો	**lakshaṇo**	signs
ધૂળ	**dhuḷ**	dust
ધુમાડો	**dhumādo**	smoke
વૃક્ષનાં થડ	**vrukshnā̃ thad**	trunks of the trees
બત્તીના થાંભલા	**battinā thā̃bhlā**	lampposts
ચોક્કસ	**chokkas**	no doubt

Key to exercises

Unit 1

Exercise 1

(a) majāmā̃; (b) garmi; (c) ṭhanḍi.

Exercise 2

(a) te kem chhe. (b) te majāmā̃ chhe. (c) āje bahu ṭhandi chhe. (d) āje garmi nathi. (e) hũ kām karũ chhũ. (f) te base chhe.

Exercise 3

(a) āje garmi chhe. (b) ājkāl ṭhanḍi bahu paḍe chhe. (c) tame paṇ āvjo. (d) ame karie chhie. (e) teo bese chhe. (f) tũ kare chhe.

Exercise 4

ghar, bājumā̃, pāchhaḷ, upar, niche, rasoḍũ, saras.

Exercise 5

(a) orḍāo; (b) nathi; (c) āvo; (d) āvjo; (e) chhie; (f) chho.

Exercise 6

(a) chhũ; (b) chho; (c) chhe; (d) chhe; (e) jāḷavjo; (f) karũ chhũ.

Exercise 7

(a) ramaṇ ahī̃ chhe. (b) nā, e ā orḍo nathi. (c) hā, ā rasoḍũ chhe. (d) gharni āgaḷ bāg chhe. (e) gitā gharmā̃ nathi. (f) ramesh bāgmā̃ chhe.

Exercise 8

hũ–chhũ; ame–chhie; tũ–chhe; tame–chho.

Exercise 9

(a) tamārũ ghar saras chhe. (b) upar be orḍāo chhe. (c) pāchhaḷ shākbhāji uge chhe. (d) ramesh gharmā̃ chhe. (e) gitā andar nathi. (f) ā tārũ shāk chhe.

Unit 2

Exercise 1

(a) ā bheṭ chhe. (b) hũ bāgkām karũ chhũ. (c) te kāle Birmingham pahÕchshe. (d) āje somvār chhe. (e) sulemān bhārat jashe. (f) rekhā gharmā̃ chhe.

Exercise 2

bheṭ–saras; ravivār–rajā; divas–rāt; ghaṇũ–thoḍũ; kām–ārām; divāḷi–tahevār.

Exercise 3

(a) tabiyat; (b) āvjo; (c) bāgmā̃; (d) āṭh vāge; (e) kāle; (f) rajā.

Exercise 4

(a) kem chho giṭāben? (b) divāḷini bheṭ chhe? (c) pārsal mokle chhe? (d) saras. āvje.

Exercise 5

Person	*Singular*	*Plural*
I	khāũ chhũ	khāie chhie
II	khāy chhe	khāo chho
III	khāy chhe	khāy chhe

Exercise 6

(a) chhũ; (b) rekhānũ; (c) sureshni; (d) shilāno; (e) hashe; (f) mināni.

Exercise 7

(a) kāle ṭhanḍi paḍshe. (b) hũ ā parsal England moklũ chhũ. (c) ame kām karie chhie. (d) rām gharni saphāi kare chhe. (e) divāḷimā̃ ghaṇũ kām chhe. (f) hũ ārām karish.

Exercise 8

phaḷ–tāju; drāksh–miṭhi; bhāv–sitter pens; mÕghi–sasti; āgaḷ–pāchhaḷ; ṭhanḍi–garmi.

Exercise 9

drāksh, keri, nāḷiyer, tarbuch.

Exercise 10

(a) sapharjan; (b) shākbhāji; (c) ṭhanḍi.

Exercise 11

(a) pestanji ane vipinbhāi. kāle. (b) kharidi. (c) ramaṇbhāine maḷshe.

Exercise 12

(a) khārũ, kaḍvũ, khāṭũ, tikhũ. (b) sapharjan, mosambi, ṭeṭi, limbu.

Exercise 13

uṭhish, karish, jamish, āvshe, joishũ, paḍshe.

Unit 3

Exercise 1

saras, kharāb; shaher, gām; shākāhāri, mā̃sāhāri; pāse, dur; savāl, javāb; ek, be.

Exercise 2

(a) shaher; (b) dharm; (c) sā̃bhaḷ.

Exercise 3

ramesh, tū kyā̃ jāy chhe? ghaṇū dur chhe? victoriani pāsej chhe. hū tyā̃ kharidi karish.

Exercise 4

ā kayū ghar chhe? pensilno sho bhāv chhe? riṭānū nāk nānū chhe pan ā̃kh moṭi chhe. tū āve chhe?

Exercise 5

(a) kayā shahernū chhe? (b) divāḷini thoḍi kharidi karishū. (c) ā kayā dharmnū mandir chhe? (d) chāl, pahelā̃ shahermā̃ jaie.

Exercise 6

(a) ahī̃ jamaṇ āpe chhe? (b) ā riṭā chhe? (c) prakāsh, gitā ane bhānu sāthe āve chhe? (d) gharthi nishāḷ dur chhe?

Exercise 7

roṭli	dāḷ	bhāt	shāk
puchhish	karish	jamish	āvish
sitār	sangit	tablā̃	bhārtiya
kyā̃	koṇ	shū	keṭli

Exercise 8

ghar, chha, āvshe, bharatni, jashe, kharidi

Exercise 9

(a) ā saras ghar chhe. (b) tame rājesh sāthe āvsho? (c) hū london jaish nahi. (d) orḍo kyā̃ chhe?

Exercise 10

(a) sulemān paisādār nathi. (b) hū kāle āvish nahī̃. (c) rādhā gharmā̃ nathi. (d) teo kāle shahermā̃ āvshe nahī̃.

Exercise 11

hũ emā samajti nathi. ghaṇā māṇas āve chhe. kāle koṇ āvshe shi khabar. āje chhokrā paṇ jashe.

Unit 4

Exercise 1

(a) hũ kāle Lanḍanmā̃ hato. (b) tũ kāle nishāḷmā̃ āvyo. (c) tamāri pāse paisā hatā. (d) latāne gher phon karyo. (e) rehmān ane sakinā sāthe bhaṇtā̃ hatā̃.

Exercise 2

chhe, shanivār, hashe, jaish, jamish.

Exercise 3

(a) mẼ mojā̃ kharidyā̃. (b) mẼ tamne kāle phon karyo hato. (c) viliyam amdāvād gayo. (d) reshmā bhāratmā̃ gujrāti bhaṇi. (e) te kagaḷ lakhshe. (f) hũ shāk ane bhāt jamyo.

Exercise 4

(a) hũ ghaṇũ kām karũ chhũ. (b) tamāri pāse e kāgal nathi. (c) kāle salmāne saras chikan khādhũ. (d) tũ kāle māre tyā̃ āvish? (e) surekhā āvi tyāre hũ gharmā̃ na hato. (f) nokre kapḍā̃ dhoyā̃ pachhi te jamyo.

Exercise 5

bajār, kharidi; khamis, pātḷun; savār, sā̃j; āj, kāl; gharmā̃, bahār.

Exercise 7

tame māri sāthe āvti kāle avsho? āpṇe bajārmā̃ jaishu. pachhi kharidi karishu ane sāthe jamishũ. majā paḍshe.

Exercise 8

The Christmas sale will start tomorrow. There will be many new sarees available at a 25 per cent discount. There was a sale last year also but then the discount was less. Even so, sales were up. This year there is a recession so people do not buy.

Exercise 10

ahī̃	tyā̃	upar	niche
āvshe	jashe	āvyo	gayo
sutrāu	reshmi	ṭerilin	ṭerikoṭan
savār	sā̃j	rāt	divas

Exercise 11

(a) mane ā rāg game chhe. (b) āje bajārmā̃ sel nathi. (c) ā nainānū̃ ghar hashe. (d) āvti kāle navin bahār jamshe. (e) ā ramaṇlālni dukān chhe? (f) dukāndār sāḍi veche chhe.

Exercise 12

(a) vipine sarlāne sāthe lidhi. (b) banne rehmānne tyā̃ gayā̃. (c) rehmānni khabar puchhvā gayā̃. (d) temṇe rehmānne phaḷ āpyā̃.

Unit 5

Exercise 1

moṭū̃, medān; ghaṇi, baheno; nāno, rasto; sārā̃, phulo; āchhā̃, rango; kāḷi, sāḍi.

Exercise 3

When I went out on Monday evening it wasn't raining. It wasn't even very cold. There were beautiful trees on both sides of the road. I had quite a long walk. Then at one place I had a coffee. It was nine o'clock at night when I returned home.

Exercise 4

MEGI āpṇe banne bahār jashū̃?
JON hā̃, jarur. chālo, paṇ kyā̃ jashū̃?
MEGI āpṇe rāṇinā mahel bāju jashū̃?

JON hā paṇ tyā̃ ghaṇā loko hashe.
MEGI to voṭfarḍnā mandirni jagā kevi chhe?
JON hā chālo. e saras ane shānt jagā chhe.

Exercise 6

(a) ek, traṇ. (b) keṭlũ. (c) ḍābi bāju. (d) kyā̃. (e) kyā̃thi.

Exercise 7

māri pāse ghar chhe. tāri pāse ghar nathi. mẼ kerino ras pidho. sita sṭeshan gai nathi? gāḍi moḍi chhe ne bas vaheli chhe. ame besishũ/ besshũ.

Exercise 8

be	chār	pā̃ch	nav
ahī̃	tyā̃	sidhũ	sāme
uttar	dakshiṇ	purva	pashchim
phar	chāl	doḍ	bes

Exercise 9

(a) āje ṭren chhe teni mane khabar nathi. (b) mane sārā̃ khamis kyā̃thi maḷshe? (c) ā deshni sundar jagāo hũ joish. (d) gujratmā̃ ramatnā̃ sārā̃ medāno chhe. (e) mārũ jamaṇ sārũ hatũ paṇ kOphi ghaṇi kharāb hati. (f) ahī̃ tamāre ghaṇo varsād hoy chhe?

Exercise 10

(a) rasto; (b) divas; (c) kāle; (d) phuṭbOl.

Exercise 11

(a) medānno rasto kayo hato? (b) ahī̃thi chār rastā ketlā dur hashe? (c) āje gāḍio bandh chhe. (d) hũ somvāre jamto nathi. (e) rasto oḷangine ḍabi bāju jasho.

Unit 6

Exercise 1

હાથ	પગ	માથું	કાન
ઊઠ	ચાલ	બેસ	દોડ
ઈકોતેર	એકસઠ	એકાવન	એકયાશી
પરચુરણ	પૈસા	નોટ	રૂપિયા

Exercise 2

પંદર, પચાસ; ગાડી, બસ; પૈસા, પરચુરણ; સામાન, બેગ; ચોક્કસ, કદાચ આપશો, લેશો.

Exercise 3

It was Sunday. I got up late. I had breakfast and switched on the television but there was nothing worth watching. I went to the shops bought a paper and returned. I read the paper but there was nothing very interesting. Then I did some gardening. Gita is coming this evening. I will go out with her and we will eat out.

Exercise 4

(a) બહેન; (b) સરકાર; (c) સોમવાર; (d) આભાર; (e) બિલાડી.

Exercise 5

(a) આ ગાડી મુંબઈ જશે? (b) વડોદરાની ટિકિટના કેટલા પૈસા થશે? (c) મારો કેટલ નંબરનો રૂમ છે? (d) મારાં ખમીસ ક્યારે મળશે? (e) ખાવાલાયક કઈ ચીજો છે?

Exercise 6

હું ભૂખ્યો હતો/ભૂખી હતી. મેં રોટલી ખાધી. શાક ખાધું. દાળભાત ખાધાં પછી પાણી પીધું. કોફી પીધી. થોડી વાર ટીવી જોયું. નિશાળનું ઘરકામ કર્યું. પછી સૂતો/સૂતી.

Exercise 8

(a) મને બે સફરજન અને થોડી દ્રાક્ષ આપો. (b) આજે કયો વાર છે? (c) આવતી કાલે હું ન્યુ યોર્ક હોઈશ. (d) આ ખમીસ ખૂબ મોંઘું છે? (e) ૧૯૯૦માં હું ભારતમ હતો.

Exercise 9

પચીસ, પાંચ, બહેન, મોજાં, ફળો, હશે, સારા.

Exercise 11

(a) મારાં ઘરનું બારણું પૂર્વ દિશામાં છે. (b) રમણલાલ ભારત જશે. (c) રમણલાલ સાથે હું થોડાં ખમીસ અને થોડી બદામ મોકલીશ. (d) મારા ભાઈ માટે મોકલીશ.

Exercise 12

(a) પશ્ચિમ; (b) દક્ષિણ.

Exercise 13

હુસેન: આજે આપણે મામાને ત્યાં જવાનું છે.
સકીના: પણ આપણે ખરીદી માટે જવાનું હતું..
હુસેન: કાલે ખરીદી કરીશું. મામાનો ફોન હતો..
સકીના: શું કાંઈ ખાસ છે?.
હુસેન: મામી માંદા છે, ખૂબ તાવ આવ્યો છે.
સકીના: તો તો ચોક્કસ જવું પડશે.
હુસેન: તું જલદી તૈયાર થા.

Unit 7

Exercise 1

(a) બર્મિંગહમથી; (b) જાપોતે; (c) ચાલશે; (d) પેલા માણસો; (e) આવ્યો, ન.

Exercise 2

Last Sunday I was in Glasgow. It was not raining but it was very cold. It is raining here in London today but it is not cold. I will visit Nitin this evening. He came from Luton yesterday. He is working there. Sometimes he himself comes down to London for the weekend. He is a good man. We will eat together.

Exercise 4

ચા	કૉફી	દૂધ	પાણી
બસો	ચારસો	છસો	આઠસો

કોણ	આ	કઈ	શું
ગરમી	ઠંડી	પવન	વરસાદ

Exercise 6

આજે મને ઠીક નથી. મને તાવ આવ્યો છે. મે ખાધું નથી. દૂધ પીધું છે. સાંજે એક ફળ લઇશ. રાતે દવા પીશ ને સૂઈ જઈશ. આવતી કાલે સવારે સારે થઈ જઈશ.

Exercise 7

(a) તાવ; (b) શરદી; (c) ઘડો; (d) વિચાર; (e) અક્કલ.

Exercise 8

(a) એની તો એ ના જ ના પાડે. (b) તમે કાંઈ ચાબા લેશો? (c) મારે રહેવાની સગવ જોઈએ છે. (d) તમે તો હમણાં દેખાતાં જ નથી. (e) કોઈ બારણે આવ્યું લાગે છે.

Exercise 10

(a) મને આ ઘર ગમ્યું. છે. (b) તમારી પાસે પૈસા છે. (c) આજે હું નિશાળે જાઉં છું (d) નીતાને ઠીક નથી. (e) રામલાલ ઘર બતાવશે.

Unit 8

Exercise 1

(a) ગઈ કાલે હું માંદો હતો/માંદી હતી. (b) મને સંગીત ગમે છે. (c) મારી પેન ખોવાઈ ગઈ છે. (d) બરાબર કરો. (e) મીરાએ ચોપડી ખોઈ નાખી.

Exercise 2

નીચે, અંદર, પહેલાં, પછી, માટે, પાસે, પછી, અંદર, વડે.

Exercise 3

(a) પડી હતી; (b) ખોઈ નાખ્યો; (c) ગમે છે; (d) બરાબર; (e) રમશે.

Exercise 4

તારી આંખ દુખે છે? આંખમાં દવા નાખી? દવા નથી નાખી? દુકાન બંધ હતી? તો બીજી દુકાને જા. પૈસા છે? કેટલા પૈસા છે? આ બીજા પૈસા રાખ..

Exercise 5

(a) I am interested in sport. (b) This headmaster is not strict. (c) This novel is good. (d) We will go shopping on Saturday afternoon. (e) I will spend time with you on Sunday.

Exercise 7

(a) વાદળું; (b) મેલેરિયા; (c) અમેરિકા; (d) યુરોપ.

Exercise 8

(a) લોકો કાલે વરસાદમાં સપડાઈ ગયા. (b) કપડાં નિચોવી પાણી કાઢી નાખ. (c) ટોની કેનેડામાં માંદો પડી ગયો. (d) મને તાવ છે એટલે હું દવા લઇશ. (e) ભજિયાં તીખાં લાગે છે પણ ભાવે છે.

Exercise 10

(a) મને તો અંગ્રેજી ગમતું નથી. (b) આજે બપોર પછી સંગીત હશે. (c) તને મેલેરિયા થઈ ગયો છે. (d) બધું મટી ગયું હતું. (e) વખત ગાળવો મને પોસાય છે.

Exercise 11

સાચું, ખોટું; સારું, ખરાબ; માંદુ, સાજું; આવ, જા; કડક, નરમ.

Exercise 12

(a) નટુભાઈ માંદા પડી ગયા. (b) તેમને તાવ આવતો હતો. (c) હવે સારું છે. (d) નટુભાઈ એકાદ અઠવાડિયું આરામ કરશે. (e) ફળ લઈ ગયાં હતાં.

Unit 9

Exercise 1

(a) એ સ્ત્રી સૌથી વધુ જાણીતી અને રૂપાળી હતી. (b) આજે વરસાદ આવે કે ન પણ આવે. (c) તેણે કહ્યું કે તેની પાસે પૈસા નથી.

Exercise 3

(a) કશી; (b) કશું; (c) કશી; (d) કશો.

Exercise 4

રહેવું છે, કરીશ, બનીશ, છું, મેળવવાની છે.

Exercise 5

(a) જવાબ; (b) પત્ર; (c) પણ; (d) બુદ્ધિ; (e) રજૂઆત.

Exercise 6

માન	અપમાન	જીવ	નિર્જીવ
નીતિ	અનીતિ	ન્યાય	અન્યાય
સત્ય	અસત્ય		

Exercise 9

આજે	કાલે	ધીમે	ઝડપથી
હમણા	પછી	ચોક્કસ	કદાચ
અહીં	ત્યાં		

Exercise 10

કીડી, મચ્છર, ઉંદર, કૂતરો, ઘોડો, સિંહ, હાથી

Exercise 11

Acting is both a hobby and a profession. The dramatist writes the play. The actors and actresses perform. People see the play. Some of them like it. Some don't like it.

Exercise 12

મીના નમસ્તે. હું સંગીતના વર્ગમાં જોડાવા માગું છું.
શિક્ષક નમસ્તે. તમારે શું શીખવું છે?
મીના મારે સિતાર શીખવી છે.
શિક્ષક સિતારની ફી મહિને પાંચસો રૂપિયા છે.
મીના ભલે. ફોર્મ ક્યાંથી મળશે?
શિક્ષક આ લો ને ભરીને સામે આપો.
મીના વર્ગ ક્યારે શરૂ થાય છે?
શિક્ષક દર શનિવારે સવારે નવ વાગે.

Exercise 13

(a) તમને શાનો શોખ છે? (b) તમે કાલે આવશો? (c) તમારે સંગીત શીખવું છે? (d) તમારા ઘરમાં કોણ ભણે છે? (e) તમારા પડોશીઓ કેવા છે? (f) ગઈ કાલે તમે ક્યાં હતા?

Exercise 14

છે, છે, હતી, છું, છીએ.

Unit 10

Exercise 1

(a) I come from Pennsylvania. (b) I don't have any currency of this country. (c) Is there a boarding house or a hotel? (d) You can clearly see the distant scenes with binoculars. (e) Do you know who is the tallest man in Britain?

Exercise 2

રામલાલભાઈ ઝાડ ઉપરથી પડી ગયા. તેમને માથામાં વાગી ગયું તેથી બેભાન થઈ ગયા. શારદાબહેન દોડતાં આવ્યાં ને ફોન કર્યો. હોસ્પિટલમાંથી ગાડી આવી. તેમને લઈ ગઈ.

Exercise 3

(a) દોડ; (b) કર; (c) રમત; (d) ઉંદર; (e) પથ્થર.

Exercise 4

(a) હું ભારત જઈશ. (b) મારાથી શાકાહારી ખોરાક લેવાય છે. (c) અહીં ઘણાં ટેબલો છે. (d) હીરાભાઈથી દોડાય છે. (e) ગાય ઘાસ ખાતી હતી..

Exercise 6

સારું, ખરાબ; ઠંડી, ગરમી; પ્રકાશ, અંધાર; ઉપર, નીચે; સગવડ, અગવડ.

Exercise 7

યુરોપ	અમેરિકા	એશિયા	આફ્રિકા
ગુજરાતી	તમિળ	અંગ્રેજી	ભાષા

કોલસા	લાકડાં	ધુમાડો	આગ
કેળવણી	કોલેજ	વર્ગ	વિદ્યાર્થી

Exercise 8

અધ્યાપક, કેળવણી; વિદ્યાર્થી, અભ્યાસ; ભોમિયો, માર્ગદર્શન; માતા, બાળઉછેર; કડિયો, બાંધકામ; માળી, બાગકામ.

Exercise 9

(a) ઘરડાંને મદદ કરવી જોઈએ. (b) આજે પૈસા ન પણ મળે. (c) આખું ઘર બંધ હતું. (d) હું સાચો નિશ્ચય કરું છું. (e) તે ઘેર જઈને પછી ઓફિસે ગયો. (f) તરતી છોકરી બહાર નીકળી. / તરતો છોકરો બહાર નીકળ્યો.

Exercise 10

(a) ઊડતાં પંખી નીચે આવ્યાં. (b) ભસતા કૂતરા કરડતા નથી. (c) કોઈએ છેતરવું ન જોઈએ. (d) જો વરસાદ પડશે તો હું નહી જાઉં. (e) ફોન કરતાં વ્યક્તિગત સંપર્ક સારો.

Exercise 12

જઈશ, રહીશ, લઈ, માટે, નથી, સુધી.

Unit 11

Exercise 1

દુર્ગેશ આજે ક્યાં બહાર જવું છે?
સુશીલા બહાર તો રોજ જ જઈએ છીએને.
દુર્ગેશ તો આજે ટીવી જોઈએ.
સુશીલા ઓહો. સરસ હિંદી ફિલ્મ છે.
દુર્ગેશ તેમાં સુનિલ દત્ત અને નરગિસ કામ કરે છે.
સુશીલા ઘણા દિવસે શાંતિથી બેસીશું.

Exercise 3

થયું, લાગ્યા, ગઈ, ગઈ, હતું, શકશે.

Exercise 4

(a) હતી, (b) છું; (c) હતા; (d) છે; (e) હશે; (f) છે.

Exercise 5

બત્તી, પ્રકાશ; દાળ, ભાત; ફિલ્મ, નાટક; માઈક, જાહેરાત; ધીમેથી, ઝડપથી; સવાર, સાંજ

Exercise 7

ફિલ્મી કળાકાર, સુંદર; પ્રોફેસર, ભૂલકણા; પ્રધાન, અભિમાની; ચિત્રકાર, ધૂની; વિદ્યાર્થી, તોફાની.

Exercise 8

(a) I don't eat in the afternoon. (b) Leela goes every day for an evening walk. (c) A famous play is not necessarily a good play. (d) This article could only be written by him. (e) I will finish this work in an hour.

Exercise 9

આનંદ	ગુસ્સો	ભય	શોક
અંગ્રેજી	મરાઠી	ગુજરાતી	ફ્રેંચ
બસ	વિમાન	ટ્રેન	સાઈકલ
ધ્વનિ	પ્રકાશ	પડદો	સેટિંગ

Exercise 10

નાટક, ટિકિટો, હતું, અભિનય, અમને, જમવા, સરસ, ભાવ્યું, ઘેર

Exercise 11

ઉપર, નીચે; અંદર, બહાર; આગળ, પાછળ; દૂર, પાસે; પહેલાં, પછી; ડાબી, જમણી.

Exercise 12

(a) નાટકનો વિષય સૌને ગમે તેવો હતો. (b) થિયેટરમાં દાખલ થયાં ને બત્તીઓનો પ્રકાશ ઘટી ગયો. (c) શકીલને માઈકમાંથી બોલેલું બરાબર ન સંભળાયું. (d) ભારતના વડા પ્રધાન હેરોમાં વિદ્યાર્થી હતા. (e) સરિતા પાસેથી ટિકિટ લઈ દીપકને આપ.

Exercise 14

(a) માથુરથી આ કામ બની શકશે. (b) સાંજનો શો પ્રોગ્રામ છે? (c) મને આ નામ ઘણું ગમે છે. (d) મારા પૈસા ધીમે ધીમે ખલાસ થઈ ગયા. (e) રજની અને સરોજ બહાર હતાં.

Exercise 15

(a) ભાનુ રમાડે છે. (b) જયા લખાવે છે. (c) ચંદ્રકાન્ત હસાવતો હતો. (d) અરજણ ઘાસ કપાવશે. (e) જહાંગીર કામ કરાવે છે.

Exercise 16

(a) હું (ગઈ) કાલે નાટક જોવા ગયો હતો. (b) જહાંગીર અગિયારીમાં જાય છે. (c) (ગયા) રવિવારે તમે ઘરની સફાઈનું કામ કરતા હતા. (d) અમે થિયેટરમાંથી નીકળશું ત્યારે સાંજ પડી ગઈ હશે. (e) નલિની ઓફીસમાંથી છૂટીને દુકાનમાં ચોપડી ખરીદતી હશે..

Unit 12

Exercise 1

(a) ગઈ કાલે તમે એથેન્સ ગયા હતા? (b) તમારું વર્ણન ઘણું સ્પષ્ટ છે. (c) આપણે શિક્ષણનું સાચું લક્ષ્ય કેમ પામી શકીએ? (d) તમારી નોંધો મને તરત આપો. (e) તમારી પાર્ટીમાં હું ન આવી શક્યો તેથી દિલગીર છું. (f) મે તાજેતરમાં જ મારી ડીગ્રી મેળવી છે.

Exercise 3

પદવીદાન, સમારંભ; પ્રોફેસર, વિદ્વાન; પરીક્ષા, ઉત્તીર્ણ; નાદુરસ્ત, તબિયત; હાજરી, ગેરહાજરી; ઝબ્બો,ટોપી.

Exercise 4

ભસતો, વાંચતી, પડતું, પડનારું, ચૂંટાનારો, કરેલું.

Exercise 6

(a) ફળ; (b) મગજ; (c) પાંદડું; (d) ગધેડાઓ; (e) જંતુ.

Exercise 9

માંદી/દો/દું; કદરૂપો/પી/પું or ખરાબ; અવ્યવસ્થા; નાનો/નાની/નાનું; અસામાન્ય.

Exercise 11

(a) કાલે મારી પાસે મકાન નહી હોય. (b) કરેલું કામ નકામું જાય છે. (c) હું યુરોપ જઈને પછી અમેરિકા જઈશ. (d) આવતી કાલે મને પેટમાં દુખતું હશે. (e) મને મોસ્કોમાં ગમે છે ને ન્યુ યોર્કમાં પણ ગમશે. (f) શીલાને કાનમાં સખત દુખાવો રહેતો હતો.

Unit 13

Exercise 1

(a) જેનનું ઘર ટેકરી ઉપર છે. (b) સુલેમાન એરપોર્ટ જવાનો હતો. (c) આ કાર માટે મેં ઘણી મોટી રકમ આપી છે. (d) તાજેતરમાં ઉદ્યોગપતિઓની એક મોટી પરિષદ દિલ્હીમાં થઈ ગઈ. (e) સૌથી સારી અને તંદુરસ્ત કસરત કઈ છે? (f) સોમનાથના દરિયાકાંઠે ઊગતા સૂર્યને જોવો મને ગમે છે.

Exercise 2

હરવું	ફરવું	ઊતરવું	ચઢવું
નાના	મોટા	મધ્યમ	વિશાળ
પ્રાણી	પક્ષી	જંતુ	પંખી
બગીચો	બાગ	વાડી	ખેતર

Exercise 4

હું મુંબઈના વિમાની મથકે ઊતર્યો ત્યારે સવાર પડી હતી. આકાશમાં સૂરજ દેખાતો ન હતો ને વરસાદ પડતો હતો. મેં એક ટેક્સી મગાવી ને ડ્રાઈવરને કહ્યું કે ચર્ચગેટ જવું છે. કેટલા પૈસા? તેણે કહ્યું, ભાઈ સાહેબ, મીટર પ્રમાણે આપજો. મેં સામાન મૂક્યો. ડ્રાઈવરે ગાડી ચલાવી.

Exercise 5

ઇંગ્લેન્ડમાં ગાંધીજી વકીલાતનું ભણવા આવ્યા હશે. તેઓ સાદાઈથી રહેતા હશે. એક રૂમમાં રહેતા હશે. સવારે ઑટમીલની પોરીજ બનાવતા હશે. સાંજે કોકો બનાવી બ્રેડ સાથે ખાતા હશે. બપોરે બહાર જમતા હશે. કામની જગાએ ચાલીને જતા હશે.

Exercise 6

હોટેલવાળો શું કરો છો સાહેબ?
સ્વામી હું ધાર્મિક વ્યાખ્યાનો આપું છું.
હોટેલવાળો સરસ. સાહેબ મને પણ ધર્મમાં રસ છે.
સ્વામી એમ. તમને એવો રસ છે તે સારું છે.
હોટેલવાળો મેં હજી ફક્ત બાઈબલ જ વાંચ્યું છે.
સ્વામી ખરું તો તેમાંનું આચરણ છે.
હોટેલવાળો આપે તદ્દન સાચી વાત કહી.
સ્વામી તમારી સાથે વાત કરીને આનંદ થયો.

Exercise 7

(a) It is not true that lawyers always lie. (b) The price of this house is approximately the same as mine. (c) It is surprising that he has never been outside Ahmedabad. (d) I love to watch nature. (e) Work done is never wasted. (f) He came out of his house and welcomed us.

Exercise 9

સાઈકલ ગાડું કાર ખટારો વિમાન

Exercise 10

સરસ, સારું; ખુશી, આનંદ; યશ, કીર્તિ; દરિયો, સમુદ્ર; વહાણ, જહાજ; ચોખ્ખું, શુદ્ધ.

Unit 15

Exercise 1

હવે વધુ વખત કોઈ કુટુંબની સાથે રહેવાને બદલે મેં જાતે જ ઓરડી રાખી રહેવાનું નક્કી કર્યું. મારા કામ પ્રમાણે જુદી જુદી જગ્યાઓ બદલતા રહેવાનું પણ નક્કી કર્યું. ઓરડી એવા ઠેકાણે પસંદ કરી કે જ્યાંથી કામની જગ્યાએ અડધા કલાકમાં ચાલીને જઈ શકાય. આથી ગાડીભાડું બચ્યું અને રોજના આઠ-દસ માઈલ ફરવાનું મળ્યું. મુખ્યત્વે આ ટેવને લીધે જ હું ઈંગ્લેન્ડમાં ભાગ્યે જ માંદો પડ્યો હોઈશ. શરીર પણ ઠીક ઠીક મજબૂત બન્યું.

Exercise 2

ગુજરાતીઓએ આખી દુનિયામાં સ્થળાંતર કર્યું છે. ગુજરાતી અને બિનગુજરાતી યુવાન પેઢી મોટી સંખ્યામાં ભાષા શીખવા માગે છે. ગુજરાતી એ ભારતમાં વધુ બોલાતી ભાષાઓમાંની એક ભાષા છે અને ગુજરાત રાજ્યની સરકારી ભાષા છે. તેમાં આશરે ૪૦ મિલિયન રહેવાસીઓ છે. દરિયાપાર વસતા ૧૫ મિલિયન ભારતીયોમાં ગુજરાતીઓની ઘણી મોટી સંખ્યા છે. માત્ર બ્રિટનમાં જ ૬ લાખ ગુજરાતીઓ વસે છે! તેઓ માત્ર ભારતમાંથી જ આવેલા નથી; બ્રિટનની પહેલાંની કોલોનીઓમાંથી પણ આવેલા છે.

Exercise 3

બ્રિટનમાં ગુજરાતી બોલનારાઓની પહેલી પેઢી પોતાના પ્રદેશમાં બોલાતી ગુજરાતી જેવી કક્ષાનું જ ગુજરાતી બોલે છે. છતાં તેમનું શબ્દભંડોળ નોંધપાત્ર છે. ભારતમાં બ્રિટિશ અમલ લાંબો સમય રહ્યો હોવાથી સ્ટેશન, ટિકિટ, પેન, કોર્ટ, કોટ, જેવા શબ્દો રોજની બોલચાલની ભાષા બની ગયા હતા. આ ઉછીના શબ્દો ચાલુ રહ્યા અને વિડીયો, ટ્યુબ, કમ્પ્યૂટર, રોકેટ જેવા શબ્દો તેમાં ઉમેરાયા. જે ગુજરાતીઓ પૂર્વે પૂર્વ આફ્રિકામાં વસ્યા હતા તેઓ જુગુ (શીંગ), કિસુ (ચાકુ), બાકુડી (વાટકી) અને મારામોજા (જલ્દી) જેવા સ્વાહિલી શબ્દો પણ વાપરતા થયા છે.

Exercise 4

દુનિયામાં કેટલી ભાષાઓ બોલાય છે? ભારતમાં કઈ કઈ ભાષાઓ બોલાય છે? કઈ ભાષાઓમાં વધુ બોલનારાઓ છે? યુરોપિયનોએ વસવાટ કર્યો ત્યાર પહેલાં ઓસ્ટ્રેલિયા અને કેલિફોર્નિયામાં કઈ ભાષાઓ બોલાતી હતી? લેટિન ક્યારથી બોલાતું બંધ થયું અને ફ્રેંચ ક્યારથી શરૂ થયું? અંગ્રેજી ભાષા દુનિયાની મહત્વની ભાષા શી રીતે બની ગઈ? (ભાષામાં) રસ ધરાવનાર સામાન્ય માણસ આ અને આવા સવાલો ઘણી વાર પૂછે છે. પહેલા સવાલના જવાબમાં કહી શકાય કે આજે આશરે ૪૦,૦૦૦ ભાષાઓ બોલાય છે. સામાન્ય માણસ આ આંકડો આટલો મોટો જોઈને નવાઈ પામે છે.

Exercise 5

The State of Gujarat is not very big in length or breadth when compared on the map of India. But one thing is striking: its sea coast is about 1,000 miles, something which no other Indian state possesses. Secondly, the land is fertile and people from all over India have migrated there, the most noteworthy of them being the Parsis, who, with their sacred fire, came by sea and mixed with the Gujaratis as 'sugar mixes with milk'. In the *Mahabharata* reference is made to this area as a province between Mount Abu and the sea, which is compared to the milk-filled udder of a cow. The ports of Dwarka, Bharuch, Khambhat and Surat developed at different times. An extensive coastal area, fertility of the land and gatherings of various peoples helped to mould the character of the Gujaratis. The Bazaar of Ahmedabad has one mantra: **kaḍ-do** – compromise, practical solution. This practicability is helping considerably in removing unnecessary conflicts and animosities.

(Umashankar Joshi)

Exercise 6

Gujarat is a beautiful land. The whole area is fertile and prosperous. Rivers and lakes, orchards and farms, villages and cities, industries and markets, temples and palatial buildings – Gujarat is rich with all these. Its history is equally glorious. Many historical monuments, religious places, industrial centres and natural beauty spots show the cultural consciousness of Gujarat. When you travel around Gujarat, reminiscences of divinities and human personalities, from Bhagwan Krishna to Mahatma Gandhi, spring to mind. We visualize an identity of Gujarat that has existed for thousands of years.

(Rajni Vyas)

Exercise 7

There is nothing more important in social life than education. Through education we obtain knowledge and may thereby become useful to society. The type of society depends upon the education we receive. With a good education we may recognize our own faults and so progress. In this way society also develops. We may be educated in many ways. As soon as a child is born, education begins. Education comes through experience. Education is also obtained through study at school; from the guidance of our elders and from reading.

(Dr N. G. Kalelkar)

Exercise 8

Gujarat is the Garden of Paradise. See the oceanlike rivers of Tapi and Narmada. See the Jain temples. See its art and the architecture of the mosques in Ahmedabad. See the ancient sun temple of Modhera. See the remains of ancient culture in Lothal. Climb the high Girnar mountain or see the grand temple of Somnath near the sea. Everywhere you will find the harmony of nature's blessings and human creation.

Exercise 9

Gujarat has a sea coast of 1,000 miles out of a total of 3,500 miles of Indian coastline. In former times world trade was carried on through ports like Dwarka, Khambhat and Surat. Gujaratis were always voyagers and remain so to the present day. They were mixing with all types of people. Courage is another name for a Gujarati. There is no corner of the world where Gujaratis have not gone and settled. Karachi or Calcutta, London or Paris, New York or Tokyo, they are everywhere. This movement constitutes a substantial part of the Gujarati character. Business is in his blood. He knows how to earn money – and how to spend it.

Exercise 10

Bombay is a large city where even the idler perspires freely. The man with no particular occupation is also in a hurry. How does one know when a city becomes a metropolis? There are two signs to look out for. When dust decreases and smoke increases one knows the city is turned into a metropolis. Again, when the trunks of trees decrease and the number of lampposts increase there is no doubt about this development.

English–Gujarati glossary

above	ઉપર	**upar** (*adv*)
above	ઉપલું	**uplũ** (*a*)
abscess	ગુમડું	**gumḍũ** (*n*)
abuse	ગાળ	**gāḷ** (*f*)
accident	અકસ્માત	**akasmāt** (*m*)
account	હિસાબ	**hisāb** (*m*)
account	ખાતું	**khātũ** (*n*)
accusation	આરોપ	**ārop** (*m*)
acting (on stage)	અભિનય	**abhinay** (*m*)
actor	નટ	**naṭ** (*m*)
AD	ઈસવિસન	**isvi san** (*f*)
addiction	વ્યસન	**vyasan** (*n*)
address	સરનામું	**sarnāmũ** (*n*)
address (residence)	ઠેકાણું	**ṭhekāṇũ** (*n*)
administration	વહિવટ	**vahivaṭ** (*m*)
advantage	ફાયદો	**phāydo** (*m*)
adventure, rashness	સાહસ	**sāhas** (*n*)
advertisement	જાહેરખબર	**jāherkhabar** (*f*)
advice	સલાહ	**salāh** (*f*)
advice	શિખામણ	**shikhāmaṇ** (*f*)
again	પાછું	**pāchhũ** (*adv*)
age	ઉંમર	**ummar** (*f*)
agree	કબુલ	**kabul** (*a*) (*adv*)
agreeable	માફક	**māphak** (*a*)
agreement	કરાર	**karār** (*m*)
all	બધું	**badhũ** (*a*)
all right	ઠીક	**ṭhik** (*a*)
alphabet	કક્કો	**kakko** (*m*)
always	હંમેશાં	**hameshā̃** (*adv*)
ambassador	એલચી	**elchi** (*m*)
and, also	વળી	**vaḷi** (*adv*)
animal	જાનવર	**jānvar** (*n*)
animosity	વેર	**ver** (*n*)

answer	જવાબ	**javāb** (*m*)
anxious	આતુર	**ātur** (*a*)
anything	કાંઈ	**kāi** (*a, pron*)
application	અરજી	**arji** (*f*)
appreciation	કદર	**kadar** (*f*)
approximately	આશરે	**āshre** (*adv*)
arithmetic	ગણિત	**gaṇit** (*n*)
army	લશ્કર	**lashkar** (*n*)
around	આસપાસ	**āspās** (*adv*)
arrow; bank (of river)	તીર	**tir** (*n*)
art	કલા	**kalā** (*f*)
as if	જાણે	**jāṇe** (*adv*)
as it is	જેવું	**jevũ** (*a*)
as much	જેટલું	**jeṭlũ** (*a*)
at this moment	અત્યારે	**atyāre** (*adv*)
attack	હલ્લો	**hallo** (*m*)
auspicious	શુભ	**shubh** (*a*)
authority	સત્તા	**sattā** (*f*)
automatically	આપોઆપ	**āpoāp** (*adv*)
awkward	કઢંગું	**kaḍhãgũ** (*a*)
bad	ખરાબ	**kharāb** (*a*)
bad omen	અપશુકન	**apshukan** (*n*)
baldness	ટાલ	**ṭāl** (*f*)
bank (of river), coast	કિનારો	**kināro** (*m*)
barren	ઉજ્જડ	**ujjaḍ** (*a*)
bathing, bath	સ્નાન	**snān** (*n*)
bazaar	બજાર	**bajār** (*f*)
beautiful	સુંદર	**sundar** (*a*)
beauty	રૂપ	**rup** (*n*)
bed sheet	ચાદર	**chādar** (*f*)
before	આગળ	**āgaḷ** (*adv*)
begging	ભીખ	**bhikh** (*f*)
beginning	શરૂઆત	**sharuāt** (*f*)
behind	પાછળ	**pāchaḷ** (*adv*)
bell	ઘંટ	**ghanṭ** (*m*)
big	મોટું	**moṭũ** (*a*)
big knife	છરો	**chharo** (*m*)
bird	પંખી	**pankhi** (*n*)
birth	જનમ,જન્મ	**janam, janma** (*m*)
bitter	કડવું	**kaḍvũ** (*a*)
blessings	આશીર્વાદ	**āshirvād** (*m*)

blind	આંધળું	**ā̃dhḷũ** (*a*)
blood	લોહી	**lohi** (*n*)
blot	ડાઘ	**ḍāgh** (*m*)
boat	હોડી	**hoḍi** (*f*)
body	શરીર	**sharir** (*n*)
book	ચોપડી	**chopḍi** (*f*)
boredom	કંટાળો	**kā̃ṭāḷo** (*m*)
borrowed	ઉછીનું	**uchhinũ** (*a*)
bottle	બાટલી	**bāṭli** (*f*)
bottle	શીશી	**shishi** (*f*)
boundary	સરહદ	**sarhad** (*f*)
box	પેટી	**peṭi** (*f*)
breakfast, snacks	નાસ્તો	**nāsto** (*m*)
breathing	શ્વાસ	**shvās** (*m*)
brick	ઈંટ	**ī̃ṭ** (*f*)
bride, wife	વહુ	**vahu** (*f*)
bridegroom	વર	**var** (*m*)
bridge	પુલ	**pul** (*m*)
broomstick	ઝાડુ	**jhāḍu** (*n*)
bucket	ડોલ	**ḍol** (*f*)
business	ધંધો	**dhandho** (*m*)
but	પણ	**paṇ** (*conj*)
butcher	કસાઈ	**kasāi** (*m*)
buttermilk	છાશ	**chhāsh** (*f*)
capital (investment)	મૂડી	**muḍi** (*f*)
car, train (depending on context)	ગાડી	**gāḍi** (*f*)
care	કાળજી	**kāḷji** (*f*)
cash	રોકડ	**rokaḍ** (*a*)
cause	કારણ	**kāraṇ** (*n*)
cautious	સાવચેત	**sāvchet** (*a*)
ceiling	છત	**chhat** (*f*)
ceremony (waving of lights before God)	આરતી	**ārti** (*f*)
certain	અમુક	**amuk** (*a*)
chair	ખુરશી	**khurshi** (*f*)
change	ફરક	**pharak** (*m*)
charity	દાન	**dān** (*n*)
chief	મુખ્ય	**mukhya** (*a*)
child	છોકરું	**chhokrũ** (*n*)
chit	ચિઠ્ઠી	**chiṭṭhi** (*f*)

city	શહેર	**shaher** (*n*)
clapping	તાળી	**tāḷi** (*f*)
clean	ચોખ્ખું	**chokkhũ** (*a*)
clean	સાફ	**sāph** (*a*)
clerk	કારકુન	**kārkun** (*m*)
climate	આબોહવા	**ābohavā** (*f*)
closed, dam	બંધ	**bandh** (*a*) (*m*)
cloth	કપડું	**kapḍũ** (*n*)
cobbler	મોચી	**mochi** (*m*)
coffin	કફન	**kaphan** (*n*)
cold	ઠંડી	**ṭhanḍi** (*f*)
collision	ટક્કર	**ṭakkar** (*f*)
comb	દાંતિયો	**dā̃tiyo** (*m*)
compassion	દયા	**dayā** (*f*)
complaint	ફરિયાદ	**phariyād** (*f*)
complete	પૂરું	**purũ** (*a*)
confidence	વિશ્વાસ	**vishvās** (*m*)
confusion, misappropriation	ગોટાળો	**goṭāḷo** (*m*)
confusion; disorder	ગરબડ	**gaḍbaḍ** (*f*)
congratulations	અભિનંદન	**abhinandan** (*n*)
connection	સંબંધ	**sambandh** (*m*)
consciousness, sense	ભાન	**bhān** (*n*)
constipation	કબજિયાત	**kabajiyāt** (*f*)
container	ડબો	**ḍabo** (*m*)
contrary	અવળું	**avḷũ** (*a*)
contrary	ઊલટું	**ulṭũ** (*a*)
control	કાબુ	**kābu** (*m*)
convenience, comfort	સગવડ	**sagvaḍ** (*f*)
cooking	રસોઈ	**rasoi** (*f*)
copy	નકલ	**nakal** (*f*)
corn	અનાજ	**anāj** (*n*)
corner	ખૂણો	**khuṇo** (*m*)
corpse	શબ	**shab** (*n*)
costly	મોંઘું	**mÕghũ** (*a*)
cotton	રૂ	**ru** (*n*)
cough	ઉધરસ	**udhras** (*f*)
counting	ગણતરી	**gaṇatri** (*f*)
country	દેશ	**desh** (*m*)
courage	હિમ્મત	**himmat** (*f*)
cowardly	કાયર	**kāyar** (*a*)
criticism	ટીકા	**ṭikā** (*f*)

crowd	ભીડ	**bhiḍ** (*f*)
crowd	ટોળું	**ṭoḷũ** (*n*)
cupboard	કબાટ	**kabāṭ** (*m, n*)
custom	રિવાજ	**rivāj** (*m*)
customer	ઘરાક	**gharāk** (*m*)
daily	રોજ	**roj** (*adv*)
darkness	અંધારું	**andhārũ** (*n*)
date	તારીખ	**tārikh** (*f*)
daughter	દીકરી	**dikri** (*f*)
day	દિવસ	**divas** (*m*)
death	મોત	**mot** (*n*)
debt	કરજ	**karaj** (*n*)
decision	ચુકાદો	**chukādo** (*m*)
deep	ઊંડું	**ũḍũ** (*a*)
definite	ચોક્કસ	**chokkas** (*a*)
description	વર્ણન	**varṇan** (*n*)
desert	રણ	**raṇ** (*n*)
devotee	ભગત	**bhagat** (*m*)
dialect	બોલી	**boli** (*f*)
diamond	હીરો	**hiro** (*m*)
dictionary	કોશ	**kosh** (*m*)
difficult	અઘરૂં	**aghrũ** (*a*)
difficulty	અડચણ	**aḍchaṇ** (*f*)
dim, unclear	ઝાંખું	**jhā̃khũ** (*a*)
direction	દીશા	**dishā** (*f*)
dirt	મેલ	**mEl** (*m*)
discount	વળતર	**vaḷtar** (*n*)
discredit	અપજશ	**apjash** (*m*)
distance	અંતર	**antar** (*n*)
distant, far off	આઘું	**āghũ** (*a*)
disturbance, riot	હુલ્લડ	**hullaḍ** (*n*)
divorce	છૂટાછેડા	**chhuṭāchheḍā** (*m pl*)
doll	ઢીંગલી	**ḍhingli** (*f*)
domestic life	સંસાર	**samsar** (*m*)
doubt	શંકા	**shankā** (*f*)
doubt	વહેમ	**vhem** (*m*)
dough	કણક	**kaṇak** (*f*)
drawer	ખાનું	**khānũ** (*n*)
dream	સ્વપ્ન	**svapna** (*n*)
drink	પીવું	**piṇũ** (*n*)

drowsiness	ઘેન	**ghen** (*n*)
dry	કોરું	**korũ** (*a*)
dry	સૂકું	**sukũ** (*a*)
dust	ધુળ	**dhuḷ** (*f*)
dustbin	કચરાપેટી	**kachrāpeṭi** (*f*)
early	વહેલું	**vhelũ** (*adv*)
earth	પૃથ્વી	**pruthvi** (*f*)
earth	માટી	**māṭi** (*f*)
economic	આર્થિક	**ārthik** (*a*)
education	કેળવણી	**keḷavṇi** (*f*)
effect	અસર	**asar** (*f*)
effective	અકસિર	**aksir** (*a*)
effort	મહેનત	**mahenat** (*f*)
egg	ઈંડું	**inḍũ** (*n*)
either, or; that	કે	**ke** (*conj*)
election	ચૂંટણી	**chũṭṇi** (*f*)
embarrassment	મૂંઝવણ	**mũjhvaṇ** (*f*)
empty	ખાલી	**khāli** (*a*)
end	અંત	**ant** (*m*)
endurance	સહન	**sahan** (*n*)
Englishman	અંગ્રેજ	**ãgrej** (*m*)
enjoyment	મજા	**majā** (*f*)
enthusiasm	ઉત્સાહ	**utsāh** (*m*)
entry	પ્રવેશ	**pravesh** (*m*)
equal	સરખું	**sarkhũ** (*a*)
et cetera	વગેરે	**vagere** (*adv*)
evening	સાંજ	**sā̃j** (*f*)
examination	પરીક્ષા	**parikshā** (*f*)
example	દાખલો	**dākhlo** (*m*)
exercise	કસરત	**kasrat** (*f*)
expense	ખરચ	**kharach** (*n*)
experience	અનુભવ	**anubhav** (*m*)
explanation	ખુલાસો	**khulāso** (*m*)
export	નિકાસ	**nikās** (*f*)
fabricated, counterfeit	બનાવટી	**banāvṭi** (*a*)
face	ચહેરો	**chahero** (*m*)
fact	હકિકત	**hakikat** (*f*)
factory	કારખાનું	**kārkhānũ** (*n*)
false	જૂઠું	**juṭhũ** (*a*)
fame	જશ	**jash** (*m*)

family	કુટુંબ	**kuṭumb** (*n*)
famine	દુકાળ	**dukāḷ** (*m*)
fan	પંખો	**pankho** (*m*)
far off, distant	દૂર	**dur** (*a*)
farm	ખેતર	**khetar** (*n*)
farming	ખેતી	**kheti** (*f*)
fat	ચરબી	**charbi** (*f*)
fat	જાડું	**jāḍũ** (*a*)
fate	નસીબ	**nasib** (*n*)
favourable	અનુકૂળ	**anukuḷ** (*a*)
feeling	લાગણી	**lāgṇi** (*f*)
feeling; rate	ભાવ	**bhāv** (*m*)
festival (generally religious)	તહેવાર	**tahevār** (*m*)
fever	તાવ	**tāv** (*m*)
finished	ખલાસ	**khalās** (*a*)
fire	આગ	**āg** (*f*)
flag	ઝંડો	**jhanḍo** (*m*)
flattery	ખુશામત	**khushāmat** (*f*)
flower	ફૂલ	**phul** (*n*)
foam	ફીણ	**phiṇ** (*n*)
fog	ધુમ્મસ	**dhummas** (*n*)
folk dance with (usually) religious songs	ગરબો	**garbo** (*m*)
food	ખોરાક	**khorāk** (*m*)
foolish	મૂરખ	**murakh** (*a*)
foot of mountain	તળેટી	**taḷeṭi** (*f*)
forest	જંગલ	**jãgal** (*n*)
forgiven	માફ	**māph** (*a*)
forgiveness	ક્ષમા	**kshamā** (*f*)
formerly	પહેલાં	**pahelã** (*adv*)
fort	ગઢ	**gaḍh** (*m*)
fraud	કપટ	**kapaṭ** (*n*)
free of charge	મફત	**maphat** (*adv*)
freedom	આઝાદી	**āzādi** (*f*)
freedom	મુક્તિ	**mukti** (*f*)
fresh	તાજું	**tājũ** (*a*)
fruit	ફળ	**phaḷ** (*n*)
fruit juice; interest	રસ	**ras** (*m*)
full moon day	પૂનમ	**punam** (*f*)
funeral pyre	ચિતા	**chitā** (*f*)
future	ભવિષ્ય	**bhavishya** (*n*)

gambling	જુગાર	**jugār** (*m*)
garden, park	બાગ	**bāg** (*m*)
gardener	માળી	**māḷi** (*m*)
garland, necklace	હાર	**hār** (*m*)
gate	ઝાંપો	**jhā̃po** (*m*)
generous	ઉદાર	**udār** (*a*)
ghost	ભૂત	**bhut** (*n*)
gift	ભેટ	**bheṭ** (*f*)
glass	કાચ	**kāch** (*m*)
glasses	ચશ્માં	**chashmā̃** (*n pl*)
god	દેવ	**dev** (*m*)
good	સારું	**sārũ** (*a*)
goodbye (*lit.* come again)	આવજો	**āvjo** (*vi*)
goods	માલ	**māl** (*m*)
government	સરકાર	**sarkār** (*f*)
grass	ઘાસ	**ghās** (*n*)
grave	કબર	**kabar** (*f*)
grief	શોક	**shok** (*m*)
ground	ભોંય	**bhÕy** (*f*)
guardian	વાલી	**vāli** (*m*)
guest	મહેમાન	**mahemān** (*m*)
guide	ભોમિયો	**bhomiyo** (*m*)
gum	ગુંદર	**gundar** (*m*)
half	અડધું	**aḍdhũ** (*a*)
handicapped	અપંગ	**apãg** (*a*)
handkerchief	રૂમાલ	**rumāl** (*m*)
hanging	ફાંસી	**phā̃si** (*f*)
happiness	આનંદ	**ānand** (*m*)
happiness	સુખ	**sukh** (*n*)
happy	ખુશ	**khush** (*a*)
hard	કઠણ	**kaṭhaṇ** (*a*)
hard	સખત	**sakhat** (*a*)
heading	મથાળું	**mathāḷũ** (*n*)
headquarters	મથક	**mathak** (*n*)
heap	ઢગલો	**ḍhaglo** (*m*)
heart	હૈયું	**haiyũ** (*n*)
heavy	ભારે	**bhāre** (*a*)
help	સહાય	**sahāy** (*f*)
here	અહીં	**ahī̃** (*adv*)
high	ઊંચું	**ũchũ** (*a*)
high in the air	અધ્ધર	**addhar** (*a, adv*)

history	ઈતિહાસ	**itihās** (*m*)
hobby, liking	શોખ	**shokh** (*m*)
hole	કાણું	**kāṇũ** (*n*)
home of married woman's parents	પિયર	**piyar** (*n*)
honest	પ્રામાણિક	**prāmāṇik** (*a*)
hope	આશા	**āshā** (*f*)
horizon	ક્ષિતિજ	**kshitij** (*n*)
host	યજમાન	**yajmān** (*m*)
hot	ગરમ	**garam** (*a*)
hot (taste)	તીખું	**tikhũ** (*a*)
hour	કલાક	**kalāk** (*m*)
house	ઘર	**ghar** (*n*)
how much	કેટલું	**keṭlũ** (*a*)
how much, how big	કેવડું	**kevḍũ** (*a*)
how, why	કેમ	**kem** (*adv*)
hunger	ભૂખ	**bhukh** (*f*)
hunting	શિકાર	**shikār** (*m*)
hurry	ઉતાવળ	**utāvaḷ** (*f*)
illiterate	અભણ	**abhaṇ** (*a*)
illness	માંદગી	**mā̃dgi** (*f*)
illusion, attachment	માયા	**māyā** (*f*)
immediately	તરત	**tarrat** (*adv*)
immortal	અમર	**amar** (*a*)
import	આયાત	**āyāt** (*f*)
imposing appearance	રૂઆબ	**ruāb** (*m*)
imprisonment	કેદ	**ked** (*f*)
in	અંદર	**andar** (*prep*)
in any way	ગમેતેમ	**game tem** (*adv*)
in between	વચ્ચે	**vachche** (*prep, adv*)
in which way	જેમ	**jem** (*adv*)
income	આવક	**āvak** (*f*)
incomplete	અધુરું	**adhurũ** (*a*)
inconvenience	અગવડ	**agvaḍ** (*f*)
increasing prices	મોંઘવારી	**mÕghvāri** (*f*)
independent	સ્વતંત્ર	**svatantra** (*a*)
India	ભારત	**bhārat** (*m*)
industrial	ઔદ્યોગિક	**audyogik** (*a*)
infection	ચેપ	**chep** (*m*)
inflation	ફુગાવો	**phugāvo** (*m*)

njustice	અન્યાય	**anyāy** (*m*)
nkpot	ખડિયો	**khaḍiyo** (*m*)
nsect	જંતુ	**jantu** (*n*)
nsistence	આગ્રહ	**āgrah** (*m*)
nsult	અપમાન	**apman** (*n*)
nsurance	વિમો	**vimo** (*m*)
ntellect	બુદ્ધિ	**buddhi** (*f*)
ntelligence	અક્કલ	**akkal** (*f*)
ntention	ઈરાદો	**irādo** (*m*)
nterview, visit	મુલાકાત	**mulākāt** (*f*)
nverted	ઊંધું	**ũdhũ** (*a*)
nvitation	આમંત્રણ	**āmantraṇ** (*n*)
nvitation (esp. marriage)	કંકોતરી	**kãkotri** (*f*)
sland	બેટ	**beṭ** (*m*)
sland	ટાપુ	**ṭāpu** (*m*)
ealousy	અદેખાઈ	**adekhāi** (*f*)
oke	મજાક	**majāk** (*f*)
ourney	પ્રવાસ	**pravās** (*m*)
oy	હરખ	**harakh** (*m*)
ump	કૂદકો	**kudko** (*m*)
ustice	ન્યાય	**nyāy** (*m*)
ey	ચાવી	**chāvi** (*f*)
ick	લાત	**lāt** (*f*)
ind	ભલું	**bhalũ** (*a*)
ingdom/capital	રાજ/રાજ્ધાની	**rāj** (*n*)/**rājdhāni** (*f*)
ite	પતંગ	**patang** (*m, f*)
not	ગાંઠ	**gā̃ṭh** (*f*)
nowledge	જ્ઞાન	**gnān** (*n*)
abourer	મજૂર	**majur** (*m*)
ake	સરોવર	**sarovar** (*n*)
amp	દીવો	**divo** (*m*)
and	જમીન	**jamin** (*f*)
anguage	ભાષા	**bhāshā** (*f*)
ap	ખોળો	**khoḷo** (*m*)
ate	મોડું	**moḍũ** (*a*)
aw	કાયદો	**kāydo** (*m*)
awyer	વકીલ	**vakil** (*m*)
aziness	આળસ	**āḷas** (*f*)
eap	છલાંગ	**chhalãg** (*f*)

learning, knowledge	વિદ્યા	**vidyā** (*f*)
left (side)	ડાબું	**ḍābũ** (*a*)
leisure	નિરાંત	**nirā̃t** (*f*)
less	કમ	**kam** (*a*)
letter (of the alphabet)	અક્ષર	**akshar** (*m*)
lid	ઢાંકણું	**ḍhā̃kṇũ** (*n*)
light	અજવાળું	**ajvāḷũ** (*n*)
light	હલકું	**halkũ** (*a*)
light (of moon, sun, etc.)	તેજ	**tej** (*n*)
lightning, electricity	વીજળી	**vijḷi** (*f*)
like this	આવું	**āvũ** (*a*)
limit (time)	મુદત	**mudat** (*f*)
line	લીટી	**liṭi** (*f*)
little	સહેજ	**sahej** (*a*)
little	થોડું	**thoḍũ** (*a*)
local	સ્થાનિક	**sthānik** (*a*)
lonely	એકલું	**eklũ** (*a*)
long	લાંબું	**lāmbũ** (*a*)
lord; honorific address	સાહેબ	**sāheb** (*m*)
lorry	ખટારો	**khaṭāro** (*m*)
loss	નુકસાન	**nuksān** (*n*)
love	હેત	**het** (*n*)
love	પ્રેમ	**prem** (*m*)
mad	ગાંડું	**gā̃ḍũ** (*a*)
magic	જાદુ	**jādu** (*m*)
maintenance	ગુજરાન	**gujrān** (*n*)
male	પુરુષ	**purush** (*m*)
many	અનેક	**anek** (*a*)
map	નકશો	**naksho** (*m*)
marriage	લગ્ન	**lagna** (*n*)
mason	કડિયો	**kaḍiyo** (*m*)
master	માલિક	**mālik** (*m*)
master, teacher	ગુરુ	**guru** (*m*)
matchstick	દીવાસળી	**divasāḷi** (*f*)
matter	બાબત	**bābat** (*f*)
mattress	ગાદલું	**gādlũ** (*n*)
meaning	અર્થ	**artha** (*m*)
measure	માપ	**māp** (*n*)
meat, flesh	માંસ	**mā̃s** (*n*)
meeting	સભા	**sabhā** (*f*)
member	સભ્ય	**sabhya** (*m*)

essage	સંદેશો	**sandesho** (*m*)
ethod	રીત	**rit** (*f*)
ilk	દૂધ	**dudh** (*n*)
ine	ખાણ	**khāṇ** (*f*)
ineral	ધાતુ	**dhātu** (*f*)
irror	અરીસો	**ariso** (*m*)
istake	ભૂલ	**bhul** (*f*)
istake	ખામી	**khāmi** (*f*)
odesty, shame	શરમ	**sharam** (*f*)
odesty; etiquette	વિવેક	**vivek** (*m*)
oney	પૈસો	**paiso** (*m*)
onsoon	ચોમાસું	**chomāsũ** (*n*)
onthly; monthly magazine	માસિક	**māsik** (*a*) (*n*)
oon	ચાંદો	**chā̃do** (*m*)
oonless night	અમાસ	**amās** (*f*)
orality	નીતિ	**niti** (*f*)
ore	વધારે	**vadhāre** (*a*)
orning	સવાર	**savār** (*f*) (*n*)
orsel	કોળિયો	**koḷiyo** (*m*)
ortgaged	ગીરો	**giro** (*a*)
otherland, fatherland	વતન	**vatan** (*n*)
ountain	ડુંગર	**ḍungar** (*m*)
ountain	પર્વત	**parvat** (*m*)
ouse	ઉંદર	**undar** (*m*)
outhful of water	કોગળો	**kOgḷo** (*m*)
r	શ્રી	**shri** (*a*)
uch	બહુ	**bahu** (*a*)
uch	ઘણું	**ghaṇũ** (*a*)
ud	કાદવ	**kādav** (*m*)
ultiplication	ગુણાકાર	**guṇākār** (*m*)
urder	ખૂન	**khun** (*n*)
usic	સંગીત	**sangit** (*n*)
utual, amongst yourselves	અરસપરસ	**arasparas** (*adv*)

ail	ખીલી	**khili** (*f*)
ame	નામ	**nām** (*n*)
arrow lane	ગલી	**gali** (*f*)
ature	કુદરત	**kudrat** (*f*)
ear, in possession of	પાસે	**pāse** (*prep, adv*)
eed	ગરજ	**garaj** (*f*)
eighbour	પડોશી	**paḍoshi** (*m*)

nevertheless	છતાં	**chhatā̃** (*adv, con*j)
new	નવું	**navũ** (*a*)
news	ખબર	**khabar** (*f*)
news	સમાચાર	**samāchār** (*m*)
newspaper	છાપું	**chhāpũ** (*n*)
not straight	વાંકું	**vā̃kũ** (*a*)
not straight, getting in the way	આડું	**āḍũ** (*a*)
now	હમણાં	**hamṇā̃** (*adv*)
now (onwards)	હવે	**have** (*adv*)
number	આંકડો	**ā̃kḍo** (*m*)
objection	વાંધો	**vā̃dho** (*m*)
obligation	ઉપકાર	**upkār** (*m*)
obstinacy, stubbornness	હાથ	**hāṭh** (*f*)
obstruction, objection	હરકત	**harkat** (*f*)
offence, crime	ગુનો	**guno** (*m*)
oh!	અરે!	**are** (*int*)
oil	તેલ	**tel** (*n*)
ointment	મલમ	**malam** (*m*)
OK, all right, correct	બરાબર	**barābar** (*adv*)
OK; expert	કુશળ	**kushaḷ** (*a*)
old	જૂનું	**junũ** (*a*)
old age	ઘડપણ	**ghaḍpaṇ** (*n*)
old woman	ડોસી	**ḍosi** (*f*)
on credit	ઉધાર	**udhār** (*a*)
open	ખુલ્લું	**khullũ** (*a*)
open ground	મેદાન	**medān** (*n*)
opinion, vote	મત	**mat** (*m*)
opportunity	તક	**tak** (*f*)
opposite	સામું	**sāmũ** (*a, adv*)
or, if	અગર	**agar** (*conj*)
orchard	વાડી	**vāḍi** (*f*)
order	હુકમ	**hukam** (*m*)
original	અસલ	**asal** (*a*)
ornament	ઘરેણું	**ghareṇũ** (*n*)
orphan	અનાથ	**anāth** (*a*)
out	બહાર	**bahār** (*adv*)
padlock	તાળું	**tāḷũ** (*n*)
page (of a book)	પાનું	**pānũ** (*n*)
pain	દરદ	**darad** (*n*)

palace	મહેલ	**mahel** (*m*)
paper, letter	કાગળ	**kāgaḷ** (*m*)
part	ભાગ	**bhāg** (*m*)
parts of the body	અવયવ	**avyav** (*m*)
patience	ધીરજ	**dhiraj** (*f*)
peak	શિખર	**shikhar** (*n*)
peg	ખીંટી	**khĩṭi** (*f*)
penalty	દંડ	**danḍ** (*m*)
pendal, large tent-like structure	મંડપ	**manḍap** (*m*)
penknife	ચપ્પુ	**chappu** (*n*)
people	જનતા	**jantā** (*f*)
people	લોક	**lok** (*m*)
permanent, constant	કાયમ	**kāyam** (*a*)
permission, leave, holiday	રજા	**rajā** (*f*)
person	માણસ	**māṇas** (*m*)
perspiration	પરસેવો	**parsevo** (*m*)
phlegm	કફ	**kaph** (*m*)
physician	વૈદ	**vaid** (*m*)
pickles	અથાણું	**athāṇũ** (*n*)
picture	ચિત્ર	**chitra** (*n*)
piece	કટકો	**kaṭko** (*m*)
pillow	ઓશીકું	**oshikũ** (*n*)
pin	ટાંકણી	**ṭā̃akṇi** (*f*)
pit	ખાડો	**khāḍo** (*m*)
place	જગા	**jagā** (*f*)
plant	છોડ	**chhoḍ** (*m*)
plate	થાળી	**thāḷi** (*f*)
play, drama	નાટક	**nāṭak** (*n*)
player	ખેલાડી	**khelāḍi** (*m*)
pocket	ગજવું	**gajvũ** (*n*)
pocket	ખીસું	**khisũ** (*n*)
poem	કવિતા	**kavitā** (*f*)
poet	કવિ	**kavi** (*m*)
poison	ઝેર	**jhEr** (*n*)
poor	ગરીબ	**garib** (*a*)
port	બંદર	**bandar** (*n*)
possession	કબજો	**kabjo** (*m*)
post, mail	ટપાલ	**ṭapāl** (*f*)
praise	વખાણ	**vakhāṇ** (*n*)
prayer	પ્રાર્થના	**prārthanā** (*f*)

prayer song	ભજન	**bhajan** (*n*)
precept	ઉપદેશ	**updesh** (*m*)
present	હાજર	**hājar** (*a*)
presented	રજૂ	**raju** (*a*)
prestige	આબરૂ	**ābru** (*f*)
pretence	ઢોંગ	**ḍhOng** (*m*)
previous	આગલું	**āglũ** (*a*)
price	કિંમત	**kimmat** (*f*)
pride	અભિમાન	**abhimān** (*n*)
printing press	છાપખાનું	**chhāpkhānũ** (*n*)
prize	ઈનામ	**inām** (*n*)
procession	સરઘસ	**sarghas** (*n*)
profit	નફો	**napho** (*m*)
progeny	સંતાન	**santān** (*n*)
promise	વચન	**vachan** (*n*)
pronunciation	ઉચ્ચાર	**uchchār** (*m*)
protection	આશરો	**āshro** (*m*)
proverb	કહેવત	**kahevat** (*f*)
pulse	કઠોળ	**kaṭhoḷ** (*n*)
pulse	નાડી	**nāḍi** (*f*)
punishment	સજા	**sajā** (*f*)
purified butter	ઘી	**ghi** (*n*)
push, jolt	ધક્કો	**dhakko** (*m*)
puzzle	કોયડો	**koyḍo** (*m*)
quarrel	ઝગડો	**jhagḍo** (*m*)
quarrel	કજિયો	**kajiyo** (*m*)
question	સવાલ	**savāl** (*m*)
quickly	જલદી	**jaldi** (*adv*)
quickly	ઝટ	**jhaṭ** (*adv*)
quiet	શાંત	**shānt** (*a*)
quietly	ગુપચુપ	**gupchup** (*adv*)
race	કુળ	**kul** (*n*)
race; bet; condition	શરત	**sharāt** (*f*)
rain	વરસાદ	**varsād** (*m*)
raw	કાચું	**kāchũ** (*a*)
ray	કિરણ	**kiraṇ** (*n*)
ready	તૈયાર	**taiyār** (*a*)
reason	હેતુ	**hetu** (*m*)
recession	મંદી	**mandi** (*f*)
recollection	યાદ	**yād** (*f*)

egular	નિયમિત	**niymit** (*a*)
eligion	ધરમ, ધર્મ	**dharam, dharma** (*m*)
emaining	બાકી	**bāki** (*a*)
emedy	ઉપાય	**upāy** (*m*)
emedy, treatment, cure	ઈલાજ	**ilāj** (*m*)
equest	વિનંતી	**vinanti** (*f*)
esolution	ઠરાવ	**ṭharāv** (*m*)
esources, tools	સાધન	**sādhan** (*n*)
espect	માન	**mān** (*n*)
est	આરામ	**ārām** (*m*)
ght	અધિકાર	**adhikār** (*m*)
ght	હક	**hak** (*m*)
ght (e.g. hand)	જમણું	**jamṇũ** (*a*)
ghteous	પુણ્ય	**puṇya** (*a*)
sk	જોખમ	**jokham** (*n*)
ver	નદી	**nadi** (*f*)
oad	રસ્તો	**rasto** (*m*)
oot	મૂળ	**muḷ** (*n*)
ound; jaggery (coarse sugar)	ગોળ	**goḷ** (*a, m*)
ubbish	ગંદકી	**gandki** (*f*)
ubbish	કચરો	**kachro** (*m*)
uffian	ગુંડો	**gunḍo** (*m*)
ule	નિયમ	**niyam** (*m*)
umour	અફવા	**aphvā** (*f*)
ad	ઉદાસ	**udās** (*a*)
afe	સલામત	**salāmat** (*a*)
age	ઋષિ	**rushi** (*m*)
ailor	ખલાસી	**khalāsi** (*m*)
aint	સાધુ	**sādhu** (*m*)
alad	કચુંબર	**kachumbar** (*f*)
alary	પગાર	**pagār** (*m*)
ample	નમૂનો	**namuno** (*m*)
atisfaction	સંતોષ	**santosh** (*m*)
carcity	તંગી	**tangi** (*f*)
cent	અત્તર	**attar** (*n*)
chool	નિશાળ	**nishāḷ** (*f*)
cience	વિજ્ઞાન	**vignān** (*n*)
cissors	કાતર	**kātar** (*f*)
cript	લિપિ	**lipi** (*f*)

sea, ocean	દરિયો	**dariyo** (*m*)
season	ઋતુ	**rutu** (*f*)
secret	છાનું	**chhānũ** (*a*)
seed	બી	**bi** (*n*)
self-interest	સ્વાર્થ	**svārtha** (*m*)
separate, different	જુદું	**judũ** (*a*)
servant	નોકર	**nokar** (*m*)
service	સેવા	**sevā** (*f*)
settlement (of dispute)	સમાધાન	**samādhān** (*n*)
shape	આકાર	**ākār** (*m*)
sharp end	અણી	**aṇi** (*f*)
ship	વહાણ	**vahāṇ** (*n*)
shop	દુકાન	**dukān** (*f*)
shout	બૂમ	**bum** (*f*)
sight	નજર	**najar** (*f*)
signature	સહી	**sahi** (*f*)
silent	ચુપ	**chup** (*a*)
simple	સાદું	**sādũ** (*a*)
sin	પાપ	**pāp** (*n*)
singer	ગાયક	**gāyak** (*m*)
size	કદ	**kad** (*n*)
skill	આવડત	**āvḍaṭ** (*f*)
sky	આકાશ	**ākāsh** (*n*)
slaughter	કતલ	**katal** (*f*)
slave	ગુલામ	**gulām** (*m*)
sleepless night	ઉજાગરો	**ujāgro** (*m*)
slope	ઢાળ	**ḍhāḷ** (*m*)
slow	ધીમું	**dhimũ** (*a*)
small	નાનું	**nānũ** (*a*)
small handbag	કોથળી	**kothḷi** (*f*)
small lake	તળાવ	**taḷāv** (*n*)
small room	ઓરડી	**orḍi** (*f*)
smoke	ધુમાડો	**dhumāḍo** (*m*)
smooth	સુંવાળું	**sũvāḷũ** (*a*)
sneeze	છીંક	**chhĩk** (*f*)
so much	આટલું	**āṭlũ** (*a*)
society	સમાજ	**samāj** (*m*)
soft	નરમ	**naram** (*a*)
soft	પોચું	**pochũ** (*a*)
solution	ઉકેલ	**ukel** (*m*)
someone	કોઈ	**koi** (*a*)
something	કશુંક	**kashũk** (*pron*, *a*)

on	દીકરો	**dikro** (*m*)
oul	પ્રાણ	**prāṇ** (*m*)
ound	અવાજ	**avāj** (*m*)
pecial	ખાસ	**khās** (*a*)
peech (lecture)	ભાષણ	**bhāshaṇ** (*n*)
peed	ઝડપ	**jhaḍap** (*f*)
pelling	જોડણી	**joḍṇi** (*f*)
table (for animals)	તબેલો	**tabelo** (*m*)
taircase	દાદર	**dādar** (*m*)
tar	તારો	**tāro** (*m*)
ticky	ચીકણું	**chikṇũ** (*a*)
ting	ડંખ	**ḍankh** (*m*)
tone	પથરો	**pathro** (*m*)
tory	વાત	**vāt** (*f*)
tory (mainly religious)	કથા	**kathā** (*f*)
traight, direct	સીધું	**sidhũ** (*a*)
trap	પટ્ટો	**paṭṭo** (*m*)
trength	જોર	**jor** (*n*)
trength	શક્તિ	**shakti** (*f*)
trict, hard	કડક	**kaḍak** (*a*)
trike	હડતાળ	**haḍtāḷ** (*f*)
tring	દોરી	**dori** (*f*)
trong	મજબૂત	**majbut** (*a*)
uch	એવું	**evũ** (*a*)
uddenly	અચાનક	**achānak** (*adv*)
ugar	ખાંડ	**khā̃ḍ** (*f*)
um	રકમ	**rakam** (*f*)
ummer	ઉનાળો	**unāḷo** (*m*)
un	સૂરજ	**suraj** (*m*)
unshine	તડકો	**taḍko** (*m*)
uperior	ઉપરી	**upri** (*m*)
upport	ટેકો	**ṭeko** (*m*)
upport, depend on	આધાર	**ādhār** (*m*)
urely	અચૂક	**achuk** (*adv*)
urname	અટક	**aṭak** (*f*)
weet	ગળ્યું	**gaḷyũ** (*a*)
weets	મીઠાઈ	**miṭhāi** (*f*)
wing	હીંચકો	**hĩchko** (*m*)

ablet	ટીકડી	**ṭikḍi** (*f*)
ablet; bullet	ગોળી	**goḷi** (*f*)
ail	પૂછડી	**puchhḍi** (*f*)

taste	સ્વાદ	**svād** (*m*)
tax	જકાત	**jakāt** (*f*)
tax	કર	**kar** (*m*)
tear	આંસુ	**ā̃su** (*n*)
temple	મંદિર	**mandir** (*n*)
ten million; spine	કરોડ	**karoḍ** (*a*, *f*)
test	કસોટી	**kasoṭi** (*f*)
than	કરતાં	**kartā̃** (*prep*, *conj*)
thanks	આભાર	**ābhār** (*m*)
therefore	એટલે	**eṭle** (*adv*)
thief	ચોર	**chor** (*m*)
thing	વસ્તુ	**vastu** (*f*)
this	આ	**ā** (*pron*)
this much	આવડું	**āvḍū̃** (*a*)
thorn	કાંટો	**kā̃ṭo** (*m*)
thousand million	અબજ	**abaj** (*a*)
thrift	કરકસર	**karkasar** (*f*)
thug, rogue	ઠગ	**ṭhag** (*m*)
tide	ભરતી	**bharti** (*f*)
till (in a shop)	ગલ્લો	**gallo** (*m*)
time	સમય	**samay** (*m*)
time	વખત	**vakhat** (*m*)
to (feel) pain	દુખવું	**dukhvū̃** (*vi*)
to accept	સ્વીકારવું	**svikārvū̃** (*vt*)
to add	ઉમેરવું	**umervū̃** (*vt*)
to adopt	અપનાવવું	**apnāvvū̃** (*vt*)
to arrange	ગોઠવવું	**goṭhavvū̃** (*vt*)
to ask	પૂછવું	**puchhvū̃** (*vt*)
to awaken	જાગવું	**jāgvū̃** (*vi*)
to bake	શેકવું	**shekvū̃** (*vt*)
to bath, bathe	નાહવું	**nāhvū̃** (*vi*)
to be	હોવું	**hovū̃** (*vi*)
to be (negative, present tense)	નથી	**nathi** (*vi*)
to be breathless	હાંફવું	**hā̃phvū̃** (*vi*)
to be defeated	હારવું	**hārvū̃** (*vi*)
to be digested	પચવું	**pachvū̃** (*vi*)
to be displeased	રીસાવું	**risāvū̃** (*vi*)
to be free	છૂટવું	**chhuṭvū̃** (*vi*)
to be hung	ટિંગાવું	**ṭĩgāvū̃** (*vi*)
to be lifted	ઊપડવું	**upaḍvū̃** (*vi*)

to be played (instrument), to be struck	વાગવું	**vāgvũ** (*vi*)
to be ripe	પાકવું	**pākvũ** (*vi*)
to be saved	બચવું	**bachvũ** (*vi*)
to be tempted	લલચાવું	**lalchāvũ** (*vi*)
to be tired	થાકવું	**thākvũ** (*vi*)
to be torn	ફાડવું	**phāḍvũ** (*vi*)
to be wet	પલળવું	**palaḷvũ** (*vi*)
to beat	મારવું	**mārvũ** (*vt*)
to become	થવું	**thavũ** (*vi*)
to become impure	અભડાવું	**abhḍāvũ** (*vi*)
to beg	કરગરવું	**kargarvũ** (*vi*)
to bend	વાળવું	**vāḷvũ** (*vi*)
to bind	બાંધવું	**bā̃dhvũ** (*vt*)
to bite	કરડવું	**karaḍvũ** (*vt*)
to blossom	ખીલવું	**khilvũ** (*vi*)
to blow	ફૂકવું	**phũkvũ** (*vt*)
to boil	ઊકળવું	**ukaḷvũ** (*vi*)
to bounce	ઊછળવું	**uchhaḷvũ** (*vi*)
to bow down	નમવું	**namvũ** (*vt*)
to break	તોડવું	**toḍvũ** (*vt*)
to break	તૂટવું	**tuṭvũ** (*vi*)
to bring	લાવવું	**lāvvũ** (*vt*)
to build	ચણવું	**chaṇvũ** (*vt*)
to burn	બળવું	**baḷvũ** (*vi*)
to burn	સળગવું	**saḷagvũ** (*vt*)
to bury	દાટવું	**dāṭvũ** (*vt*)
to catch	ઝીલવું	**jhilvũ** (*vt*)
to cheat	છેતરવું	**chhetarvũ** (*vt*)
to check	તપાસવું	**tapāsvũ** (*vt*)
to chew	ચાવવું	**chāvvũ** (*vt*)
to climb	ચડવું	**chaḍvũ** (*vi, t*)
to climb down	ઊતરવું	**utarvũ** (*vi*)
to collide, dash against	અથડાવું	**athḍāvũ** (*vi*)
to colour	રંગવું	**rangvũ** (*vt*)
to come	આવવું	**āvvũ** (*vi*)
to compare	સરખાવવું	**sarkhāvvũ** (*vt*)
to count	ગણવું	**gaṇvũ** (*vt*)
to cover	ઢાંકવું	**ḍhā̃kvũ** (*vt*)
to cut	કાપવું	**kāpvũ** (*vt*)
to dance	નાચવું	**nāchvũ** (*vi*)
to dash violently	અફળાવું	**aphāḷvũ** (*vt*)

to decorate	શણગારવું	**shaṇgārvũ** (*vt*)
to decrease	ઘટવું	**ghaṭvũ** (*vi*)
to develop	વિકસવું	**vikasvũ** (*vi*)
to die	મરવું	**marvũ** (*vi*)
to dig	ખોદવું	**khodvũ** (*vt*)
to do	કરવું	**karvũ** (*vt*)
to draw (a line)	આંકવું	**ā̃kvũ** (*vt*)
to draw (lines), paint (picture)	દોરવું	**dorvũ** (*vt*)
to drink	પીવું	**pivũ** (*vt*)
to drip	ટપકવું	**ṭapakvũ** (*vi*)
to dwell	વસવું	**vasvũ** (*vi*)
to earn	કમાવું	**kamāvũ** (*vt*)
to eat	જમવું	**jamvũ** (*vt*)
to eat	ખાવું	**khāvũ** (*vt*)
to fall	પડવું	**paḍvũ** (*vi*)
to fall down	ખરવું	**kharvũ** (*vi*)
to fear	ગભરાવું	**gabhrāvũ** (*vi*)
to fear, be afraid of	ડરવું	**ḍarvũ** (*vi*)
to feel	લાગવું	**lāgvũ** (*vi*)
to fight	લડવું	**laḍvũ** (*vi*)
to fill, to pay	ભરવું	**bharvũ** (*vt*)
to find	જડવું	**jaḍvũ** (*vi*)
to fly	ઊડવું	**uḍvũ** (*vi*)
to forget	ભૂલવું	**bhulvũ** (*vi*)
to get separated	ઊખડવું	**ukhaḍvũ** (*vi*)
to get up	ઊઠવું	**uṭhvũ** (*vi*)
to give	આપવું	**āpvũ** (*vt*)
to go	જવું	**javũ** (*vi*)
to graze	ચરવું	**charvũ** (*vi*)
to hang	લટકવું	**laṭakvũ** (*vi*)
to happen	બનવું	**banvũ** (*vi*)
to hold	પકડવું	**pakaḍvũ** (*vt*)
to improve	સુધારવું	**sudharvũ** (*vi*)
to join	જોડવું	**joḍvũ** (*vt*)
to jump	કૂદવું	**kudvũ** (*vi*)
to keep	રાખવું	**rākhvũ** (*vt*)
to know	જાણવું	**jāṇvũ** (*vt*)
to know how to do	આવડવું	**āvaḍvũ** (*vi*)
to laugh	હસવું	**hasvũ** (*vi*)
to learn	શિખવું	**shikhvũ** (*vi*)
to let go	છોડવું	**chhoḍvũ** (*vt*)
to lick	ચાટવું	**chāṭvũ** (*vt*)

to lift	ઊંચકવું	**uchakvũ** (*vt*)
to like (used only for food)	ભાવવું	**bhāvvũ** (*vi*)
to live	જીવવું	**jivvũ** (*vi*)
to marry	પરણવું	**paraṇvũ** (*vt*)
to meet; to find	મળવું	**maḷvũ** (*vi*)
to melt	ઓગળવું	**ogaḷvũ** (*vi*)
to melt	પીગળવું	**pigaḷvũ** (*vi*)
to memorize by repetition	ગોખવું	**gokhvũ** (*vt*)
to move	ખસવું	**khasvũ** (*vi*)
to note	નોંધવું	**nÕdhvũ** (*vt*)
to obtain	મેળવવું	**meḷavvũ** (*vt*)
to open	ખૂલવું	**khulvũ** (*vi*)
to open	ઊઘડવું	**ughaḍvũ** (*vi*)
to paint (picture)	ચીતરવું	**chitarvũ** (*vt*)
to pay	ચુકવવું	**chukavvũ** (*vt*)
to pick	વીણવું	**viṇvũ** (*vt*)
to plan	યોજવું	**yojvũ** (*vt*)
to play	રમવું	**ramvũ** (*vi*)
to press	દાબવું	**dābvũ** (*vt*)
to print	છાપવું	**chhāpvũ** (*vt*)
to pull	ખેંચવું	**khẼchvũ** (*vt*)
to purchase	ખરીદવું	**kharidvũ** (*vt*)
to push in	ઘુસવું	**ghusvũ** (*vi*)
to put, to leave	મૂકવું	**mukvũ** (*vt*)
to read	વાંચવું	**vā̃chvũ** (*vt*)
to recognize	ઓળખવું	**oḷakhvũ** (*vt*)
to remain till last	ટકવું	**ṭakvũ** (*vt*)
to rise, grow	ઊગવું	**ugvũ** (*vi*)
to roar	ગરજવું	**garajvũ** (*vi*)
to rob	લૂંટવું	**lũṭvũ** (*vt*)
to roll, tumble	ગબડવું	**gabaḍvũ** (*vi*)
to rub	ઘસવું	**ghasvũ** (*vt*)
to run	દોડવું	**doḍvũ** (*vi*)
to run away; to divide (maths)	ભાગવું	**bhāgvũ** (*vi*)
to say	કહેવું	**kahevũ** (*vt*)
to scold	વઢવું	**vaḍhvũ** (*vt*)
to scrutinize	ચકાસવું	**chakāsvũ** (*vt*)
to see	જોવું	**jovũ** (*vt*)
to sell	વેચવું	**vechvũ** (*vt*)
to send	મોકલવું	**mokalvũ** (*vt*)
to serve food	પીરસવું	**pirasvũ** (*vt*)

to sing	ગાવું	**gāvũ** (*vt*)
to sit	બેસવું	**besvũ** (*vi*)
to sleep	સુવું	**suvũ** (*vi*)
to sleep	ઊંઘવું	**ũghvũ** (*vi*)
to slip	લપસવું	**lapasvũ** (*vi*)
to smell	સુંઘવું	**sũghvũ** (*vt*)
to speak	બોલવું	**bolvũ** (*vt*)
to spill	ઢોળવું	**ḍholvũ** (*vt*)
to spin	કાંતવું	**kā̃tvũ** (*vt*)
to split	ચીરવું	**chirvũ** (*vt*)
to squeeze	નિચોવવું	**nichovvũ** (*vt*)
to stand	ઊભવું	**ubhvũ** (*vi*)
to stay	રહેવું	**rahevũ** (*vi*)
to stick	ચોડવું	**choḍvũ** (*vt*)
to stop	થોભવું	**thobhvũ** (*vi*)
to stop	રોકવું	**rokvũ** (*vt*)
to study	ભણવું	**bhaṇvũ** (*vt*)
to suppose	ધારવું	**dhārvũ** (*vt*)
to surround	ઘેરવું	**ghervũ** (*vt*)
to swim	તરવું	**tarvũ** (*vt*)
to swing	ડોલવું	**ḍolvũ** (*vi*)
to take	લેવું	**levũ** (*vt*)
to take out, draw	કાઢવું	**kāḍhvũ** (*vt*)
to teach	શિખવવું	**shikhavvũ** (*vt*)
to think	વિચારવું	**vichārvũ** (*vt*)
to throw	નાખવું	**nākhvũ** (*vt*)
to touch	અડવું	**aḍvũ** (*vt*)
to tremble	ધ્રુજવું	**dhrujvũ** (*vi*)
to tremble	કંપવું	**kampvũ** (*vi*)
to try	અજમાવવું	**ajmāvvũ** (*vt*)
to walk	ચાલવું	**chālvũ** (*vi*)
to walk, stroll	ફરવું	**pharvũ** (*vi*)
to wander	રખડવું	**rakhaḍvũ** (*vi*)
to wash	ધોવું	**dhovũ** (*vt*)
to wear	પહેરવું	**pahervũ** (*vt*)
to weep	રડવું	**raḍvũ** (*vi*)
to win	જીતવું	**jitvũ** (*vt*)
to wither	કરમાવું	**karmāvũ** (*vi*)
to write	લખવું	**lakhvũ** (*vt*)
today	આજ	**āj** (*f*)
tools	ઓજાર	**ojār** (*n*)
trade	વેપાર	**vepār** (*m*)
treachery	દગો	**dago** (*m*)

tree	ઝાડ	**jhāḍ** (*n*)
trial (experiment)	અખતરો	**akhatro** (*m*)
trick	યુક્તિ	**yukti** (*f*)
trouble	તકલીફ	**takliph** (*f*)
trouble	ઉપાધિ	**upādhi** (*f*)
true	ખરું	**kharũ** (*a*)
true, correct	સાચું	**sāchũ** (*a*)
trunk (of tree)	થડ	**thaḍ** (*n*)
turn	વારો	**vāro** (*m*)
ugly	કદરૂપું	**kadrupũ** (*a*)
umbrella	છત્રી	**chhatri** (*f*)
unanimous	એકમત	**ekmat** (*a*)
understanding	સમજણ	**samjaṇ** (*f*)
unexpected	ઓચિંતું	**ochintũ** (*a*)
unmarried girl	કન્યા	**kanyā** (*f*)
use	ઉપયોગ	**upyog** (*m*)
useless	નકામું	**nakāmũ** (*a*)
valley	ખીણ	**khiṇ** (*f*)
veil	ઘુમટો	**ghumṭo** (*m*)
very good	સરસ	**saras** (*a*)
very much	ખૂબ	**khub** (*a*)
village	ગામ	**gām** (*n*)
violence	હિંસા	**hinsā** (*f*)
virtue, quality	ગુણ	**guṇ** (*m*)
vomit	ઊલટી	**ulṭi** (*f*)
washerman	ધોબી	**dhobi** (*m*)
watch, clock	ઘડિયાળ	**ghaḍiyāḷ** (*f*) (*n*)
watchman	ચોકીદાર	**chokidār** (*m*)
water	પાણી	**pāṇi** (*n*)
wax	મીણ	**miṇ** (*n*)
weapon	હથિયાર	**hathiyār** (*n*)
weekly	અઠવાડિક	**aṭhvāḍik** (*a, n*)
weight	વજન	**vajan** (*n*)
welcome	આવકાર	**āvkār** (*m*)
well	કૂવો	**kuvo** (*m*)
well, fine, OK	ભલે	**bhale** (*int*)
wet	ભીનું	**bhinũ** (*a*)
what	શું	**shũ** (*pron*)
what type	કેવું	**kevũ** (*a*)
when	ક્યારે	**kyāre** (*adv*)

where	જ્યાં	**jyā̃** (*adv*)
where	ક્યાં	**kyā̃** (*adv*)
whereas	જેથી	**jethi** (*conj*)
white, shining	ઊજળું	**ujḷũ** (*a*)
who	કોણ	**koṇ** (*pron*)
whole	આખું	**ākhũ** (*a*)
wholesale	જથ્થાબંધ	**jatthābandh** (*adv*)
whose	કોનું	**konũ** (*pron*)
widow	વિધવા	**vidhvā** (*f*)
wind	પવન	**pavan** (*m*)
wind, air	હવા	**havā** (*f*)
wine, liquor; gunpowder	દારૂ	**dāru** (*m*)
wing	પાંખ	**pā̃kh** (*f*)
winter	શિયાળો	**shiyāḷo** (*m*)
wish	ઈચ્છા	**ichchhā** (*f*)
wish	મરજી	**marji** (*f*)
without reason	અમથું	**amthũ** (*a*)
woman, wife	સ્ત્રી	**stri** (*f*)
wood	લાકડું	**lākḍũ** (*n*)
wool	ઊન	**un** (*n*)
word, sound	શબ્દ	**shabda** (*m*)
work	કામ	**kām** (*n*)
world	દુનિયા	**duniyā** (*f*)
world	જગત	**jagat** (*n*)
worry	ચિંતા	**chintā** (*f*)
worship	પૂજા	**pujā** (*f*)
wound	ઘા	**ghā** (*m*)
wrinkle	કરચલી	**karachli** (*f*)
wrong	ખોટું	**khoṭũ** (*a*)
yarn; telegram	તાર	**tār** (*m*)
yawn	બગાસું	**bagāsũ** (*n*)
year	વરસ	**varas** (*n*)
yesterday, tomorrow (depending on context)	કાલ	**kāl** (*f*)
yoghurt, curds	દહીં	**dahī̃** (*n*)
you (honorific)	આપ	**āp** (*pron*)
youth (male)	યુવક	**yuvak** (*m*)
youth (female)	યુવતી	**yuvati** (*f*)
zinc, alloy of tin and lead	કથીર	**kathir** (*n*)

Thematic English–Gujarati vocabulary

Days of the week અઠવાડિયાના દિવસો

Sunday	રવિવાર	**ravivār**
Monday	સોમવાર	**somvār**
Tuesday	મંગળવાર	**mangaḷvār**
Wednesday	બુધવાર	**budhvār**
Thursday	ગુરુવાર	**guruvār**
Friday	શુક્રવાર	**shukravār**
Saturday	શનિવાર	**shanivār**

Time સમય

moment	પળ	**paḷ** (*f*)	evening	સાંજ	**sā̃j** (*f*)
second	સેકંડ	**sekanḍ** (*f*)	week	અઠવાડિયું	**aṭhvāḍiyũ** (*n*)
minute	મિનિટ	**miniṭ** (*f*)	fortnight	પખવાડિયું	**pakhvaḍiyu** (*n*)
hour	કલાક	**kalāk** (*m*)	month	મહિનો	**mahino** (*m*)
day	દિવસ	**divas** (*m*)	year	વરસ	**varas** (*n*)
night	રાત	**rāt** (*f*)	full moon day	પુનમ	**punam** (*f*)
morning	સવાર	**savār** (*f*)	no moon day	અમાસ	**amās** (*f*)
noon	બપોર	**bapor** (*f*)			

Seasons and weather ઋતુઓ અને હવામાન

atmosphere	વાતાવરણ	**vātāvaran**
autumn	પાનખર	**pānkhar**
climate		**ābohavā**

cloud	વાદળ	**vādal**
fog	ધુમ્મસ	**dhummas**
frost	હિમ, ઝાકળ	**him, jhākaḷ**
hailstones	કરા	**karā**
lightning	વીજળી	**vijḷi**
maximum	મહત્તમ	**mahattam**
minimum	અલ્પતમ	**alpatam**
monsoon	ચોમાસું	**chomāsũ**
rain	વરસાદ	**varsād**
spring	વસંત	**vasant**
storm	તોફાન	**tophān**
summer	ઉનાળો	**unāḷo**
sunshine	તડકો	**taḍko**
thunder	ગાજવીજ	**gājvij**
wind	પવન	**pavan**
winter	શિયાળો	**shiyāḷo**

Directions દિશાઓ

north	ઉત્તર	**uttar**
north-east	ઈશાન	**ishān**
east	પૂર્વ	**purva**
south-east	અગ્નિ	**agni**
south	દક્ષિણ	**dakshiṇ**
south-west	નૈઋત્ય	**nairutya**
west	પશ્ચિમ	**pashchim**
north-west	વાયવ્ય	**vāyavya**

Family કુટુંબ

brother	ભાઈ	**bhāi**
brother's wife	ભાભી	**bhābhi**
cousin (brother's daughter)	ભત્રીજી	**bhatriji**
cousin (brother's son)	ભત્રીજો	**bhatrijo**
cousin (sister's son/daughter)	ભાણેજ	**bhānej**
daughter	દીકરી	**dikri**
daughter-in-law	વહુ,પુત્રવધૂ	**vahu, putrāvadhu**
father	પિતા,બાપા	**pitā, bāpā**
father-in-law	સસરા	**sasrā**

husband	પતિ, વર	**pati, var**
husband of maternal aunt	માસા	**māsā**
husband of paternal aunt	ફૂઆ	**phuā**
maternal aunt	માસી	**māsi**
maternal uncle	મામા	**māmā**
mother	બા	**bā**
mother-in-law	સાસુ	**sāsu**
paternal aunt	કાકી	**kāki**
paternal uncle	કાકા	**kākā**
relative	સગું	**sagũ**
sister	બહેન	**bahen**
son	દીકરો,પુત્ર	**dikro, putra**
son-in-law	જમાઈ	**jamāi**
step-(father, mother, etc.)	સાવકા	**sāvkā**
wife	વહુ, પત્ની	**vahu, patni**
wife of maternal uncle	મામી	**māmi**
wife's brother	સાળો	**sāḷo**
wife's sister	સાળી	**sāḷi**

The body શરીર

hair	વાળ	**vāḷ** (*m*)	back	પીઠ	**piṭh** (*f*)
forehead	કપાળ	**kapāḷ** (*n*)	spine	કરોડ	**karoḍ** (*f*)
eyebrow	ભ્રમર	**bhramar** (*f*)	shoulder	ખભો	**khabho** (*m*)
eye	આંખ	**ā̃kh** (*f*)	hand	હાથ	**hāth** (*m*)
eyelid	પોપચું	**popchũ** (*n*)	armpit	બગલ	**bagal** (*f*)
eyelash	પાંપણ	**pā̃paṇ** (*f*)	elbow	કોણી	**koṇi** (*f*)
nose	નાક	**nāk** (*n*)	wrist	કાંડું	**kā̃ḍũ** (*n*)
ear	કાન	**kān** (*m*)	palm	હથેળી	**hatheḷi** (*f*)
cheek	ગાલ	**gāl** (*m*)	finger	આંગળી	**ā̃gḷi** (*f*)
lip	હોઠ	**hoṭh** (*m*)	thumb	અંગુઠો	**anguṭho** (*m*)
tooth	દાંત	**dā̃t** (*m*)	nail	નખ	**nakh** (*m*)
tongue	જીભ	**jibh** (*f*)	waist	કમર/કેડ	**kamar/keḍ** (*f*)
mouth	મોં	**mÕ** (*n*)	leg	પગ	**pag** (*m*)
head	માથું	**māthũ** (*n*)	thigh	સાથળ	**sāthaḷ** (*m*)
brain	મગજ	**magaj** (*n*)	knee	ઘૂંટણ	**ghũṭaṇ** (*n*)
face	ચહેરો	**chahero** (*m*)	calf	પીંડી	**pinḍi** (*f*)
throat	ગળું	**gaḷũ** (*n*)	ankle	ઘૂંટી	**ghũṭi** (*f*)
neck	ડોક	**ḍok** (*f*)	heel	પાની	**pāni** (*f*)
chin, beard	દાઢી	**dāḍhi** (*f*)	skin	ચામડી	**chāmḍi** (*f*)

moustache	મૂછ	**muchh** (*f*)	flesh	માંસ	**mā̃s** (*n*)
chest	છાતી	**chhāti** (*f*)	bone	હાડકું	**hāḍkũ** (*n*)
heart	હૃદય	**hruday** (*n*)	blood	લોહી	**lohi** (*n*)
lung	ફેફસું	**phephsũ** (*n*)	body	શરીર	**sharir** (*n*)
rib	પાંસળી	**Pā̃sḷi** (*f*)	pulse	નાડી	**nāḍi** (*f*)
stomach	પેટ	**peṭ** (*n*)			

Illnesses માંદગી

indigestion	અપચો	**apacho**
migraine	આધાશીશી	**ādhāshishi**
cough	ઉધરસ	**udḥras**
nausea	ઊલટી	**ulṭi**
measles	ઓરી	**Ori**
constipation	કબજીયાત	**kabajiyāt**
tuberculosis	ક્ષય	**kshya**
diarrhoea	ઝાડા	**jhāḍā**
malaria	ટાઢીયો તાવ	**tāḍḥiyo tāv**
fever	તાવ	**tāv**
medicine	દવા	**davā**
surgery, clinic	દવાખાનું	**davākhānũ**
pain	દુખાવો	**dukhāvo**
dysentery	મરડો	**marḍo**
headache	માથાનો દુખાવો	**māthāno dukhāvo**
paralysis	લકવો, પક્ષઘાત	**lakvo, pakshghāt**
cold	શરદી	**shardi**
heart attack	હ્રદયરોગનો હુમલો	**hrudayrogno humlo**

Professions ધંધાદારી

actor	નટ	**naṭ**
actress	નટી	**naṭi**
astrologer	જોશી	**joshi**
barber	હજામ	**hajām**
blacksmith	લુહાર	**luhār**
butcher	કસાઈ	**kasāi**
carpenter	સુથાર	**suthḥār**
clerk	કારકુન	**kārkun**
cobbler	મોચી	**mochi**

cook	રસોઇયો	**rasoio**
dancer (*m*)	નર્તક	**nartak**
dancer (*f*)	નર્તિકા	**nartikā**
diamond merchant	ઝવેરી	**jhaveri**
doctor	ડોક્ટર	**ḍoktar**
dyer	રંગારો	**rãgāro**
farmer	ખેડૂત	**kheḍut**
fisherman	માછીમાર	**māchhimār**
gardener	માળી	**māḷi**
goldsmith	સોની	**soni**
journalist	પત્રકાર	**patrakār**
labourer	મજૂર	**majur**
lawyer	વકીલ	**vakil**
magician	જાદુગર	**jādugar**
mason	કડીયો	**kaḍio**
milkman	દૂધવાળો	**dudhvālo**
painter	ચિત્રકાર	**chitrakār**
professor	પ્રોફેસર, પ્રાધ્યાપક	**prophesar, prādhyāpak**
sculptor	શિલ્પી	**shilpi**
singer (*m*)	ગાયક	**gāyak**
singer (*f*)	ગાયિકા	**gāyikā**
student (*m*)	વિદ્યાર્થી	**vidyārthi**
student (*f*)	વિદ્યાર્થિની	**vidyārthini**
tailor	દરજી	**darji**
teacher (*m*)	શિક્ષક	**shikshak**
teacher (*f*)	શિક્ષિકા	**shikshikā**
washerwoman/man	ધોબણ/ધોબી	**dhoban/dhobi**
worker	કર્મચારી	**karmachāri**
writer (*m*)	લેખક	**lekhak**
writer (*f*)	લેખિકા	**lekhikā**

Birds and animals પક્ષીઓ અને પ્રાણીઓ

bear	રીંછ	**rī̃chh** (*n*)
buffalo	ભેંસ	**bhẼs** (*f*)
camel	ઊંટ	**ū̃ṭ** (*n*)
cat	બિલાડી બિલાડો બિલાડું	**bilāḍi** (*f*), **bilāḍo** (*m*), **bilāḍū̃** (*n*)
cobra	નાગ	**nāg** (*m*)
cow	ગાય	**gāy** (*f*)

crab	કરચલો	**karachlo** (*m*)
crane	બગલો	**baglo** (*m*),
	બગલી	**bagli** (*f*)
crocodile	મગર	**magar** (*m*),
	મગરી	**magri** (*f*)
crow	કાગડો	**kāgḍo** (*m*),
	કાગડી	**kāgḍi** (*f*)
cuckoo	કોયલ	**koyal** (*f*)
deer	હરણ	**haraṇ** (*n*)
dog	કૂતરો	**kutro** (*m*),
	કૂતરી	**kutri** (*f*),
	કૂતરું	**kutrũ** (*n*)
donkey	ગધેડો	**gadḥeḍo** (*m*),
	ગધેડી	**gadḥeḍi** (*f*),
	ગધેડું	**gadḥeḍũ** (*n*)
duck	બતક	**batak** (*n*)
eagle	ગરુડ	**garuḍ** (*n*)
elephant	હાથી	**hāthi** (*m*)
fish	માછલી	**māchhli** (*f*)
frog	દેડકો	**deḍko** (*m*)
goat	બકરો	**bakro** (*m*),
	બકરી	**bakri** (*f*)
horse	ઘોડો	**gḥoḍo** (*m*),
	ઘોડી	**gḥoḍi** (*f*),
	ઘોડું	**gḥoḍũ** (*n*)
jackal	શિયાળ	**shiyāl** (*n*)
kite	સમડી	**samḍi** (*f*)
lamb	ઘેટું	**ghẽtũ** (*n*)
lion	સિંહ	**sĩh** (*m*)
	સિંહણ	**sĩhaṇ** (*f*)
owl	ઘુવડ	**ghuvaḍ** (*n*)
ox	બળદ	**baḷad** (*m*)
parrot	પોપટ	**popaṭ** (*m*)
peacock	મોર	**mor** (*m*)
pig	ડુક્કર	**ḍukkar** (*n*)
pigeon	કબૂતર	**kabutar** (*n*)
pony	ટટ્ટુ	**ṭaṭṭu** (*n*)
rabbit	સસલું	**saslũ** (*n*)
serpent	સાપ	**sāp** (*m*)
sparrow	ચકલી	**chakli** (*f*),
	ચકલો	**chaklo** (*m*),
	ચકલું	**chaklũ** (*n*)

wan	હંસ	**hãs** (*m*),
	હંસી	**hãsi** (*f*)
ger	વાઘ	**vāgh** (*m*),
	વાઘણ	**vāghan** (*f*)
ortoise	કાચબો	**kāchbo** (*m*),
	કાચબી	**kāchbi** (*f*)
ulture	ગીધ	**gidh** (*n*)
olf	વરુ	**varu** (*n*)
oodpecker	લક્કડખોદ	**lakkaḍkhod** (*n*)

nsects જીવજંતુઓ

nt	કીડી	**kiḍi** (*f*)
edbug	માકડ	**mākaḍ** (*m*)
ee (honey)	મધમાખી	**madhmākhi** (*f*)
utterfly	પતંગિયું	**patangiũ** (*n*)
ockroach	વાંદો	**vā̃do** (*m*)
arthworm	અળસિયું	**aḷsiũ** (*n*)
refly	આગિયો	**āgiyo** (*m*)
y	માખી	**mākhi** (*f*)
rge black ant	મંકોડો	**mankoḍo** (*m*)
cust	તીડ	**tiḍ** (*n*)
use	જૂ	**ju** (*f*)
osquito	મચ્છર	**machchhar** (*n*)
corpion	વીંછી	**vĩchi** (*m*)
pider	કરોળિયો	**karoḷio** (*m*)
rmite	ઉધ્ધઈ	**uddhai** (*f*)
asp	ભમરી	**bhamri** (*f*)

ood ખોરાક

arley	જવ	**jav** (*m*)
uttermilk and gram flour soup	કઢી	**kaḍhi** (*f*)
apati	રોટલી	**roṭli** (*f*)
hutney	ચટણી	**chaṭṇi** (*f*)
ooked rice	ભાત	**bhāt** (*m*)
ce and pulse cooked together	ખીચડી	**khichḍi** (*f*)

corn	મકાઈ	**makāi** (*f*)
egg	ઈંડું	**ĩḍũ** (*n*)
fish	માછલી	**māchhli** (*f*)
leaf vegetables	ભાજી	**bhāji** (*f*)
pickle	અથાણું	**athāṇũ** (*n*)
pulse	કઠોળ	**kaṭhoḷ** (*n*)
pulse	દાળ	**dāḷ** (*f*)
pulses (soup)	દાળ	**dāḷ** (*f*)
purified butter	ઘી	**ghi** (*n*)
rice	ચોખા	**chokhā** (*m*, *pl*)
tea	ચા	**chā** (*f*, *m*)
type of mixed salad	કચુંબર	**kachũbar** (*f*)
vegetables	શાક	**shāk** (*n*)
water	પાણી	**pāṇi** (*n*)
wheat	ઘઉં	**ghaũ** (*m*, *pl*)
wine, liquor	દારૂ	**dāru** (*m*)

Vegetables શાકભાજી

cabbage	કોબી	**kobi** (*f*)
carrot	ગાજર	**gājar** (*n*)
cauliflower	ફ્લાવર	**flāvar** (*n*)
coriander	કોથમીર	**kothmir** (*f*)
aubergine	રીંગણું	**Rĩgnũ** (*n*)
garlic	લસણ	**lasaṇ** (*n*)
ginger	આદુ	**ādũ** (*n*)
leaf vegetables	ભાજી	**bhāji** (*f*)
lemon/lime	લીંબુ	**lĩbu** (*n*)
okra/ladies' fingers	ભીંડા	**bhĩḍā** (*m*)
onion	ડુંગળી	**ḍungli** (*f*)
potato	બટાટું	**baṭāṭũ** (*n*)
radish	મૂળા	**mulā** (*m*)
spinach	પાલખ	**pālakh** (*f*)
tomato	ટમેટું	**ṭameṭũ** (*n*)

Fruit and nuts ફળો અને સૂકો મેવો

walnut	અખરોટ	**akhroṭ** (*n*)
pineapple	અનાનસ	**ananas** (*n*)

g	અંજીર	**anjir** (*n*)
:ashew nuts	કાજુ	**kāju** (*m*)
aisin	કિસમિસ	**kismis** (*f*)
nango	કેરી	**keri** (*f*)
)anana	કેળું	**keḷũ** (*n*)
late	ખજૂર	**khajur** (*f*)
:pricot	જરદાળુ	**jardāḷu** (*n*)
uava	જામફળ	**jāmphaḷ** (*n*)
nelon	ટેટી	**ṭeṭi** (*f*)
vatermelon	તરબુચ	**tarbuch** (*n*)
)omegranate	દાડમ	**dāḍam** (*n*)
rapes	દ્રાક્ષ	**draksh** (*f*)
)istachio	પિસ્તા	**pistā** (*n*)
lmond	બદામ	**badām** (*f*)
range	મોસંબી	**mosambi** (*n*)
)eanuts	શીંગ	**shing** (*f*)
pple	સફરજન	**sapharjan** (*n*)

\Numbers આંકડાઓ

1	૧	**ek**	એક	11	૧૧	**agiyār**	અગિયાર
2	૨	**be**	બે	12	૧૨	**bār**	બાર
3	૩	**traṇ**	ત્રણ	13	૧૩	**ter**	તેર
4	૪	**chār**	ચાર	14	૧૪	**chaud**	ચૌદ
5	૫	**pā̃ch**	પાંચ	15	૧૫	**pandar**	પંદર
6	૬	**chha**	છ	16	૧૬	**soḷ**	સોળ
7	૭	**sāt**	સાત	17	૧૭	**sattar**	સત્તર
8	૮	**āṭh**	આઠ	18	૧૮	**aḍhār**	અઢાર
9	૯	**nav**	નવ	19	૧૯	**ogṇis**	ઓગણીસ
0	૧૦	**das**	દસ	20	૨૦	**vis**	વીસ
1	૨૧	**ekvis**	એકવીસ	31	૩૧	**ekatris**	એકત્રીસ
2	૨૨	**bāvis**	બાવીસ	32	૩૨	**batris**	બત્રીસ
3	૨૩	**tevis**	તેવીસ	33	૩૩	**tetris**	તેત્રીસ
4	૨૪	**chovis**	ચોવીસ	34	૩૪	**chotris**	ચોત્રીસ
5	૨૫	**pachis**	પચીસ	35	૩૫	**pā̃tris**	પાંત્રીસ
6	૨૬	**chhavvis**	છવીસ	36	૩૬	**chhatris**	છત્રીસ
7	૨૭	**sattāvis**	સત્તાવીસ	37	૩૭	**sāḍatris**	સાડત્રીસ
8	૨૮	**aṭṭhāvis**	અઠાવીસ	38	૩૮	**aḍatris**	આડત્રીસ
9	૨૯	**ogaṇtris**	ઓગણત્રીસ	39	૩૯	**ogaṇchālis**	ઓગણચાલીસ
0	૩૦	**tris**	ત્રીસ	40	૪૦	**chālis**	ચાલીસ

You will notice that the ending **-vis** (meaning 20) is common to all the number from 21 to 28, with the exception of 25 (**pachis**); **tris** (30) is common to a the numbers from 31 to 38, and including 35.

41	૪૧	**ektālis**	એકતાલીસ	61	૬૧	**eksaṭh**	એકસઠ
42	૪૨	**betālis**	બેતાલીસ	62	૬૨	**bāsaṭh**	બાસઠ
43	૪૩	**tetālis**	તેતાલીસ	63	૬૩	**tesaṭh**	તેસઠ
44	૪૪	**chummālis**	ચુમ્માલીસ	64	૬૪	**chosaṭh**	ચોસઠ
45	૪૫	**pistālis**	પીસ્તાલીસ	65	૬૫	**pā̃saṭh**	પાંસઠ
46	૪૬	**chhetālis**	છેતાલીસ	66	૬૬	**chhāsaṭh**	છાસઠ
47	૪૭	**suḍtālis**	સુડતાલીસ	67	૬૭	**saḍsaṭh**	સડસઠ
48	૪૮	**aḍtālis**	ઉડતાલીસ	68	૬૮	**aḍsaṭh**	અડસઠ
49	૪૯	**oganpachās**	ઓગણપચાસ	69	૬૯	**oganṣitter**	ઓગણસિત્તે
50	૫૦	**pachās**	પચાસ	70	૭૦	**sitter**	સિત્તેર
51	૫૧	**ekāvan**	એકાવન	71	૭૧	**ikoter**	એકોતેર
52	૫૨	**bāvan**	બાવન	72	૭૨	**bõter**	બોતેર
53	૫૩	**tepan**	તેપન	73	૭૩	**tõter**	તોંતેર
54	૫૪	**chopan**	ચોપન	74	૭૪	**chummoter**	ચુમ્મોતેર ચુંમોતેર
55	૫૫	**panchāvan**	પંચાવન	75	૭૫	**panchoter**	પંચોતેર
56	૫૬	**chhappan**	છપ્પન	76	૭૬	**chhÕter**	છોંતેર
57	૫૭	**sattāvan**	સત્તાવન	77	૭૭	**sitoter**	સિતોતેર
58	૫૮	**aṭṭhāvan**	અઠ્ઠાવન	78	૭૮	**iṭhoter**	ઈઠોતેર
59	૫૯	**oganṣāth**	ઓગણસાઠ	79	૭૯	**oganẼshi**	ઓગણએંશી
60	૬૦	**sāṭh**	સાઠ	80	૮૦	**Ẽshi**	એંશી

81	૮૧	**Ekyāshi**	એકયાશી	91	૯૧	**ekānũ**	એકાણું
82	૮૨	**byāshi**	બ્યાશી	92	૯૨	**bāṇũ**	બાણું
83	૮૩	**tryāshi**	ત્રાશી	93	૯૩	**trāṇũ**	ત્રાણું
84	૮૪	**choryāshi**	ચોર્યાશી	94	૯૪	**chorāṇũ**	ચોરાણું
85	૮૫	**panchyāshi**	પંચાશી	95	૯૫	**panchāṇũ**	પંચાણું
86	૮૬	**chhyāshi**	છ્યાશી	96	૯૬	**chhannu**	છન્નું
87	૮૭	**satyāshi**	સત્તાશી	97	૯૭	**sattāṇũ**	સત્તાણું
88	૮૮	**aṭṭhyāshi**	અઠ્ઠાશી	98	૯૮	**aṭṭhāṇũ**	અઠ્ઠાણું
89	૮૯	**nevyāshi**	નેવ્યાશી	99	૯૯	**navvāṇũ**	નવાણું
90	૯૦	**nevũ**	નેવું	100	૧૦૦	**so**	સો

100	૧૦૦	**ek so**	એકસો	600	૬૦૦	**chhaso**	છસો
200	૨૦૦	**baso**	બસો	700	૭૦૦	**sātso**	સાતસો
300	૩૦૦	**transo**	ત્રણસો	800	૮૦૦	**āṭhso**	આઠસો
400	૪૦૦	**chārso**	ચારસો	900	૯૦૦	**navso**	નવસો
500	૫૦૦	**pā̃chso**	પાંચસો	1,000	૧૦૦૦	**hajār**	હજાર

With the exception of 200 (**baso**), the hundreds are formed in the same way as English with **ek, be, traṇ**, etc. placed before **so** (hundred). Other examples:

1,240	૧,૨૪૦	એક હજાર બસો ચાલીસ	**ek hajār baso chālis**
3,399	૩,૩૯૯	ત્રણ હજાર ત્રણસો નવ્વાણું	**traṇ hajār traṇso navvāṇũ**

Colours રંગ

blue	વાદળી	**vādḷi**	black	કાળો	**kāḷo**
green	લીલો	**lilo**	golden	સોનેરી	**soneri**
pink	ગુલાબી	**gulābi**	dark	ઘેરો	**ghEro**
red	લાલ	**lāl**	orange	નારંગી	**nārangi**
violet	જાંબુડીઓ	**jāmbuḍio**	light	આછો	**āchho**
white	સફેદ/ધોળો	**saphed/dhoḷo**	purple	જાંબલી	**jāmbli**
yellow	પીળો	**piḷo**			

Shapes આકાર

circle	ગોળ	**goḷ** (*m*)
hexagon	ષટકોણ	**shaṭkoṇ** (*m*)
rectangle	લંબચોરસ	**lambchoras** (*m*)
square	ચોરસ	**choras** (*m*)
triangle	ત્રિકોણ	**trikoṇ** (*m*)

Metals ધાતુઓ

brass	પિત્તળ	**pittal** (*n*)
bronze	કાંસું	**kāsũ** (*n*)
copper	તાંબું	**tābũ** (*n*)
gold	સોનું	**sonũ** (*n*)
iron	લોઢું, લોખંડ	**lodhũ lokhand** (*n*)
minerals	ખનિજ	**khanij** (*f*)
silver	રૂપું ચાંદી	**roopu** (*n*)
		chā̃di (*f*)
steel	પોલાદ	**polād** (*n*)
zinc	જસત	**jasat** (*n*)

Gujarati–English glossary

અક્કલ	**akkal** (*f*)	intelligence
અકસીર	**aksir** (*a*)	effective
અકસ્માત	**akasmāt** (*m*)	accident
અક્ષર	**akshar** (*m*)	letter (of the alphabet)
અખતરો	**akhatro** (*m*)	trial (experiment)
અગર	**agar** (*conj*)	or, if
અગવડ	**agvaḍ** (*f*)	inconvenience
અઘરૂં	**aghrũ** (*a*)	difficult
અચાનક	**achānak** (*adv*)	suddenly
અચૂક	**achuk** (*adv*)	surely
અજમાવવું	**ajmāvvũ** (*vt*)	to try
અજવાળું	**ajvāḷũ** (*n*)	light
અટક	**aṭak** (*f*)	surname
અઠવાડિક	**aṭhvāḍik** (*a*, *n*)	weekly
અડચણ	**aḍchaṇ** (*f*)	difficulty
અડધું	**aḍdhũ** (*a*)	half
અડવું	**aḍvũ** (*vt*)	to touch
અણી	**aṇi** (*f*)	sharp end
અત્તર	**attar** (*n*)	scent
અત્યારે	**atyāre** (*adv*)	at this moment
અથડાવું	**athḍāvũ** (*vi*)	to collide, dash against
અથાણું	**athāṇũ** (*n*)	pickles
અદેખાઈ	**adekhāi** (*f*)	jealousy
અધિકાર	**adhikār** (*m*)	right
અધુરું	**adhurũ** (*a*)	incomplete
અધ્ધર	**addhar** (*a*, *adv*)	high in the air
અનાજ	**anāj** (*n*)	corn
અનાથ	**anāth** (*a*)	orphan
અનુકૂળ	**anukuḷ** (*a*)	favourable
અનુભવ	**anubhav** (*m*)	experience
અનેક	**anek** (*a*)	many
અન્યાય	**anyāy** (*m*)	injustice
અપજશ	**apjash** (*m*)	discredit

અપનાવવું	**apnāvvũ** (*vt*)	to adopt
અપમાન	**apman** (*n*)	insult
અપશુકન	**apshukan** (*n*)	bad omen
અપંગ	**apãg** (*a*)	handicapped
અફવા	**aphvā** (*f*)	rumour
અફળાવું	**aphāḷvũ** (*vt*)	to dash violently
અબજ	**abaj** (*a*)	thousand million
અભડાવું	**abhḍāvũ** (*vi*)	to become impure
અભણ	**abhaṇ** (*a*)	illiterate
અભિનય	**abhinay** (*m*)	acting (on stage)
અભિનંદન	**abhinandan** (*n*)	congratulations
અભિમાન	**abhimān** (*n*)	pride
અમથું	**amthũ** (*a*)	without reason
અમર	**amar** (*a*)	immortal
અમાસ	**amās** (*f*)	moonless night
અમુક	**amuk** (*a*)	certain
અરજી	**arji** (*f*)	application
અરસપરસ	**arasparas** (*adv*)	mutual, amongst yourselves
અરીસો	**ariso** (*m*)	mirror
અરે!	**are** (*int*)	oh!
અર્થ	**artha** (*m*)	meaning
અવયવ	**avyav** (*m*)	parts of the body
અવળું	**avḷũ** (*a*)	contrary
અવાજ	**avāj** (*m*)	sound
અસર	**asar** (*f*)	effect
અસલ	**asal** (*a*)	original
અહીં	**ahĩ** (*adv*)	here
અંગ્રેજ	**ãgrej** (*m*)	Englishman
અંત	**ant** (*m*)	end
અંતર	**antar** (*n*)	distance
અંદર	**andar** (*prep*)	in
અંધારું	**andhārũ** (*n*)	darkness
આ	**ā** (*pron*)	this
આકાર	**ākār** (*m*)	shape
આકાશ	**ākāsh** (*n*)	sky
આખું	**ākhũ** (*a*)	whole
આગ	**āg** (*f*)	fire
આગલું	**āglũ** (*a*)	previous
આગળ	**āgaḷ** (*adv*)	before
આગ્રહ	**āgrah** (*m*)	insistence
આઘું	**āghũ** (*a*)	distant, far off
આજ	**āj** (*f*)	today

આઝાદી	**āzādi** (*f*)	freedom
આટલું	**āṭlũ** (*a*)	so much
આડું	**āḍũ** (*a*)	not straight, getting in the way
આતુર	**ātur** (*a*)	anxious
આધાર	**ādhār** (*m*)	support, depend on
આનંદ	**ānand** (*m*)	happiness
આપ	**āp** (*pron*)	you (honorific)
આપ	**āvũ** (*vt*)	to give
આપોઆપ	**āpoāp** (*adv*)	automatically
આબરૂ	**ābru** (*f*)	prestige
આબોહવા	**ābohavā** (*f*)	climate
આભાર	**ābhār** (*m*)	thanks
આમંત્રણ	**āmantraṇ** (*n*)	invitation
આયાત	**āyāt** (*f*)	import
આરતી	**ārti** (*f*)	ceremony (waving of lights before God)
આરામ	**ārām** (*m*)	rest
આરોપ	**ārop** (*m*)	accusation
આર્થિક	**ārthik** (*a*)	economic
આવક	**āvak** (*f*)	income
આવકાર	**āvkār** (*m*)	welcome
આવજો	**āvjo** (*vi*)	goodbye (*lit.* come again)
આવડત	**āvḍaṭ** (*f*)	skill
આવડવું	**āvaḍvũ** (*vi*)	to know how to do
આવડું	**āvḍũ** (*a*)	this much
આવવું	**āvvũ** (*vi*)	to come
આવું	**āvũ** (*a*)	like this
આશરે	**āshre** (*adv*)	approximately
આશરો	**āshro** (*m*)	protection
આશા	**āshā** (*f*)	hope
આશીર્વાદ	**āshirvād** (*m*)	blessings
આસપાસ	**āspās** (*adv*)	around
આળસ	**āḷas** (*f*)	laziness
આંકડો	**ā̃kḍo** (*m*)	number
આંકવું	**ā̃kvũ** (*vt*)	to draw (a line)
આંધળું	**ā̃dhḷũ** (*a*)	blind
આંસુ	**ā̃su** (*n*)	tear
ઈચ્છા	**ichchhā** (*f*)	wish
ઈતિહાસ	**itihās** (*m*)	history
ઈનામ	**inām** (*n*)	prize
ઈરાદો	**irādo** (*m*)	intention
ઈલાજ	**ilāj** (*m*)	remedy, treatment, cure

ઈસવિસન	**isvi san** (*f*)	AD
ઈંટ	**ĩṭ** (*f*)	brick
ઈંડું	**inḍũ** (*n*)	egg
ઉકેલ	**ukel** (*m*)	solution
ઉચ્ચાર	**uchchār** (*m*)	pronunciation
ઉછીનું	**uchhinũ** (*a*)	borrowed
ઉજાગરો	**ujāgro** (*m*)	sleepless night
ઉજ્જડ	**ujjaḍ** (*a*)	barren
ઉતાવળ	**utāvaḷ** (*f*)	hurry
ઉત્સાહ	**utsāh** (*m*)	enthusiasm
ઉદાર	**udār** (*a*)	generous
ઉદાસ	**udās** (*a*)	sad
ઉધરસ	**udhras** (*f*)	cough
ઉધાર	**udhār** (*a*)	on credit
ઉનાળો	**unāḷo** (*m*)	summer
ઉપકાર	**upkār** (*m*)	obligation
ઉપદેશ	**updesh** (*m*)	precept
ઉપયોગ	**upyog** (*m*)	use
ઉપર	**upar** (*adv*)	above
ઉપરી	**upri** (*m*)	superior
ઉપલું	**uplũ** (*a*)	above
ઉપાધિ	**upādhi** (*f*)	trouble
ઉપાય	**upāy** (*m*)	remedy
ઉમેરવું	**umervũ** (*vt*)	to add
ઉંદર	**undar** (*m*)	mouse
ઉંમર	**ummar** (*f*)	age
ઊકળવું	**ukaḷvũ** (*vi*)	to boil
ઊખડવું	**ukhaḍvũ** (*vi*)	to get separated
ઊગવું	**ugvũ** (*vi*)	to rise, grow
ઊઘડવું	**ughaḍvũ** (*vi*)	to open
ઊંચકવું	**uchakvũ** (*vt*)	to lift
ઊછળવું	**uchhaḷvũ** (*vi*)	to bounce
ઊજળું	**ujḷũ** (*a*)	white, shining
ઊઠવું	**uṭhvũ** (*vi*)	to get up
ઊડવું	**uḍvũ** (*vi*)	to fly
ઊતરવું	**utarvũ** (*vi*)	to climb down
ઊન	**un** (*n*)	wool
ઊપડવું	**upaḍvũ** (*vi*)	to be lifted
ઊભવું	**ubhvũ** (*vi*)	to stand
ઊલટી	**ulṭi** (*f*)	vomit
ઊલટું	**ulṭũ** (*a*)	contrary
ઊંઘવું	**ũghvũ** (*vi*)	to sleep

ઊંચું	**ũchũ** (*a*)	high
ઊંડું	**ũḍũ** (*a*)	deep
ઊંધું	**ũdhũ** (*a*)	inverted
ઋતુ	**rutu** (*f*)	season
ઋષિ	**rushi** (*m*)	sage
એકમત	**ekmat** (*a*)	unanimous
એકલું	**eklũ** (*a*)	lonely
એટલે	**eṭle** (*adv*)	therefore
એલચી	**elchi** (*m*)	ambassador
એવું	**evũ** (*a*)	such
ઓગળવું	**ogaḷvũ** (*vi*)	to melt
ઓચિંતું	**ochintũ** (*a*)	unexpected
ઓજાર	**ojār** (*n*)	tools
ઓરડી	**orḍi** (*f*)	small room
ઓશીકું	**oshikũ** (*n*)	pillow
ઓળખવું	**oḷakhvũ** (*vt*)	to recognize
ઔદ્યોગિક	**audyogik** (*a*)	industrial
કક્કો	**kakko** (*m*)	alphabet
કચરાપેટી	**kachrāpeṭi** (*f*)	dustbin
કચરો	**kachro** (*m*)	rubbish
કચુંબર	**kachumbar** (*f*)	salad
કજિયો	**kajiyo** (*m*)	quarrel
કટકો	**kaṭko** (*m*)	piece
કઠણ	**kaṭhaṇ** (*a*)	hard
કઠોળ	**kaṭhoḷ** (*n*)	pulse
કડક	**kaḍak** (*a*)	strict, hard
કડવું	**kaḍvũ** (*a*)	bitter
કડિયો	**kaḍiyo** (*m*)	mason
કઢંગું	**kaḍhãgũ** (*a*)	awkward
કણક	**kaṇak** (*f*)	dough
કતલ	**katal** (*f*)	slaughter
કથા	**kathā** (*f*)	story (mainly religious)
કથીર	**kathir** (*n*)	zinc; alloy of tin and lead
કદ	**kad** (*n*)	size
કદર	**kadar** (*f*)	appreciation
કદરૂપું	**kadrupũ** (*a*)	ugly
કન્યા	**kanyā** (*f*)	unmarried girl
કપટ	**kapaṭ** (*n*)	fraud
કપડું	**kapḍũ** (*n*)	cloth
કફ	**kaph** (*m*)	phlegm
કફન	**kaphan** (*n*)	coffin

કબજિયાત	**kabajiyāt** (*f*)	constipation
કબજો	**kabjo** (*m*)	possession
કબર	**kabar** (*f*)	grave
કબાટ	**kabāṭ** (*m*, *n*)	cupboard
કબુલ	**kabul** (*a*) (*adv*)	agree
કમ	**kam** (*a*)	less
કમાવું	**kamāvũ** (*vt*)	to earn
કર	**kar** (*m*)	tax
કરકસર	**karkasar** (*f*)	thrift
કરગરવું	**kargarvũ** (*vi*)	to beg
કરચલી	**karachli** (*f*)	wrinkle
કરજ	**karaj** (*n*)	debt
કરડવું	**karaḍvũ** (*vt*)	to bite
કરતાં	**kartā̃** (*prep*, *conj*)	than
કરમાવું	**karmāvũ** (*vi*)	to wither
કરવું	**karvũ** (*vt*)	to do
કરાર	**karār** (*m*)	agreement
કરોડ	**karoḍ** (*a*, *f*)	ten million; spine
કલા	**kalā** (*f*)	art
કલાક	**kalāk** (*m*)	hour
કવિ	**kavi** (*m*)	poet
કવિતા	**kavitā** (*f*)	poem
કશુંક	**kashũk** (*pron*, *a*)	something
કસરત	**kasrat** (*f*)	exercise
કસાઈ	**kasāi** (*m*)	butcher
કસોટી	**kasoṭi** (*f*)	test
કહેવત	**kahevat** (*f*)	proverb
કહેવું	**kahevũ** (*vt*)	to say
કાંઈ	**kā̃i** (*a*, *pron*)	anything
કંકોતરી	**kãkotri** (*f*)	invitation (esp. marriage)
કંટાળો	**kãṭāḷo** (*m*)	boredom
કંપવું	**kampvũ** (*vi*)	to tremble
કાગળ	**kāgaḷ** (*m*)	paper, letter
કાચ	**kāch** (*m*)	glass
કાચું	**kāchũ** (*a*)	raw
કાઢવું	**kāḍhvũ** (*vt*)	to take out, draw
કાતર	**kātar** (*f*)	scissors
કાણું	**kāṇũ** (*n*)	hole
કાદવ	**kādav** (*m*)	mud
કાપવું	**kāpvũ** (*vt*)	to cut
કાબુ	**kābu** (*m*)	control
કામ	**kām** (*n*)	work

કાયદો	**kāydo** (*m*)	law
કાયમ	**kāyam** (*a*)	permanent, constant
કાયર	**kāyar** (*a*)	cowardly
કારકુન	**kārkun** (*m*)	clerk
કારખાનું	**kārkhānũ** (*n*)	factory
કારણ	**kāraṇ** (*n*)	cause
કાલ	**kāl** (*f*)	yesterday, tomorrow (depending on context)
કાળજી	**kāḷji** (*f*)	care
કાંટો	**kā̃ṭo** (*m*)	thorn
કાંતવું	**kā̃tvũ** (*vt*)	to spin
કિનારો	**kināro** (*m*)	bank (of river), coast
કિરણ	**kiraṇ** (*n*)	ray
કિંમત	**kimmat** (*f*)	price
કુટુંબ	**kuṭumb** (*n*)	family
કુદરત	**kudrat** (*f*)	nature
કુળ	**kuḷ** (*n*)	race
કુશળ	**kushaḷ** (*a*)	OK; expert
કૂદકો	**kudko** (*m*)	jump
કૂદવું	**kudvũ** (*vi*)	to jump
કૂવો	**kuvo** (*m*)	well
કે	**ke** (*conj*)	either, or; that
કેટલું	**keṭlũ** (*a*)	how much
કેદ	**ked** (*f*)	imprisonment
કેમ	**kem** (*adv*)	how, why
કેવડું	**kevḍũ** (*a*)	how much, how big
કેવું	**kevũ** (*a*)	what type
કેળવણી	**keḷavṇi** (*f*)	education
કોઈ	**koi** (*a*)	someone
કોગળો	**kOgḷo** (*m*)	mouthful of water
કોણ	**koṇ** (*pron*)	who
કોથળી	**kothḷi** (*f*)	small handbag
કોનું	**konũ** (*pron*)	whose
કોયડો	**koyḍo** (*m*)	puzzle
કોરું	**korũ** (*a*)	dry
કોશ	**kosh** (*m*)	dictionary
કોળિયો	**koḷiyo** (*m*)	morsel
ક્યારે	**kyāre** (*adv*)	when
ક્યાં	**kyā̃** (*adv*)	where
ક્ષમા	**kshamā** (*f*)	forgiveness
ક્ષિતિજ	**kshitij** (*n*)	horizon

ખટારો	**khaṭāro** (*m*)	lorry
ખડિયો	**khaḍiyo** (*m*)	inkpot
ખબર	**khabar** (*f*)	news
ખરચ	**kharach** (*n*)	expense
ખરવું	**kharvũ** (*vi*)	to fall down
ખરાબ	**kharāb** (*a*)	bad
ખરીદવું	**kharidvũ** (*vt*)	to purchase
ખરું	**kharũ** (*a*)	true
ખલાસ	**khalās** (*a*)	finished
ખલાસી	**khalāsi** (*m*)	sailor
ખસવું	**khasvũ** (*vi*)	to move
ખાડો	**khāḍo** (*m*)	pit
ખાણ	**khāṇ** (*f*)	mine
ખાતું	**khātũ** (*n*)	account
ખાનું	**khānũ** (*n*)	drawer
ખામી	**khāmi** (*f*)	mistake
ખાલી	**khāli** (*a*)	empty
ખાવું	**khāvũ** (*vt*)	to eat
ખાસ	**khās** (*a*)	special
ખાંડ	**khā̃ḍ** (*f*)	sugar
ખીણ	**khiṇ** (*f*)	valley
ખીલવું	**khilvũ** (*vi*)	to blossom
ખીલી	**khili** (*f*)	nail
ખીસું	**khisũ** (*n*)	pocket
ખીંટી	**khĩṭi** (*f*)	peg
ખુરશી	**khurshi** (*f*)	chair
ખુલાસો	**khulāso** (*m*)	explanation
ખુલ્લું	**khullũ** (*a*)	open
ખુશ	**khush** (*a*)	happy
ખુશામત	**khushāmat** (*f*)	flattery
ખૂણો	**khuṇo** (*m*)	corner
ખૂન	**khun** (*n*)	murder
ખૂબ	**khub** (*a*)	very much
ખૂલવું	**khulvũ** (*vi*)	to open
ખેતર	**khetar** (*n*)	farm
ખેતી	**kheti** (*f*)	farming
ખેલાડી	**khelāḍi** (*m*)	player
ખેંચવું	**khẼchvũ** (*vt*)	to pull
ખોટું	**khoṭũ** (*a*)	wrong
ખોદવું	**khodvũ** (*vt*)	to dig
ખોરાક	**khorāk** (*m*)	food
ખોળો	**khoḷo** (*m*)	lap

ગજવું	**gajvũ** (*n*)	pocket
ગરબડ	**garbaḍ** (*f*)	confusion; disorder
ગઢ	**gaḍh** (*m*)	fort
ગણતરી	**gaṇatri** (*f*)	counting
ગણવું	**gaṇvũ** (*vt*)	to count
ગણિત	**gaṇit** (*n*)	arithmetic
ગબડવું	**gabaḍvũ** (*vi*)	to roll, tumble
ગભરાવું	**gabhrāvũ** (*vi*)	to fear
ગમે તેમ	**game tem** (*adv*)	in any way
ગરજ	**garaj** (*f*)	need
ગરજવું	**garajvũ** (*vi*)	to roar
ગરબો	**garbo** (*m*)	folk dance with (usually) religious songs
ગરમ	**garam** (*a*)	hot
ગરીબ	**garib** (*a*)	poor
ગલી	**gali** (*f*)	narrow lane
ગલ્લો	**gallo** (*m*)	till (in a shop)
ગળ્યું	**gaḷyũ** (*a*)	sweet
ગંદકી	**gandki** (*f*)	rubbish
ગાડી	**gāḍi** (*f*)	car, train (depending on context)
ગાદલું	**gādlũ** (*n*)	mattress
ગામ	**gām** (*n*)	village
ગાયક	**gāyak** (*m*)	singer
ગાવું	**gāvũ** (*vt*)	to sing
ગાળ	**gāḷ** (*f*)	abuse
ગાંઠ	**gā̃ṭh** (*f*)	knot
ગાંડું	**gā̃ḍũ** (*a*)	mad
ગીરો	**giro** (*a*)	mortgaged
ગુજરાન	**gujrān** (*n*)	maintenance
ગુણ	**guṇ** (*m*)	virtue, quality
ગુણાકાર	**guṇākār** (*m*)	multiplication
ગુનો	**guno** (*m*)	offence, crime
ગુપચુપ	**gupchup** (*adv*)	quietly
ગુરૂ	**guru** (*m*)	master, teacher
ગુલામ	**gulām** (*m*)	slave
ગુંડો	**gunḍo** (*m*)	ruffian
ગુંદર	**gundar** (*m*)	gum
ગુમડું	**gumḍũ** (*n*)	abscess
ગોખવું	**gokhvũ** (*vt*)	to memorize by repetition
ગોટાળો	**goṭāḷo** (*m*)	confusion, misappropriation
ગોઠવવું	**goṭhavvũ** (*vt*)	to arrange
ગોળ	**goḷ** (*a*, *m*)	round; jaggery (coarse sugar)

ગોળી	**goḷi** (*f*)	tablet; bullet
જ્ઞાન	**gnān** (*n*)	knowledge

ઘટવું	**ghaṭvũ** (*vi*)	to decrease
ઘડપણ	**ghaḍpaṇ** (*n*)	old age
ઘડિયાળ	**ghaḍiyāḷ** (*f*) (*n*)	watch, clock
ઘણું	**ghaṇũ** (*a*)	much
ઘર	**ghar** (*n*)	house
ઘરાક	**gharāk** (*m*)	customer
ઘરેણું	**ghareṇũ** (*n*)	ornament
ઘસવું	**ghasvũ** (*vt*)	to rub
ઘંટ	**ghanṭ** (*m*)	bell
ઘા	**ghā** (*m*)	wound
ઘાસ	**ghās** (*n*)	grass
ઘી	**ghi** (*n*)	purified butter
ઘૂમટો	**ghumṭo** (*m*)	veil
ઘૂસવું	**ghusvũ** (*vi*)	to push in
ઘેન	**ghen** (*n*)	drowsiness
ઘેરવું	**ghervũ** (*vt*)	to surround

ચકાસવું	**chakāsvũ** (*vt*)	to scrutinize
ચડવું	**chaḍvũ** (*vi*, *t*)	to climb
ચણવું	**chaṇvũ** (*vt*)	to build
ચપ્પુ	**chappu** (*n*)	penknife
ચરબી	**charbi** (*f*)	fat
ચરવું	**charvũ** (*vi*)	to graze
ચશ્માં	**chashmā̃** (*n pl*)	glasses
ચહેરો	**chahero** (*m*)	face
ચાટવું	**chāṭvũ** (*vt*)	to lick
ચાદર	**chādar** (*f*)	bed sheet
ચાલવું	**chālvũ** (*vi*)	to walk
ચાવવું	**chāvvũ** (*vt*)	to chew
ચાવી	**chāvi** (*f*)	key
ચાંદો	**chā̃do** (*m*)	moon
ચિઠ્ઠી	**chiṭṭhi** (*f*)	chit
ચિતા	**chitā** (*f*)	funeral pyre
ચિત્ર	**chitra** (*n*)	picture
ચિંતા	**chintā** (*f*)	worry
ચીકણું	**chikṇũ** (*a*)	sticky
ચીતરવું	**chitarvũ** (*vt*)	to paint (picture)
ચીરવું	**chirvũ** (*vt*)	to split
ચુકાદો	**chukādo** (*m*)	decision

ચુપ	**chup** (*a*)	silent
ચુકવવું	**chukavvũ** (*vt*)	to pay
ચૂંટણી	**chũṭṇi** (*f*)	election
ચેપ	**chep** (*m*)	infection
ચોકીદાર	**chokidār** (*m*)	watchman
ચોક્કસ	**chokkas** (*a*)	definite
ચોખ્ખું	**chokkhũ** (*a*)	clean
ચોડવું	**choḍvũ** (*vt*)	to stick
ચોપડી	**chopḍi** (*f*)	book
ચોમાસું	**chomāsũ** (*n*)	monsoon
ચોર	**chor** (*m*)	thief
છત	**chhat** (*f*)	ceiling
છતાં	**chhatā̃** (*adv, conj*)	nevertheless
છત્રી	**chhatri** (*f*)	umbrella
છરો	**chharo** (*m*)	big knife
છલાંગ	**chhalā̃g** (*f*)	leap
છાનું	**chhānũ** (*a*)	secret
છાપખાનું	**chhāpkhānũ** (*n*)	printing press
છાપવું	**chhāpvũ** (*vt*)	to print
છાપું	**chhāpũ** (*n*)	newspaper
છાસ	**chhāsh** (*f*)	buttermilk
છીંક	**chhĩk** (*f*)	sneeze
છૂટવું	**chhuṭvũ** (*vi*)	to be free
છૂટાછેડા	**chhuṭāchheḍā** (*m pl*)	divorce
છેતરવું	**chhetarvũ** (*vt*)	to cheat
છોકરું	**chhokrũ** (*n*)	child
છોડ	**chhoḍ** (*m*)	plant
છોડવું	**chhoḍvũ** (*vt*)	to let go
જકાત	**jakāt** (*f*)	tax
જગત	**jagat** (*n*)	world
જગા	**jagā** (*f*)	place
જડવું	**jaḍvũ** (*vi*)	to find
જથ્થાબંધ	**jatthābandh** (*adv*)	wholesale
જનતા	**jantā** (*f*)	people
જનમ,જન્મ	**janam, janma** (*m*)	birth
જમણું	**jamṇũ** (*a*)	right (e.g. hand)
જમવું	**jamvũ** (*vt*)	to eat
જમીન	**jamin** (*f*)	land

રા	**jarā** (*a*, *adv*)	little
લદી	**jaldi** (*adv*)	quickly
વાબ	**javāb** (*m*)	answer
વું	**javũ** (*vi*)	to go
શ	**jash** (*m*)	fame
ગલ	**jãgal** (*n*)	forest
તુ	**jantu** (*n*)	insect
ગવું	**jāgvũ** (*vi*)	to awaken
ડું	**jāḍũ** (*a*)	fat
ણવું	**jāṇvũ** (*vt*)	to know
ણે	**jāṇe** (*adv*)	as if
દુ	**jādu** (*m*)	magic
નવર	**jānvar** (*n*)	animal
હેરખબર	**jāherkhabar** (*f*)	advertisement
તવું	**jitvũ** (*vt*)	to win
વવું	**jivvũ** (*vi*)	to live
ગાર	**jugār** (*m*)	gambling
દું	**judũ** (*a*)	separate, different
ઠું	**juṭhũ** (*a*)	false
નું	**junũ** (*a*)	old
ટલું	**jeṭlũ** (*a*)	as much
થી	**jethi** (*conj*)	whereas
મ	**jem** (*adv*)	in which way
વું	**jevũ** (*a*)	as it is
ખમ	**jokham** (*n*)	risk
ડણી	**joḍṇi** (*f*)	spelling
ડવું	**joḍvũ** (*vt*)	to join
ર	**jor** (*n*)	strength
વું	**jovũ** (*vt*)	to see
યાં	**jyā̃** (*adv*)	where
ગડો	**jhagḍo** (*m*)	quarrel
ટ	**jhaṭ** (*adv*)	quickly
ડપ	**jhaḍap** (*f*)	speed
ડો	**jhanḍo** (*m*)	flag
ડ	**jhāḍ** (*n*)	tree
ડુ	**jhāḍu** (*n*)	broomstick
ખું	**jhā̃khũ** (*a*)	dim, unclear
પો	**jhā̃po** (*m*)	gate
લવું	**jhilvũ** (*vt*)	to catch
ર	**jhEr** (*n*)	poison

ટકવું	**ṭakvũ** (*vt*)	to remain till last
ટક્કર	**ṭakkar** (*f*)	collision
ટપકવું	**ṭapakvũ** (*vi*)	to drip
ટપાલ	**ṭapāl** (*f*)	mail, post
ટાલ	**ṭāl** (*f*)	baldness
ટાપુ	**ṭāpu** (*m*)	island
ટાંકણી	**ṭā̃kṇi** (*f*)	pin
ટિંગાવું	**ṭĩgāvũ** (*vi*)	to be hung
ટીકડી	**ṭikḍi** (*f*)	tablet
ટીકા	**ṭikā** (*f*)	criticism
ટેકો	**ṭeko** (*m*)	support
ટોળું	**ṭoḷũ** (*n*)	crowd
ઠગ	**ṭhag** (*m*)	thug, rogue
ઠરાવ	**ṭharāv** (*m*)	resolution
ઠંડી	**ṭhanḍi** (*f*)	cold
ઠીક	**ṭhik** (*a*)	all right
ઠેકાણું	**ṭhekāṇũ** (*n*)	address (residence)
ડબો	**ḍabo** (*m*)	container
ડરવું	**ḍarvũ** (*vi*)	to fear, be afraid of
ડંખ	**ḍankh** (*m*)	sting
ડાઘ	**ḍāgh** (*m*)	blot
ડાબું	**ḍābũ** (*a*)	left (side)
ડુંગર	**ḍungar** (*m*)	mountain
ડોલ	**ḍol** (*f*)	bucket
ડોલવું	**ḍolvũ** (*vi*)	to swing
ડોસી	**ḍosi** (*f*)	old woman
ઢગલો	**ḍhaglo** (*m*)	heap
ઢાળ	**ḍhāḷ** (*m*)	slope
ઢાંકણું	**ḍhā̃kṇũ** (*n*)	lid
ઢાંકવું	**ḍhā̃kvũ** (*vt*)	to cover
ઢીંગલી	**ḍhingli** (*f*)	doll
ઢોળવું	**ḍhoḷvũ** (*vt*)	to spill
ઢોંગ	**ḍhOng** (*m*)	pretence
તક	**tak** (*f*)	opportunity
તકલીફ	**takliph** (*f*)	trouble
તડકો	**taḍko** (*m*)	sunshine
તપાસવું	**tapāsvũ** (*vt*)	to check
તબેલો	**tabelo** (*m*)	stable (for animals)

રત	**tarat** (*adv*)	immediately
રવું	**tarvũ** (*vt*)	to swim
હેવાર	**tahevār** (*m*)	festival (generally religious)
ળાવ	**taḷāv** (*n*)	small lake
ળેટી	**taḷeṭi** (*f*)	foot of mountain
ગી	**tangi** (*f*)	scarcity
જું	**tājũ** (*a*)	fresh
ર	**tār** (*m*)	yarn; telegram
રીખ	**tārikh** (*f*)	date
રો	**tāro** (*m*)	star
વ	**tāv** (*m*)	fever
ળી	**tāḷi** (*f*)	clapping
ળું	**tāḷũ** (*n*)	padlock
ખું	**tikhũ** (*a*)	hot (taste)
ર	**tir** (*n*)	arrow; bank (of river)
ટવું	**tuṭvũ** (*vi*)	to break
જ	**tej** (*n*)	light (of moon, sun, etc.)
લ	**tel** (*n*)	oil
યાર	**taiyār** (*a*)	ready
ડવું	**toḍvũ** (*vt*)	to break

ડ	**thaḍ** (*n*)	trunk (of tree)
વું	**thavũ** (*vi*)	to become
કવું	**thākvũ** (*vi*)	to be tired
ળી	**thāḷi** (*f*)	plate
ડું	**thoḍũ** (*a*)	little
ભવું	**thobhvũ** (*vi*)	to stop

ગો	**dago** (*m*)	treachery
યા	**dayā** (*f*)	compassion
દ	**darad** (*n*)	pain
રિયો	**dariyo** (*m*)	sea, ocean
હીં	**dahĩ** (*n*)	yoghurt, curds
ડ	**danḍ** (*m*)	penalty
ખલો	**dākhlo** (*m*)	example
ટવું	**dāṭvũ** (*vt*)	to bury
દર	**dādar** (*m*)	staircase
ન	**dān** (*n*)	charity
બવું	**dābvũ** (*vt*)	to press
રૂ	**dāru** (*m*)	wine, liquor; gunpowder
તિયો	**dā̃tiyo** (*m*)	comb
વસ	**divas** (*m*)	day

દિશા	**dishā** (*f*)	direction
દીકરો	**dikro** (*m*)	son
દીકરી	**dikri** (*f*)	daughter
દીવાસળી	**divāsaḷi** (*f*)	matchstick
દીવો	**divo** (*m*)	lamp
દુકાન	**dukān** (*f*)	shop
દુકાળ	**dukāḷ** (*m*)	famine
દુખવું	**dukhvũ** (*vi*)	to (feel) pain
દુનિયા	**duniyā** (*f*)	world
દૂધ	**dudh** (*n*)	milk
દૂર	**dur** (*a*)	far off, distant
દેવ	**dev** (*m*)	god
દેશ	**desh** (*m*)	country
દોડવું	**doḍvũ** (*vi*)	to run
દોરવું	**dorvũ** (*vt*)	to draw (lines), paint (picture)
દોરી	**dori** (*f*)	string
ધક્કો	**dhakko** (*m*)	push, jolt
ધર્મ,ધરમ	**dharma, dharam** (*m*)	religion
ધંધો	**dhandho** (*m*)	business
ધાતુ	**dhātu** (*f*)	mineral
ધારવું	**dhārvũ** (*vt*)	to suppose
ધીમું	**dhimũ** (*a*)	slow
ધીરજ	**dhiraj** (*f*)	patience
ધુમાડો	**dhumāḍo** (*m*)	smoke
ધુમ્મસ	**dhummas** (*n*)	fog
ધુળ	**dhuḷ** (*f*)	dust
ધોબી	**dhobi** (*m*)	washerman
ધોવું	**dhovũ** (*vt*)	to wash
ધ્રુજવું	**dhrujvũ** (*vi*)	to tremble
નકલ	**nakal** (*f*)	copy
નકશો	**naksho** (*m*)	map
નકામું	**nakāmũ** (*a*)	useless
નજર	**najar** (*f*)	sight
નટ	**naṭ** (*m*)	actor
નથી	**nathi** (*vi*)	to be (negative, present tense), n
નદી	**nadi** (*f*)	river
નફો	**napho** (*m*)	profit
નમવું	**namvũ** (*vt*)	to bow down
નમૂનો	**namuno** (*m*)	sample
નરમ	**naram** (*a*)	soft

વું	**navũ** (*a*)	new
સીબ	**nasib** (*n*)	fate
ાખવું	**nākhvũ** (*vt*)	to throw
ાચવું	**nāchvũ** (*vi*)	to dance
ાટક	**nāṭak** (*n*)	play, drama
ાડી	**nāḍi** (*f*)	pulse
ાનું	**nānũ** (*a*)	small
ામ	**nām** (*n*)	name
ાસ્તો	**nāsto** (*m*)	breakfast, snacks
ાહવું	**nāhvũ** (*vi*)	to bath, bathe
ેકાસ	**nikās** (*f*)	export
ેચોવવું	**nichovvũ** (*vt*)	to squeeze
ેયમ	**niyam** (*m*)	rule
ેયમિત	**niymit** (*a*)	regular
ેરાંત	**nirā̃t** (*f*)	leisure
ેશાળ	**nishāḷ** (*f*)	school
ીતિ	**niti** (*f*)	morality
ુકસાન	**nuksān** (*n*)	loss
ોકર	**nokar** (*m*)	servant
ોંધવું	**nÕdhvũ** (*vt*)	to note
યાય	**nyāy** (*m*)	justice
કડવું	**pakaḍvũ** (*vt*)	to hold
ગાર	**pagār** (*m*)	salary
ચવું	**pachvũ** (*vi*)	to be digested
ટ્ટો	**paṭṭo** (*m*)	strap
ડવું	**paḍvũ** (*vi*)	to fall
ડોશી	**paḍoshi** (*m*)	neighbour
ણ	**paṇ** (*conj*)	but
તંગ	**patang** (*m, f*)	kite
થરો	**pathro** (*m*)	stone
રણવું	**paraṇvũ** (*vt*)	to marry
રસેવો	**parsevo** (*m*)	perspiration
રીક્ષા	**parikshā** (*f*)	examination
ર્વત	**parvat** (*m*)	mountain
લળવું	**palaḷvũ** (*vi*)	to be wet
વન	**pavan** (*m*)	wind
હેરવું	**pahervũ** (*vt*)	to wear
હેલાં	**pahelā̃** (*adv*)	formerly
ખી	**pankhi** (*n*)	bird
ખો	**pankho** (*m*)	fan
ાકવું	**pākvũ** (*vi*)	to be ripe

પાછળ	**pāchaḷ** (*adv*)	behind
પાછું	**pāchhũ** (*adv*)	again
પાણી	**pāṇi** (*n*)	water
પાનું	**pānũ** (*n*)	page (of a book)
પાપ	**pāp** (*n*)	sin
પાસે	**pāse** (*prep*, *adv*)	near, in possession of
પાંખ	**pā̃kh** (*f*)	wing
પિયર	**piyar** (*n*)	home of married woman's parent
પીગળવું	**pigaḷvũ** (*vi*)	to melt
પીણું	**piṇũ** (*n*)	drink
પીરસવું	**pirasvũ** (*vt*)	to serve food
પીવું	**pivũ** (*vt*)	to drink
પુણ્ય	**puṇya** (*a*)	righteous
પુરુષ	**purush** (*m*)	male
પુલ	**pul** (*m*)	bridge
પૂંછડી	**pũchhḍi** (*f*)	tail
પૂછવું	**puchhvũ** (*vt*)	to ask
પૂજા	**pujā** (*f*)	worship
પૂનમ	**punam** (*f*)	full moon day
પૂરું	**purũ** (*a*)	complete
પૃથ્વી	**pruthvi** (*f*)	earth
પેટી	**peṭi** (*f*)	box
પૈસો	**paiso** (*m*)	money
પોચું	**pochũ** (*a*)	soft
પ્રવાસ	**pravās** (*m*)	journey
પ્રવેશ	**pravesh** (*m*)	entry
પ્રાણ	**prāṇ** (*m*)	soul
પ્રામાણિક	**prāmāṇik** (*a*)	honest
પ્રાર્થના	**prārthanā** (*f*)	prayer
પ્રેમ	**prem** (*m*)	love
ફરક	**pharak** (*m*)	change
ફરવું	**pharvũ** (*vi*)	to walk, stroll
ફરિયાદ	**phariyād** (*f*)	complaint
ફળ	**phaḷ** (*n*)	fruit
ફાટવું	**phāṭvũ** (*vi*)	to be torn
ફાયદો	**phāydo** (*m*)	advantage
ફાંસી	**phā̃si** (*f*)	hanging
ફીણ	**phiṇ** (*n*)	foam
ફુગાવો	**phugāvo** (*m*)	inflation
ફૂલ	**phul** (*n*)	flower
ફૂંકવું	**phũkvũ** (*vt*)	to blow

બગાસું	**bagāsũ** (*n*)	yawn
બચવું	**bachvũ** (*vi*)	to be saved
બજાર	**bajār** (*f*)	bazaar
બધું	**badhũ** (*a*)	all
બનવું	**banvũ** (*vi*)	to happen
બનાવટી	**banāvṭi** (*a*)	fabricated, counterfeit
બરાબર	**barābar** (*adv*)	OK, all right, correct
બહાર	**bahār** (*adv*)	out
બહુ	**bahu** (*a*)	much
બળવું	**baḷvũ** (*vi*)	to burn
બંદર	**bandar** (*n*)	port
બંધ	**bandh** (*a*) (*m*)	closed, dam
બાકી	**bāki** (*a*)	remaining
બાગ	**bāg** (*m*)	garden, park
બાટલી	**bāṭli** (*f*)	bottle
બાબત	**bābat** (*f*)	matter
બાંધવું	**bā̃dhvũ** (*vt*)	to bind
બી	**bi** (*n*)	seed
બુદ્ધિ	**buddhi** (*f*)	intellect
બૂમ	**bum** (*f*)	shout
બેટ	**beṭ** (*m*)	island
બેસવું	**besvũ** (*vi*)	to sit
બોલવું	**bolvũ** (*vt*)	to speak
બોલી	**boli** (*f*)	dialect
ભગત	**bhagat** (*m*)	devotee
ભજન	**bhajan** (*n*)	prayer song
ભણવું	**bhaṇvũ** (*vt*)	to study
ભરતી	**bharti** (*f*)	tide
ભરવું	**bharvũ** (*vt*)	to fill, to pay
ભલું	**bhalũ** (*a*)	kind
ભલે	**bhale** (*int*)	well, fine, OK
ભવિષ્ય	**bhavishya** (*n*)	future
ભાગ	**bhāg** (*m*)	part
ભાગવું	**bhāgvũ** (*vi*)	to run away; to divide (maths)
ભાન	**bhān** (*n*)	consciousness, sense
ભારત	**bhārat** (*m*)	India
ભારે	**bhāre** (*a*)	heavy
ભાવ	**bhāv** (*m*)	feeling; rate
ભાવવું	**bhāvvũ** (*vi*)	to like (used only for food)
ભાષણ	**bhāshaṇ** (*n*)	speech (lecture)
ભાષા	**bhāshā** (*f*)	language

ભીખ	**bhikh** (*f*)	begging
ભીડ	**bhiḍ** (*f*)	crowd
ભીનું	**bhinũ** (*a*)	wet
ભૂખ	**bhukh** (*f*)	hunger
ભૂત	**bhut** (*n*)	ghost
ભૂલ	**bhul** (*f*)	mistake
ભૂલવું	**bhulvũ** (*vi*)	to forget
ભેટ	**bheṭ** (*f*)	gift
ભોમિયો	**bhomiyo** (*m*)	guide
ભોંય	**bhÕy** (*f*)	ground
મજબૂત	**majbut** (*a*)	strong
મજા	**majā** (*f*)	enjoyment
મજાક	**majāk** (*f*)	joke
મજૂર	**majur** (*m*)	labourer
મત	**mat** (*m*)	opinion, vote
મથક	**mathak** (*n*)	headquarters
મથાળું	**mathāḷũ** (*n*)	heading
મફત	**maphat** (*adv*)	free of charge
મરજી	**marji** (*f*)	wish
મરવું	**marvũ** (*vi*)	to die
મલમ	**malam** (*m*)	ointment
મહેનત	**mahenat** (*f*)	effort
મહેમાન	**mahemān** (*m*)	guest
મહેલ	**mahel** (*m*)	palace
મળવું	**maḷvũ** (*vi*)	to meet; to find
મંડપ	**manḍap** (*m*)	pendal, large tent-like structure
મંદિર	**mandir** (*n*)	temple
મંદી	**mandi** (*f*)	recession
માટી	**māṭi** (*f*)	earth
માણસ	**māṇas** (*m*)	person
માન	**mān** (*n*)	respect
માપ	**māp** (*n*)	measure
માફ	**māph** (*a*)	forgiven
માફક	**māphak** (*a*)	agreeable
માયા	**māyā** (*f*)	illusion, attachment
મારવું	**mārvũ** (*vt*)	to beat
માલ	**māl** (*m*)	goods
માલિક	**mālik** (*m*)	master
માસિક	**māsik** (*a*) (*n*)	monthly; monthly magazine
માળી	**māḷi** (*m*)	gardener
માંદગી	**mā̃dgi** (*f*)	illness

માંસ	**mā̃s** (*n*)	meat, flesh
મીઠાઈ	**miṭhāi** (*f*)	sweets
મીણ	**miṇ** (*n*)	wax
મુક્તિ	**mukti** (*f*)	freedom
મુખ્ય	**mukhya** (*a*)	chief
મુદત	**mudat** (*f*)	limit (time)
મુલાકાત	**mulākāt** (*f*)	interview, visit
મૂકવું	**mukvũ** (*vt*)	to put, to leave
મૂડી	**muḍi** (*f*)	capital (investment)
મૂરખ	**murakh** (*a*)	foolish
મૂળ	**muḷ** (*n*)	root
મૂંઝવણ	**mũjhvaṇ** (*f*)	embarrassment
મેદાન	**medān** (*n*)	open ground
મેલ	**mEl** (*m*)	dirt
મેળવવું	**meḷavvũ** (*vt*)	to obtain
મોકલવું	**mokalvũ** (*vt*)	to send
મોચી	**mochi** (*m*)	cobbler
મોટું	**moṭũ** (*a*)	big
મોડું	**moḍũ** (*a*)	late
મોત	**mot** (*n*)	death
મોંઘવારી	**mÕghvāri** (*f*)	increasing prices
મોંઘું	**mÕghũ** (*a*)	costly
યજમાન	**yajmān** (*m*)	host
યાદ	**yād** (*f*)	recollection
યુક્તિ	**yukti** (*f*)	trick
યુવક	**yuvak** (*m*)	youth (male)
યોજવું	**yojvũ** (*vt*)	to plan
રકમ	**rakam** (*f*)	sum
રખડવું	**rakhaḍvũ** (*vi*)	to wander
રજા	**rajā** (*f*)	permission, leave, holiday
રજૂ	**raju** (*a*)	presented
રડવું	**raḍvũ** (*vi*)	to weep
રણ	**raṇ** (*n*)	desert
રમવું	**ramvũ** (*vi*)	to play
રસ	**ras** (*m*)	fruit juice; interest
રસોઈ	**rasoi** (*f*)	cooking
રસ્તો	**rasto** (*m*)	road
રહેવું	**rahevũ** (*vi*)	to stay
રંગવું	**rangvũ** (*vt*)	to colour
રાખવું	**rākhvũ** (*vt*)	to keep

રાજ/રાજધાની	**rāj** (*n*)/**rājdhāni** (*f*)	kingdom/capital
રિવાજ	**rivāj** (*m*)	custom
રીસાવું	**risāvũ** (*vi*)	to be displeased
રીત	**rit** (*f*)	method
રૂઆબ	**ruāb** (*m*)	imposing appearance
રૂ	**ru** (*n*)	cotton
રૂપ	**rup** (*n*)	beauty
રૂમાલ	**rumāl** (*m*)	handkerchief
રોકડ	**rokaḍ** (*a*)	cash
રોકવું	**rokvũ** (*vt*)	to stop; engage; invest
રોજ	**roj** (*adv*)	daily
લખવું	**lakhvũ** (*vt*)	to write
લગ્ન	**lagna** (*n*)	marriage
લટકવું	**laṭakvũ** (*vi*)	to hang
લડવું	**laḍvũ** (*vi*)	to fight
લપસવું	**lapasvũ** (*vi*)	to slip
લલચાવું	**lalchāvũ** (*vi*)	to be tempted
લશ્કર	**lashkar** (*n*)	army
લાકડું	**lākḍũ** (*n*)	wood
લાગણી	**lāgṇi** (*f*)	feeling
લાગવું	**lāgvũ** (*vi*)	to feel
લાત	**lāt** (*f*)	kick
લાવવું	**lāvvũ** (*vt*)	to bring
લાંબુ	**lāmbũ** (*a*)	long
લિપિ	**lipi** (*f*)	script
લીટી	**liṭi** (*f*)	line
લૂંટવું	**lũṭvũ** (*vt*)	to rob
લેવું	**levũ** (*vt*)	to take
લોક	**lok** (*m*)	people
લોહી	**lohi** (*n*)	blood
વકીલ	**vakil** (*m*)	lawyer
વખત	**vakhat** (*m*)	time
વખાણ	**vakhāṇ** (*n*)	praise
વગેરે	**vagere** (*adv*)	et cetera
વચન	**vachan** (*n*)	promise
વચ્ચે	**vachche** (*prep*, *adv*)	in between
વજન	**vajan** (*n*)	weight
વઢવું	**vaḍhvũ** (*vt*)	to scold
વતન	**vatan** (*n*)	motherland, fatherland
વધારે	**vadhāre** (*a*)	more

વર	**var** (*m*)	bridegroom
વરસ	**varas** (*n*)	year
વરસાદ	**varsād** (*m*)	rain
વર્ણન	**varṇan** (*n*)	description
વસવું	**vasvũ** (*vi*)	to dwell
વસ્તુ	**vastu** (*f*)	thing
વહાણ	**vahāṇ** (*n*)	ship
વહીવટ	**vahivaṭ** (*m*)	administration
વહુ	**vahu** (*f*)	bride, wife
વહેમ	**vhem** (*m*)	doubt
વહેલું	**vhelũ** (*adv*)	early
વળતર	**vaḷtar** (*n*)	discount
વાળવું	**vāḷvũ** (*vi*)	to bend
વળી	**vaḷi** (*adv*)	and, also
વાગવું	**vāgvũ** (*vi*)	to be played (instrument), to be struck
વાડી	**vāḍi** (*f*)	orchard
વાત	**vāt** (*f*)	story
વારો	**vāro** (*m*)	turn
વાલી	**vāli** (*m*)	guardian
વાંકું	**vā̃kũ** (*a*)	not straight
વાંચવું	**vā̃chvũ** (*vt*)	to read
વાંધો	**vā̃dho** (*m*)	objection
વિકસવું	**vikasvũ** (*vi*)	to develop
વિચારવું	**vichārvũ** (*vt*)	to think
વિજ્ઞાન	**vignān** (*n*)	science
વિદ્યા	**vidyā** (*f*)	learning, knowledge
વિધવા	**vidhvā** (*f*)	widow
વિનંતી	**vinanti** (*f*)	request
વિવેક	**vivek** (*m*)	modesty; etiquette
વિશ્વાસ	**vishvās** (*m*)	confidence
વીજળી	**vijḷi** (*f*)	lightning, electricity
વીણવું	**viṇvũ** (*vt*)	to pick
વીમો	**vimo** (*m*)	insurance
વેચવું	**vechvũ** (*vt*)	to sell
વેપાર	**vepār** (*m*)	trade
વેર	**ver** (*n*)	animosity
વૈદ	**vaid** (*m*)	physician
વ્યસન	**vyasan** (*n*)	addiction
શકવું	**shakvũ**	able (*inf*, to be able)
શક્તિ	**shakti** (*f*)	strength

શણગારવું	**shaṇgārvũ** (*vt*)	to decorate
શબ	**shab** (*n*)	corpse
શબ્દ	**shabda** (*m*)	word, sound
શરત	**sharāt** (*f*)	race; bet; condition
શરમ	**sharam** (*f*)	modesty, shame
શરીર	**sharir** (*n*)	body
શરૂઆત	**sharuāt** (*f*)	beginning
શહેર	**shaher** (*n*)	city
શંકા	**shankā** (*f*)	doubt
શાંત	**shānt** (*a*)	quiet
શિકાર	**shikār** (*m*)	hunting
શિખર	**shikhar** (*n*)	peak
શિખામણ	**shikhāmaṇ** (*f*)	advice
શિયાળો	**shiyāḷo** (*m*)	winter
શીખવવું	**shikhavvũ** (*vt*)	to teach
શીખવું	**shikhvũ** (*vi*)	to learn
શીશી	**shishi** (*f*)	bottle
શુભ	**shubh** (*a*)	auspicious
શું	**shũ** (*pron*)	what
શેકવું	**shekvũ** (*vt*)	to bake
શોક	**shok** (*m*)	grief
શોખ	**shOkh** (*m*)	hobby, liking
શ્રી	**shri** (*a*)	Mr
શ્વાસ	**shvās** (*m*)	breathing
સખત	**sakhat** (*a*)	hard
સગવડ	**sagvaḍ** (*f*)	convenience, comfort
સજા	**sajā** (*f*)	punishment
સત્તા	**sattā** (*f*)	authority
સભા	**sabhā** (*f*)	meeting
સભ્ય	**sabhya** (*m*)	member
સમજણ	**samjaṇ** (*f*)	understanding
સમય	**samay** (*m*)	time
સમાચાર	**samāchār** (*m*)	news
સમાજ	**samāj** (*m*)	society
સમાધાન	**samādhān** (*n*)	settlement (of dispute)
સરકાર	**sarkār** (*f*)	government
સરખાવવું	**sarkhāvvũ** (*vt*)	to compare
સરખું	**sarkhũ** (*a*)	equal
સરઘસ	**sarghas** (*n*)	procession
સરનામું	**sarnāmũ** (*n*)	address
સરસ	**saras** (*a*)	very good

સરહદ	**sarhad** (*f*)	boundary
સરોવર	**sarovar** (*n*)	lake
સલામત	**salāmat** (*a*)	safe
સલાહ	**salāh** (*f*)	advice
સવાર	**savār** (*f*) (*n*)	morning
સવાલ	**savāl** (*m*)	question
સહન	**sahan** (*n*)	endurance
સહાય	**sahāy** (*f*)	help
સહી	**sahi** (*f*)	signature
સહેજ	**sahej** (*a*)	little
સળગવું	**saḷagvũ** (*vt*)	to burn
સંગીત	**sangit** (*n*)	music
સંતાન	**santān** (*n*)	progeny
સંતોષ	**santosh** (*m*)	satisfaction
સંદેશો	**sandesho** (*m*)	message
સંબંધ	**sambandh** (*m*)	connection
સંસાર	**samsar** (*m*)	domestic life
સાચું	**sāchũ** (*a*)	true, correct
સાદું	**sādũ** (*a*)	simple
સાધન	**sādhan** (*n*)	resources, tools
સાધુ	**sādhu** (*m*)	saint
સાફ	**sāph** (*a*)	clean
સામું	**sāmũ** (*a, adv*)	opposite
સારું	**sārũ** (*a*)	good
સાવચેત	**sāvchet** (*a*)	cautious
સાહસ	**sāhas** (*n*)	adventure, rashness
સાહેબ	**sāheb** (*m*)	lord; honorific address
સાંજ	**sā̃j** (*f*)	evening
સીધું	**sidhũ** (*a*)	straight, direct
સુખ	**sukh** (*n*)	happiness
સુધરવું	**sudharvũ** (*vi*)	to improve
સુંદર	**sundar** (*a*)	beautiful
સુંવાળું	**sũvāḷũ** (*a*)	smooth
સૂકું	**sukũ** (*a*)	dry
સૂરજ	**suraj** (*m*)	sun
સૂવું	**suvũ** (*vi*)	to sleep
સૂંઘવું	**sũghvũ** (*vt*)	to smell
સેવા	**sevā** (*f*)	service
સ્ત્રી	**stri** (*f*)	woman, wife
સ્થાનિક	**sthanik** (*a*)	local
સ્નાન	**snān** (*n*)	bathing, bath
સ્વતંત્ર	**svatantra** (*a*)	independent

સ્વપ્ન	**svapna** (*n*)	dream
સ્વાદ	**svād** (*m*)	taste
સ્વાર્થ	**svārtha** (*m*)	self-interest
સ્વીકારવું	**svikārvũ** (*vt*)	to accept
હક	**hak** (*m*)	right
હકીકત	**hakikat** (*f*)	fact
હઠ	**haṭh** (*f*)	obstinacy, stubbornness
હડતાળ	**haḍtāḷ** (*f*)	strike
હથિયાર	**hathiyār** (*n*)	weapon
હમણાં	**hamṇā̃** (*adv*)	now
હમેશાં	**hameshā̃** (*adv*)	always
હરકત	**harkat** (*f*)	obstruction, objection
હરખ	**harakh** (*m*)	joy
હલકું	**halkũ** (*a*)	light
હલ્લો	**hallo** (*m*)	attack
હવા	**havā** (*f*)	wind, air
હવે	**have** (*adv*)	now (onwards)
હસવું	**hasvũ** (*vi*)	to laugh
હાજર	**hājar** (*a*)	present
હાર	**hār** (*m*)	garland, necklace
હારવું	**hārvũ** (*vi*)	to be defeated
હાંફવું	**hā̃phvũ** (*vi*)	to be breathless
હિસાબ	**hisāb** (*m*)	account
હિમ્મત	**himmat** (*f*)	courage
હિંસા	**hinsā** (*f*)	violence
હીરો	**hiro** (*m*)	diamond
હીંચકો	**hĩchko** (*m*)	swing
હુકમ	**hukam** (*m*)	order
હુલ્લડ	**hullaḍ** (*n*)	disturbance, riot
હેત	**het** (*n*)	love
હેતુ	**hetu** (*m*)	reason
હૈયું	**haiyũ** (*n*)	heart
હોડી	**hoḍi** (*f*)	boat
હોવું	**hovũ** (*vi*)	to be

Thematic Gujarati–English vocabulary

Days of the week અઠવાડિયાના દિવસો

રવિવાર	Sunday	**ravivār**
સોમવાર	Monday	**somvār**
મંગળવાર	Tuesday	**mangaḷvār**
બુધવાર	Wednesday	**budhvār**
ગુરુવાર	Thursday	**guruvār**
શુક્રવાર	Friday	**shukravār**
શનિવાર	Saturday	**shanivār**

Time સમય

પળ	moment	**paḷ** (*f*)	સાંજ	evening	**sā̃j** (*f*)
સેકંડ	second	**sekanḍ** (*f*)	અઠવાડિયું	week	**aṭhvāḍiyũ** (*n*)
મિનિટ	minute	**miniṭ** (*f*)	પખવાડિયું	fortnight	**pakhvaḍiyũ** (*n*)
કલાક	hour	**kalāk** (*m*)	મહિનો	month	**mahino** (*m*)
દિવસ	day	**divas** (*m*)	વરસ	year	**varas** (*n*)
રાત	night	**rāt** (*f*)	પુનમ	full moon day	**punam** (*f*)
સવાર	morning	**savār** (*f*)	અમાસ	no moon day	**amās** (*f*)
બપોર	noon	**bapor** (*f*)			

Seasons and weather ઋતુઓ અને હવામાન

આબોહવા	climate	**ābohavā**
ઉનાળો	summer	**unāḷo**
કરા	hailstones	**karā**
ગાજવીજ	thunder	**gājvij**
ચોમાસું	monsoon	**chomāsũ**

તડકો	sunshine	**taḍko**
તોફાન	storm	**tophān**
ધુમ્મસ	fog	**dhummas**
પવન	wind	**pavan**
પાનખર	autumn	**pānkhar**
વરસાદ	rain	**varsād**
વસંત	spring	**vasant**
વાતાવરણ	atmosphere	**vātāvaraṇ**
વીજળી	lightning	**vijḷi**
શિયાળો	winter	**shiyāḷo**
હિમ, ઝાકળ	frost	**him, jhākaḷ**
મહત્તમ	maximum	**mahattam**
અલ્પતમ	minimum	**alpatam**
વાદળ	cloud	**vādaḷ**

Directions દિશાઓ

ઉત્તર	north	**uttar**
ઈશાન	north-east	**ishān**
પૂર્વ	east	**purva**
અગ્નિ	south-east	**agni**
દક્ષિણ	south	**dakshiṇ**
નૈઋત્ય	south-west	**nairutya**
પશ્ચિમ	west	**pashchim**
વાયવ્ય	north-west	**vāyavya**

Family કુટુંબ

કાકા	paternal uncle	**kākā**
કાકી	paternal aunt	**kāki**
જમાઈ	son-in-law	**jamāi**
દીકરી	daughter	**dikri**
દીકરો,પુત્ર	son	**dikro, putra**
પતિ, વર	husband	**pati, var**
પિતા,બાપા	father	**pitā, bāpā**
ફૂઆ	husband of paternal aunt	**phuā**
બહેન	sister	**bahen**
બા	mother	**bā**
ભત્રીજી	cousin (brother's daughter)	**bhatriji**

ત્રીજો	cousin (brother's son)	**bhatrijo**
ઈ	brother	**bhāi**
ણેજ	cousin (sister's son/daughter)	**bhāṇej**
ભી	brother's wife	**bhābhi**
મા	maternal uncle	**māmā**
મી	wife of maternal uncle	**māmi**
સા	husband of maternal aunt	**māsā**
સી	maternal aunt	**māsi**
હુ, પત્ની	wife	**vahu, patni**
હુ,પુત્રવધૂ	daughter-in-law	**vahu, putrāvadhu**
ગું	relative	**sagũ**
સરા	father-in-law	**sasrā**
વકા	step (father, mother, etc.)	**sāvkā**
સુ	mother-in-law	**sāsu**
ળી	wife's sister	**sāḷi**
ળો	wife's brother	**sāḷo**

he body શરીર

ગૂઠો	thumb	**anguṭho** (*m*)
ખ	eye	**ā̃kh** (*f*)
ંગળી	finger	**ā̃gḷi** (*f*)
પાળ	forehead	**kapāḷ** (*n*)
મર/કેડ	waist	**kamar/keḍ** (*f*)
રોડ	spine	**karoḍ** (*f*)
ડું	wrist	**kā̃ḍũ** (*n*)
ન	ear	**kān** (*m*)
ણી	elbow	**koṇi** (*f*)
ભો	shoulder	**khabho** (*m*)
ળું	throat	**gaḷũ** (*n*)
લ	cheek	**gāl** (*m*)
ૂંટણ	knee	**ghũṭaṇ** (*n*)
ટી	ankle	**ghũṭi** (*f*)
હેરો	face	**chahero** (*m*)
ામડી	skin	**chāmḍi** (*f*)
તી	chest	**chhāti** (*f*)
ભ	tongue	**jibh** (*f*)
ક	neck	**ḍok** (*f*)
ઢી	chin, beard	**dāḍhi** (*f*)
ત	tooth	**dā̃t** (*m*)
ખ	nail	**nakh** (*m*)

નાક	nose	**nāk** (*n*)
નાડી	pulse	**nāḍi** (*f*)
પગ	leg	**pag** (*m*)
પેટ	stomach	**peṭ** (*n*)
પાની	heel	**pāni** (*f*)
પાંપણ	eyelash	**pā̃paṇ** (*f*)
પાંસળી	rib	**pā̃sḷi** (*f*)
પીઠ	back	**piṭh** (*f*)
પીંડી	calf	**pinḍi** (*f*)
પોપચું	eyelid	**popchũ** (*n*)
ફેફસું	lung	**phephsũ** (*n*)
બગલ	armpit	**bagal** (*f*)
ભ્રમર	eyebrow	**bhramar** (*f*)
મગજ	brain	**magaj** (*n*)
મૂછ	moustache	**muchh** (*f*)
માથું	head	**māthũ** (*n*)
માંસ	flesh	**mā̃s** (*n*)
મોં	mouth	**mÕ** (*n*)
લોહી	blood	**lohi** (*n*)
વાળ	hair	**vāḷ** (*m*)
શરીર	body	**sharir** (*n*)
સાથળ	thigh	**sāthaḷ** (*m*)
હથેળી	palm	**hatheḷi** (*f*)
હૃદય	heart	**hruday** (*n*)
હાડકું	bone	**hāḍkũ** (*n*)
હાથ	hand	**hāth** (*m*)
હોઠ	lip	**hoṭh** (*m*)

Illnesses માંદગી

અપચો	indigestion	**apacho**
આધાશીશી	migraine	**ādhāshishi**
ઉધરસ	cough	**udḥras**
ઊલટી	nausea	**ulṭi**
ઓરી	measles	**Ori**
કબજીયાત	constipation	**kabajiyāt**
ક્ષય	tuberculosis	**kshya**
ઝાડા	diarrhoea	**jhāḍā**
ટાઢીયો તાવ	malaria	**tāḍhiyo tāv**
તાવ	fever	**tāv**
દવા	medicine	**davā**

વાખાનું	surgery, clinic	**davākhānũ**
ખાવો	pain	**dukhāvo**
રડો	dysentery	**marḍo**
થાનો દુખાવો	headache	**māthāno dukhāvo**
કવો, પક્ષઘાત	paralysis	**lakvo, pakshghāt**
રદી	cold	**shardi**
દયરોગનો હુમલો	heart attack	**hrudayrogno humlo**
મ	asthma	**dam**
ધિવા	arthritis	**sandhivā**
રોગ	cancer	**karkrog**
ધુમેહ	diabetes	**madhumeh**

Professions ધંધાદારી

ડિયો	mason	**kaḍio**
ર્મચારી	worker	**karmachāri**
સાઈ	butcher	**kasāi**
રકુન	clerk	**kārkun**
ડૂત	farmer	**kheḍut**
ાયક	singer	**gāyak** (*m*),
ાયિકા		**gāyikā** (*f*)
ત્રકાર	painter	**chitrakār**
દુગર	magician	**jādugar**
શી	astrologer	**joshi**
વેરી	diamond merchant	**jhaveri**
ક્ટર	doctor	**ḍokṭar**
ર્જી	tailor	**darji**
ધવાળો	milkman	**dudhvāḷo**
બણ/ધોબી	washerwoman/man	**dhobaṇ/dhobi**
ટ	actor	**naṭ**
ટી	actress	**naṭi**
ર્તક	dancer	**nartak** (*m*),
ર્તિકા		**nartikā** (*f*)
ત્રકાર	journalist	**patrakār**
ફેસર પ્રાધ્યાપક	professor	**prophesor** **prādhyāpak**
જૂર	labourer	**majur**
છીમાર	fisherman	**māchhimār**
ળી	gardener	**māḷi**
ચી	cobbler	**mochi**
ોઇયો	cook	**rasoio**

રંગારો	dyer	**rāgāro**
લુહાર	blacksmith	**luhār**
લેખક	writer	**lekhak** (*m*),
લેખિકા		**lekhikā** (*f*)
વકીલ	lawyer	**vakil**
વિદ્યાર્થી	student	**vidyārthi** (*m*),
વિદ્યાર્થિની		**vidyārthini** (*f*)
શિક્ષક	teacher	**shikshak** (*m*),
શિક્ષિકા		**shikshikā** (*f*)
શિલ્પી	sculptor	**shilpi**
સુથાર	carpenter	**suthār**
સોની	goldsmith	**soni**
હજામ	barber	**hajām**

Birds and animals પક્ષીઓ અને પ્રાણીઓ

ઊંટ	camel	**ū̃ṭ** (*n*)
કબૂતર	pigeon	**kabutar** (*n*)
કરચલો	crab	**karachlo** (*m*)
કાગડો	crow	**kāgḍo** (*m*),
કાગડી		**kāgḍi** (*f*)
કાચબો	tortoise	**kāchbo** (*m*),
કાચબી		**kāchbi** (*f*)
કૂતરો	dog	**kutro** (*m*),
કૂતરી		**kutri** (*f*),
કૂતરું		**kutrũ** (*n*)
કોયલ	cuckoo	**koyal** (*f*)
ગધેડો	donkey	**gadhẹḍo** (*m*),
ગધેડી		**gadhẹḍi** (*f*),
ગધેડું		**gadhẹḍũ** (*n*)
ગરુડ	eagle	**garuḍ** (*n*)
ગાય	cow	**gāy** (*f*)
ગીધ	vulture	**gidh** (*n*)
ઘુવડ	owl	**ghuvaḍ** (*n*)
ઘેટું	lamb	**ghẽṭũ** (*n*)
ઘોડો	horse	**ghoḍo** (*m*),
ઘોડી		**ghoḍi** (*f*),
ઘોડું		**ghoḍũ** (*n*)
ચકલી	sparrow	**chakli** (*f*),
ચકલો		**chaklo** (*m*),
ચકલું		**chaklũ** (*n*)

ટ્ટુ	pony	**taṭṭu** (*n*)
ક્કર	pig	**ḍukkar** (*n*)
ડકો	frog	**deḍko** (*m*)
ાગ	cobra	**nāg** (*m*)
ોપટ	parrot	**popaṭ** (*m*)
કરો	goat	**bakro** (*m*),
કરી		**bakri** (*f*)
ગલો	crane	**baglo** (*m*),
ગલી		**bagli** (*f*)
તક	duck	**batak** (*n*)
ળદ	ox	**baḷad** (*m*)
ેલાડી	cat	**bilāḍi** (*f*),
ેલાડો		**bilāḍo** (*m*),
ેલાડું		**bilāḍũ** (*n*)
ેંસ	buffalo	**bhẼs** (*f*)
ગર	crocodile	**magar** (*m*),
ગરી		**magri** (*f*)
ાછલી	fish	**māchhli** (*f*)
ોર	peacock	**mor** (*m*)
ીંછ	bear	**rĩchh** (*n*)
ક્કડખોદ	woodpecker	**lakkaḍkhod** (*n*)
રુ	wolf	**varu** (*n*)
ાઘ	tiger	**vāgh** (*m*),
ાઘણ		**vāghaṇ** (*f*)
ોયાળ	jackal	**shiyāl** (*n*)
મડી	kite	**samḍi** (*f*)
સલું	rabbit	**saslũ** (*n*)
ાપ	serpent	**sāp** (*m*)
ેંહ	lion	**sĩh** (*m*)
ેંહણ		**sĩhaṇ** (*f*)
રણ	deer	**haraṇ** (*n*)
સ	swan	**hãs** (*m*),
સી		**hãsi** (*f*)
થી	elephant	**hāthi** (*m*)

nsects જીવજંતુઓ

ળસિયું	earthworm	**aḷsiũ** (*n*)
ાગિયો	firefly	**āgiyo** (*m*)
ધઈ	termite	**udhai** (*f*)
રોળિયો	spider	**karoḷio** (*m*)

કીડી	ant	**kiḍi** (*f*)
જૂ	louse	**ju** (*f*)
તીડ	locust	**tiḍ** (*n*)
પતંગિયું	butterfly	**patangiũ** (*n*)
ભમરી	wasp	**bhamri** (*f*)
મચ્છર	mosquito	**machchhar** (*n*)
મધમાખી	bee (honey)	**madhmākhi** (*f*)
મંકોડો	large black ant	**mankoḍo** (*m*)
માકડ	bed bug	**mākaḍ** (*m*)
માખી	fly	**mākhi** (*f*)
વાંદો	cockroach	**vā̃do** (*m*)
વીંછી	scorpion	**vĩchi** (*m*)

Food ખોરાક

અથાણું	pickle	**athāṇũ** (*n*)
ઈંડું	egg	**ĩḍũ** (*n*)
કચુંબર	type of mixed salad	**kachũbar** (*f*)
કઠોળ	pulse	**kaṭhoḷ** (*n*)
કઢી	buttermilk and gram flour soup	**kaḍhi** (*f*)
ખીચડી	rice and pulse cooked together	**khichḍi** (*f*)
ઘઉં	wheat	**ghaũ** (*m pl*)
ઘી	purified butter	**ghi** (*n*)
ચટણી	chutney	**chaṭṇi** (*f*)
ચા	tea	**chā** (*f*, *m*)
ચોખા	rice	**chokhā** (*m pl*)
જવ	barley	**jav** (*m*)
દારૂ	wine, liquor	**dāru** (*m*)
દાળ	pulse	**dāḷ** (*f*)
દાળ	pulses (soup)	**dāḷ** (*f*)
પાણી	water	**pāṇi** (*n*)
ભાજી	leaf vegetables	**bhāji** (*f*)
ભાત	cooked rice	**bhāt** (*m*)
મકાઈ	corn	**makāi** (*f*)
માછલી	fish	**māchhli** (*f*)
રોટલી	chapati	**roṭli**
શાક	vegetables	**shāk** (*n*)

Vegetables શાકભાજી

આદુ	ginger	**ādu** (*n*)
કોથમીર	coriander	**kothmir** (*f*)
કોબી	cabbage	**kobi** (*f*)
ગાજર	carrot	**gājar** (*n*)
ટમેટું	tomato	**ṭameṭũ** (*n*)
ડુંગળી	onion	**ḍungḷi** (*f*)
પાલખ	spinach	**pālakh** (*f*)
ફ્લાવર	cauliflower	**flāvar** (*n*)
બટાટું	potato	**baṭāṭũ** (*n*)
ભાજી	leaf vegetables	**bhāji** (*f*)
ભીંડા	okra/ladies' fingers	**bhĩḍā** (*m*)
મૂળા	radish	**muḷā** (*m*)
રીંગણું	aubergine	**rĩgṇũ** (*n*)
લસણ	garlic	**lasaṇ** (*n*)
લીંબુ	lemon/lime	**lĩbu** (*n*)

Fruit and nuts ફળો અને સૂકો મેવો

અખરોટ	walnut	**akhroṭ** (*n*)
અનાનસ	pineapple	**anānas** (*n*)
અંજીર	fig	**anjir** (*n*)
કાજુ	cashew nuts	**kāju** (*m*)
કિસમિસ	raisin	**kismis** (*f*)
કેરી	mango	**keri** (*f*)
કેળું	banana	**keḷũ** (*n*)
ખજૂર	date	**khajur** (*f*)
જરદાળુ	apricot	**jardāḷu** (*n*)
જામફળ	guava	**jāmphaḷ** (*n*)
ટેટી	melon	**ṭeṭi** (*f*)
તરબુચ	watermelon	**tarbuch** (*n*)
દાડમ	pomegranate	**dāḍam** (*n*)
દ્રાક્ષ	grapes	**draksh** (*f*)
પિસ્તા	pistachio	**pistā̃** (*n*)
બદામ	almond	**badām** (*f*)
મોસંબી	orange	**mosambi** (*n*)
શીંગ	peanuts	**shing** (*f*)
સફરજન	apple	**sapharjan** (*n*)

Numbers આંકડાઓ

૧	1	**ek**	એક	૧૧	11	**agiyār**	અગિયાર
૨	2	**be**	બે	૧૨	12	**bār**	બાર
૩	3	**traṇ**	ત્રણ	૧૩	13	**ter**	તેર
૪	4	**chār**	ચાર	૧૪	14	**chaud**	ચૌદ
૫	5	**pā̃ch**	પાંચ	૧૫	15	**pandar**	પંદર
૬	6	**chha**	છ	૧૬	16	**soḷ**	સોળ
૭	7	**sāt**	સાત	૧૭	17	**sattar**	સત્તર
૮	8	**āṭh**	આઠ	૧૮	18	**aḍhār**	અઢાર
૯	9	**nav**	નવ	૧૯	19	**ogṇis**	ઓગણીસ
૧૦	10	**das**	દસ	૨૦	20	**vis**	વીસ

૨૧	21	**ekvis**	એકવીસ	૩૧	31	**ekatris**	એકત્રીસ
૨૨	22	**bāvis**	બાવીસ	૩૨	32	**batris**	બત્રીસ
૨૩	23	**tevis**	તેવીસ	૩૩	33	**tetris**	તેત્રીસ
૨૪	24	**chovis**	ચોવીસ	૩૪	34	**chotris**	ચોત્રીસ
૨૫	25	**pachis**	પચીસ	૩૫	35	**pā̃tris**	પાંત્રીસ
૨૬	26	**chhavvis**	છવ્વીસ	૩૬	36	**chhatris**	છત્રીસ
૨૭	27	**sattāvvis**	સત્તાવીસ	૩૭	37	**sāḍatris**	સાડત્રીસ
૨૮	28	**aṭṭhāvis**	અઠ્ઠાવીસ	૩૮	38	**aḍatris**	આડત્રીસ
૨૯	29	**ogaṇtris**	ઓગણત્રીસ	૩૯	39	**ogaṇchālis**	ઓગણચાલીસ
૩૦	30	**tris**	ત્રીસ	૪૦	40	**chālis**	ચાલીસ

You will notice that the ending **-vis** (meaning 20) is common to all the numbers from 21 to 28, with the exception of 25 (**pachis**); **tris** (30) is common to a the numbers from 31 to 38, and including 35.

૪૧	41	**ektālis**	એકતાલીસ	૫૫	55	**panchāvan**	પંચાવન
૪૨	42	**betālis**	બેતાલીસ	૫૬	56	**chhappan**	છપ્પન
૪૩	43	**tetālis**	તેતાલીસ	૫૭	57	**sattāvan**	સત્તાવન
૪૪	44	**chummālis**	ચુમાલીસ	૫૮	58	**aṭṭhāvan**	અઠ્ઠાવન
૪૫	45	**pistālis**	પીસ્તાલીસ	૫૯	59	**ogaṇsāṭh**	ઓગણસાઠ
૪૬	46	**chhetālis**	છેતાલીસ	૬૦	60	**sāṭh**	સાઠ
૪૭	47	**suḍtālis**	સુડતાલીસ	૬૭	61	**eksaṭh**	એકસઠ
૪૮	48	**aḍtālis**	અડતાલીસ	૬૮	62	**bāsaṭh**	બાસઠ
૪૯	49	**ogaṇpachās**	ઓગણપચાસ	૬૯	63	**tesaṭh**	તેસઠ
૫૦	50	**pachās**	પચાસ	૭૦	64	**chosaṭh**	ચોસઠ
૫૧	51	**ekāvan**	એકાવન	૭૧	65	**pā̃saṭh**	પાંસઠ
૫૨	52	**bāvan**	બાવન	૭૨	66	**chhāsaṭh**	છાસઠ
૫૩	53	**tepan**	તેપન	૭૩	67	**saḍsaṭh**	સડસઠ
૫૪	54	**chopan**	ચોપન	૭૪	68	**aḍsaṭh**	અડસઠ

૬૯	69	**oganṣitter**	ઓગણોસિત્તેર	૭૫	75	**panchoter**	પંચોતેર
૭૦	70	**sitter**	સિત્તેર	૭૬	76	**chhÕter**	છોંતેર
૭૧	71	**ekoter**	એકોતેર	૭૭	77	**sitoter**	સિતોતેર
૭૨	72	**bÕter**	બોતેર	૭૮	78	**iṭhoter**	ઈઠોતેર
૭૩	73	**tÕter**	તોંતેર	૭૯	79	**oganẼshi**	ઓગણએંસી
૭૪	74	**chummoter**	ચુમ્મોતેર	૮૦	80	**Ẽshi**	એંસી
૮૧	81	**Ekyāshi**	એકયાશી	૯૧	91	**ekānũ**	એકાણું
૮૨	82	**byāshi**	બ્યાશી	૯૨	92	**bāṇũ**	બાણું
૮૩	83	**tryāshi**	ત્રાશી	૯૩	93	**trāṇũ**	ત્રાણું
૮૪	84	**choryāshi**	ચોર્યાશી	૯૪	94	**chorāṇũ**	ચોરાણું
૮૫	85	**panchyāshi**	પંચાશી	૯૫	95	**panchāṇũ**	પંચાણું
૮૬	86	**chhyāshi**	છાશી	૯૬	96	**chhannu**	છન્નું
૮૭	87	**satyāshi**	સત્તાશી	૯૭	97	**sattāṇũ**	સત્તાણું
૮૮	88	**aṭṭhyāshi**	અઠ્ઠાશી	૯૮	98	**aṭṭhāṇũ**	અઠ્ઠાણું
૮૯	89	**nevyāshi**	નેવ્યાશી	૯૯	99	**navvāṇũ**	નવાણું
૯૦	90	**nevũ**	નેવું	૧૦૦	100	**so**	સો
૧૦૦	100	**ekso**	એકસો	૬૦૦	600	**chhaso**	છસો
૨૦૦	200	**baso**	બસો	૭૦૦	700	**sātso**	સાતસો
૩૦૦	300	**traṇso**	ત્રણસો	૮૦૦	800	**āṭhso**	આઠસો
૪૦૦	400	**chārso**	ચારસો	૯૦૦	900	**navso**	નવસો
૫૦૦	500	**pā̃chso**	પાંચસો	૧૦૦૦	1,000	**hajār**	હજાર

With the exception of 200 (**baso**), the hundreds are formed in the same way as English with **ek, be, traṇ**, etc. placed before **so** (hundred). Other examples:

૧,૨૪૦	1,240	એક હજાર બસો ચાલીસ	**ek hajār baso chālis**
૩,૩૯૯	3,399	ત્રણ હજાર ત્રણસો નવાણું	**traṇ hajār traṇso navvāṇũ**

Colours રંગ

આછો	light	**āchho**
કાળો	black	**kāḷo**
ગુલાબી	pink	**gulābi**
ઘેરો	dark	**ghEro**
જાંબુડીઓ	violet	**Jāmbuḍio**
જાંબલી	purple	**jāmbli**
નારંગી	orange	**nārangi**
પીળો	yellow	**piḷo**
લાલ	red	**lāl**
લીલો	green	**lilo**

વાદળી	blue	**vādḷi**
સફેદ/ધોળો	white	**saphed/dhoḷo**
સોનેરી	golden	**soneri**

Shapes આકાર

ગોળ	circle	**goḷ** (*m*)
ચોરસ	square	**choras** (*m*)
ત્રિકોણ	triangle	**trikoṇ** (*m*)
લંબચોરસ	rectangle	**lambchoras** (*m*)
ષટકોણ	hexagon	**shaṭkoṇ** (*m*)

Metals ધાતુઓ

કાંસું	bronze	**kāsũ** (*n*)
ખનિજ	minerals	**khanij** (*f*)
જસત	zinc	**jasat** (*n*)
તાંબું	copper	**tā̃bũ** (*n*)
પિત્તળ	brass	**pittaḷ** (*n*)
પોલાદ	steel	**polād** (*n*)
રૂપું ચાંદી	silver	**roopũ** (*n*)
		chā̃di (*f*)
લોઢું,	iron	**loḍhũ** (*n*)
લોખંડ		**lokhanḍ** (*n*)
સોનું	gold	**sonũ** (*n*)

Gujarati references and further reading

Websites

http://www.sandesh.com/
http://www.samachar.com/
www.gujaratilexicon.com
www.mavjibhai.com
www.youtube.com
http://www.abplgroup.com/
http://www.gg2.net/
http://www.chitralekha.com/

Further reading

gujarātni asmitā, rajni vyās, published by Gurjar Sahitya Bhavan, Gandhi Road, Ahmedābād.

videsh yātrānā prerak prasãgo, Swami Sacchidānand, published by Gurjar Sahitya Bhavan, Gandhi Road, Ahmedābād.

Gujarāti Bhashā Pravesh Pt. 2, 3, 4, published by Navbhārat Sāhitya Mandir, Ahmedābād.

Learning Gujarati video, Gamtech, London.

britanmā̃ gujrātio, Pravin Sheth and Jagdish Dave, Gujarāt Sāhitya Academy, Gandhinagar, Gujarāt.

Atmakathā, M. K. Gāndhi, Navjivan Prakashan Mandir, Ahmedābād.

Grammatical index